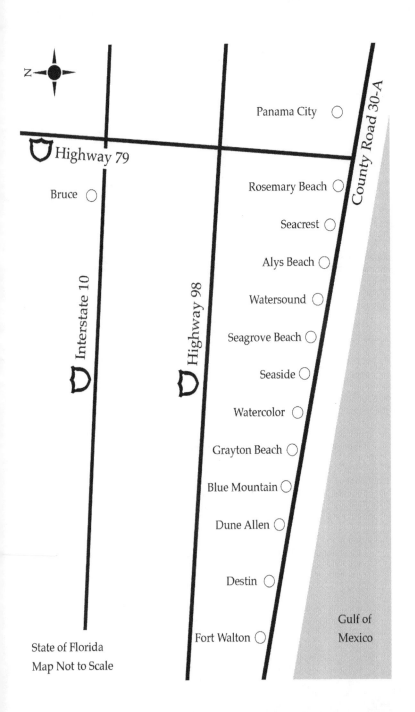

30-A Supper Club

Liza Elliott

Red Camel Press | Birmingham, Alabama

2012 Red Camel Press

Published by Red Camel Press, Birmingham, AL, USA

ISBN 978-1-937014-00-1

Printed in the United States

www.redcamelpress.com

Library of Congress Control Number 2011913960
Library of Congress subject headings
Southern Fiction
Mystery
U.S. Civil War

Home Depot Kind'a Man, music and lyrics © by E.Elliott
Book cover design by Mazy Holiday
Book Design by David Porter

This is a work of fiction. Names, characters, places, and all incidents are the products of the author's imagination or are used fictitiously. Any resemblance to actual events, locales, or persons, living or dead, is coincidental.

To the Pirates and Sirens of

San Juan Avenue

Seagrove Beach, Florida

and

The Forest Park Supper Club

Birmingham, Alabama

Table of Contents

Members of 30-A Supper Club

Harley McBride and Marco Polo	Seagrove Beach
Eliza Blackmon and Wilson Garrett	Alys Beach
Patricia and Spencer Dell	Seagrove Beach
Fern and Bobby Carlyle	Grayton Beach
Consuela and Guillermo Martinez	Blue Mountain
Chantal Carter and Darius Jawara	Seacrest Beach
Dana and Mario Obstbaum	Watersound
Marie Justine and Jean Louis Junot	Seagrove Beach
Adelaide and Brantley Vernon	Seaside
Reese and Walter McElwain	Rosemary Beach
Brenda and Glen Royal	Dune Allen
Meg and Colin Coffee	Watercolor

Menu

Cranberry and Sausage Stuffed Mushrooms

Scallion Dip with Jarlsburg and Creme Fraîche

* * *

Tomato Basil Soup topped with Parmesan and
White Popcorn

Green Leaf Salad with Pan Fried Squash

* * *

Caramelized Carrots tossed with Snow Peas and Walnuts

Garlic and Herb Crusted Lamb Chops

Cottage Loaf Bread

* * *

Persimmon Tart topped with Homemade Mint Ice Cream

Macadamia Nut Thimble Cookies

* * *

Malbec

September

"He lifted himself off of her with a sigh of exasperation and rolled over to grab the ringing phone. She shivered as cool air met her warm sweaty breasts. Damp wisps of golden brown hair clung to her cheeks. Starr Elliott pondered her position. She did not typically sleep with agents from MI6. But they were longtime mutual informants and Skype could never replace personal contact. What else could a responsible FBI agent do?

She watched him ease back over to her. He ran his fingers through her curls. Against all policy, she had fallen in love with him. That was the real danger."

"Harley, let's go."

"Okay, okay. Coming."

Marco always calls me right when it's the best part. I leaned back, exasperated like the MI6 agent. I marked the page with a folded corner then stashed the latest book of the *Starr Elliott, Undercover Agent* series under the seat cushion. Marco teases me no end about my addiction to trashy novels and I hate being caught red-handed with them. I tiptoed from my chair to the screen door and out, shutting it without a bang. Our cats snoozed on, safe in the screened porch.

Marco took my hand. We headed south. I gazed up at the cool blue sky and took a deep breath. What a place.

The sun shines differently here. It rules the Gulf of Mexico beaches, steaming the air and bleaching the sugary sand that borders the slightly teal deep. Yellow sunrises and red sunsets frame the days on County Road 30-A along the coast of the Florida Panhandle, where adventures lurk in sand dunes dotted with thick palmettos and history hides in the foam of scattered waves crashing ashore.

But sometimes history won't hide. It seeks us out. On the last day of August, almost a year ago, I tumbled into the turquoise waves unrolling on the porcelain beach. My right hand gouged the seabed as I struggled to right myself. When once again standing steady against the waves, water and sand drained away from my hand exposing a crusty lump of ocean junk.

Marco Polo had surged ahead of me, oblivious to my fall. His long gait gained ground along the line where seawater disappears leaving only soaked sand and scattered tiny shells. He didn't see me slip it into my hidden pocket along with my now-drenched secret stash of M&M almonds, bleeding sticky color down my soaked shorts. A few hours later, we headed home.

Lollygagging on our street, surveying a neighbor's new flowers, petting the dog next door, I didn't know that from the moment the chunk emerged from the cover of the waves and found me, my life had converged with an unsettled remnant of history, a destiny still yearning to happen. I was drawn in simply by taking possession of it, unaware of what lay ahead. Once home, Marco took a nap and I began to chip at the barnacles. My fingers felt hot, maybe reacting to bacteria in the grooves. A round, flat object took shape. Just a coin hidden beneath layers of sea crud, yet I couldn't take my eyes off of it. My chest began to feel tight with an angst that was not mine. I dismissed this odd sensation, attributing it to an overdose of blue and violet M&M almonds, or a pulled muscle from belly dancing class. At any rate, I would have to come clean to Marco about my newfound coin.

That next morning, the throaty groan of the coffee grinder sent our grey tabby, Daisy, scurrying for cover. Marco cooed for her to come back then opened the sports page in front of him. Against an occasional hiss from the coffee maker, she crept back to her waiting bowl. Meanwhile, Tulip, our impatient calico, began to poke her paw at the gold object near her tail. The coin, wiped free of the elements and melted chocolate still sat on the rag I used to clean it.

"Can't explain why I didn't say anything until now."

"Harley McBride. I thought we shared everything." Marco eyed the coin.

"We do. I am sharing right now. Telling you about the coin. Does it matter that it's the next morning?" In truth, I enjoyed the short period of time that the coin was just mine. When you grow up in a big family on the South Side of Chicago, you hold on tightly to what's yours, whether it's space or stuff. Especially the stuff.

He slid the coin over away from the cat's paw. "She'll carry it off to the island of lost things under the couch."

"Don't be angry. It's no big deal." I shoved the front page of the paper toward him, pointing to the article headlined *Antique Robberies Up In Panhandle*. "A maritime museum in Apalachicola was robbed last week. This week, an antique mall in Destin. The thieves targeted all things Confederate. Uniforms, weapons, antebellum teacups. Any maps, paper money and especially coins."

"You think this a Civil War gold coin?"

"Of course not. I'm only pointing out that Confederate artifacts are in demand at the moment. This coin may not even be gold or an antique, but somebody is after old coins."

"Maria loves this sort of thing. She'd say the coin is proof of Atlantis." Marco glanced at his watch and set the phone to speaker. "She'll be calling about now."

Right on cue, the phone rang. "How's my favorite little girl?" He slid his hand along Tulip, from the top of her head to the tip of her tail.

"Hi, sweetie," I called.

"Hi, there. Another sunny afternoon in Tunisia. I'm off to the countryside to meet with village elders. There's a recent uptick in cross border smuggling. Always ends up on my desk as a security issue."

"Heady stuff for a little girl from Chicago," said Marco. "Nothing new here. Your mother found a gold coin washed up at the beach."

"Well, gold colored. It's probably brass," I said.

"Maybe it is jewelry," replied Maria. "Lots of old coins here end up in necklaces, earrings or even sewn into dresses. Anyway, Mom, got something to ask you."

"Sure, anything."

"I met a guy here that says he knew you in Cairo before you were married."

I snatched the phone from the counter top and turned off the speaker. "It's off the speaker because it is so crackly. This is much better." Marco rolled his eyes and went back to the sports page.

"Okay. I get it. Dad isn't supposed to hear. Don't you think he gets it too?"

"You are probably right but go ahead." I picked up my coffee mug and walked toward Daisy on the couch.

"Hmm. He has salt and pepper hair, is a little bit tanned, almond eyes, shall I continue? He works with the Ministry of Foreign Affairs in Egypt, an archeologist by trade. His name is Gamal."

"Look, you meet many people over the years. It was so long ago. I am sure he's confused. All of us foreign girls looked alike to them way back then."

"He said you had a coquette's smile and ringlet curly hair. Good thing we are not on speaker phone."

"Don't know about that first part. Yes, the connection is better without the speaker on." Marco did not move, surely listening to every word. I felt my once adventurous youth in her voice, the restlessness, the energy. And I would never forget Gamal's weary dark eyes, bearing the weight of a secret he would never reveal.

"But Mom, some people here say I look like his daughter."

"That's absurd. What's he doing in Tunisia?"

"Ah, so you do know him! Careful, Dad always listens. He's here because weapons smuggling is getting worse. Antiquities are used as cover. He's meeting with INTERPOL."

"Hmm. Antiquities and weapons smuggling."

"Hey, the drivers are signaling to me. Just wanted to check about my parentage. Love those emails. Keep' em coming. Bye for now."

"Bye, sweetie." I clicked off and put the phone back on its stand.

Without looking up Marco said, "She's so far away but doing what she loves. A renegade, like her mother. Now she's catching smugglers."

He didn't ask anything about the long ago acquaintance. We both knew lots of people from many places, the trappings of long careers. They didn't matter. Marco and I are solid. We are Great Lakes people, sturdy, alert, and aware of the world. Ours was a passionate love match between the daughter of a Southside Irish saloon owner and his French Canadian wife, and the grandson of the personal chef at Al Capone's Couderay hideout in Wisconsin.

It was a rather unlikely match, in retrospect. I had my bags packed to see the world as early as I could remember. Although the only girl in a family with six brothers, I was not the spoiled one. On the contrary, I was treated as one of the guys. But I was different. For the boys, the family trips to Montreal to see our mother's relatives meant skiing and eating croissants. For me it was practicing French and watching the ships make way on the St. Lawrence Seaway toward the Atlantic Ocean. I wanted what was out there. I wanted it all.

Eventually I got to college and grad school majoring in sociology, the study of societies, of organizations, of cities, of people. Why, it is the study of everything. On the plane descending through the clouds above the Mediterranean Sea, peeking out the window to see the Nile River snake through the desert to the capitol city, I vowed never to go back. Sociology held the ticket to the world. This semester of fieldwork in Cairo, Egypt, would launch my future.

Months later, home from my fieldwork term to meet with my dissertation chairman, fate intervened. Exhausted from travel and academic meetings, I did what any daughter of a saloon keeper would do. I stopped at a bar for a whiskey. Not just any bar, but the Rosebud Café, Chicago's old mob hangout, now quite respectable.

There he sat at a small side table, a massive book opened to the middle. He flicked the pages, searching for something. The young medical intern ran one hand through his thick black hair and looked at me. I balanced on a bar stool nearby and flirted with him. He looked up.

"What's your name?" He swirled the beer in his mug, catching the dim light from antique chandeliers above.

"Harley, after the motorcycle." I shook my long curly hair away from my face. "What's yours?"

"Marco Polo, after the explorer."

That's all it took. That wit. It grabbed me just as sure as his hands did around my waist. We fell fast and into bed that night. Our first date. Naive and idealistic in those early years, we grappled with our chosen careers: emergency medicine for him, sociology for me, soon with baby Maria in tow.

All grown up now, Maria's short call had reminded me of a time before Marco. I was eager and free. Everything was open to me, the inquisitive grad student in Egypt. From the clatter of the donkey carts to the muezzin's call to prayer, ageless Cairo sang to me of endless possibilities in exotic places. And love. Gamal enchanted me and I wanted to stay. But he broke my heart. Choices made are choices lived. There is some Egyptian proverb to that effect.

Anyway, today marked the annual start of the new academic year, the end of summer, the beginning of autumn. A day of promise, of shifting light, of new frontiers. It is one of my favorite days of the year. After that call from Maria, I needed this favorite day.

Marco fidgeted with the calendar on the screen of his cell phone while folding the latest issue of his local fishing magazine back to a page of fancy rods and reels. He pulled his hospital ID out of his pocket and clipped it to the pocket of his blue scrubs. With another sip of hot coffee he looked at his watch. "Meant to ask you earlier, who is hosting Supper Club next week?"

"Eliza and Wilson." I refilled my mug.

"Good. Bet he'll be serving a Malbec from Argentina?"

"He does cultivate himself as the wine guru. Just a trust fund baby, you know, and what's with those worn-out boat shoes and faded Izod shirts?" I pointed to the page of rods and reels. "Darling, why not tell me, now, that you'll be stopping by Yellowfin Ocean Sports after your shift."

He grinned as he tapped the big, red reel under consideration with his fingers. For big fish I assumed. The man whose sunny disposition filled the hole in my heart long ago tore out the page and folded it. He winked as he slid it into his pocket.

"I'll be home by suppertime."

With a sweet kiss he was off. I was grateful he didn't pry about my chat with Maria. I hadn't conjured up an image of Gamal in many years. About 26 years to be exact. Those enigmatic eyes and sly smile. Tan from the desert sun. Coal black hair. I shook it away while watching Marco's British racing green Miata speed away.

The Thrillmobile. That's what Eliza Powell Blackmon, my best friend, dubbed his little green car. I concentrated on Marco, the reality of his life and my life with him. Twelve years have passed since we moved from Chicago to Seagove Beach along Highway 30-A. Our cinder block love shack is all we need.

I smiled at Tulip and stroked her downy fur. I ran my fingers over the embossed turtle on the coin next to her. It drew me in, like a phantom force promising a story if I only bothered to listen. I took a deep breath, and cleared my head. I grabbed the sack of cheese straws and stuffed it into my briefcase next to the fresh bag of M&M almonds, the ultimate health food. Protein and fat from the almond, antioxidants from the chocolate.

I quit listening to diet experts long ago. It's just about the calories. Doesn't matter which ones. Just eat to your limit and that's it. If one bag of potato chips is a thousand calories, then there's your quota for the day. Don't eat anything else. But you must exercise. As long as I don't go over my allotted 1000 calories a day, no matter what I eat, plus put in a half hour of cardio and half an hour of Pilates, I can fit any of my clothes. Truth be told, it is a struggle for me most of the time.

I took one last look at the shiny coin and pushed it behind the coffee maker. Loaded with my provisions, my assortment of journals and lists of things to do, I struck out for the world of work, speeding east on County Road 30-A. The golden September sun brightened the wide sky ahead, the backdrop to Eliza's new neighborhood, Alys Beach, just ahead.

Some years ago, she of peaches and cream skin, full lips, and the mane of a thoroughbred, collided into me at Sundog Bookstore as we both reached for the lone copy of *Cold Mountain*.

"Excuse me. Oh, go ahead, you take it," I said.

"No, you take it."

"Please, you take it." I glanced around the store.

"Well, for heaven's sake, somebody take it." We both turned towards the voice. A sales woman at the cash register glared at us, pursed lips and all. In the end, we bought it together. Eliza read it first and then handed it off to me. Thus began many a chat about books and everything else, either with a cup of French roast black coffee or a bottle of Zinfandel nearby.

As for the 30-A Supper Club, Marco and I joined thanks to her nomination over 10 years ago. She and Wilson were longtime residents of the 30-A area but only six months ago made a new villa in Alys Beach their permanent base. Alys Beach is not for the faint of heart. The latest version of Euro-fusion chic architecture, it is the polar opposite of the indigenous Panhandle beach town over grown with scrub oak and wild flowers. The best old beach towns have wooden beach shacks or cinder block bungalows scattered willy nilly around an old sandy trail leading to the beach.

I rounded a curve in advance of the Alys Beach sign. This

neighborhood erupts out of the flat Florida coast with blinding white stucco dwellings uniformly sculpted with curved Spanish trim and militantly ridged roofs. The most luxurious villas surround private ultramarine blue-tiled courtyards with their own decorative pools. Some pools contain water features, a verdigris flamingo or dolphins leaping into the pool. Rumor has it you need a cool five million to even get started.

Retired date palm trees imported from a distant, exotic tree farm line the stretch of County Road 30-A that slices through Alys Beach. Driving beneath them reminds me of the main drag in Pasadena where the Rose Bowl Parade takes place. At each end of this segment stand two butteries, towering pointed structures, not quite obelisks, more like pyramids on a box that are lit by thousands of tiny white bulbs at night. They announce in the rich grey of nighttime that this is a very special place. Gamal's face suddenly flashed before me: nighttime at the majestically lit Pyramids of Giza was one of our favorite haunts. I willed his face away.

I sped up near Eliza and Wilson's house, which boasts a water feature of a little boy who proudly tee-tees all day and night. The orange and yellow koi lounging near water lilies in the pond don't seem to mind. Once, I asked her why she didn't get a little girl to tee-tee instead of the boy.

"What an appalling idea. It just isn't done," she replied.

"Why couldn't a little girl be sitting on a leaf?"

"No decent little Southern girl would want to be caught dead tee teeing in public. What ever would she do for toilet paper?" Eliza's haughty southern accent always ends a sentence with a breathy lilt. Almost like punctuation.

"Touché." I conceded the victory to her.

I conjured up an image of her fountain, searching for coins that might have been tossed in. Maybe a penny. But no gold sovereigns or silver doubloons. No extraordinary gold coin like mine. Even without checking, I knew the coin was at least 24 carat gold. The color, a dense, warm yellow, gave it away. New coins had less gold and more copper creating a lighter, cooler shade of color. I learned about gold from Gamal during the days we strolled the gold markets at Khan el Khalili in Cairo. I didn't dare let on to Marco how I came to know all this.

All of a sudden, I passed by Eliza's street and remembered I had to call her for my Supper Club assignment. And please let it not be too complicated. She could brew, sizzle, and whip most any ingredient into submission. She was the Master Chef of 30-A Supper Club. Her unremarkable husband, Wilson, on the other hand, ate anything set in front of him with complete disregard as long as he started the meal with a Guinness.

I reached my office and unloaded my briefcase and laptop with only minutes to spare before a faculty meeing. Once powered up, I found Eliza's assignment in an email containing the complete menu. She asked me to orient the two new couples to the rules of Supper Club, and bring white popcorn as the garnish for the tomato and basil soup. With most things, food, fashion, or art, Eliza was very experimental. Whatever popcorn on soup tasted like, I'd gotten off easy this month.

The next week whipped by as I focused on the new school year. Any thoughts about my gold coin retreated, lying in uneasy wait for now. By week two of the new semester, my classes settled in with the familiarity of well-worn driving gloves. Sociology is an endless expedition, I warn my students, "so you will never arrive to there." It's a quest toward understanding the social action of societies or more simply put, what's up with that thing you do. I show up every fall to see where the journey leads next.

*

Before I knew it, the evening of the second Thursday of the month arrived. Supper Club. It always comes up fast in September. The two new couples, like everyone else, had to live in one of the communities along the 30-A corridor.

There is no official dress code for Supper Club. Casual is the mantra of beach fashion year round, but 30-A demands it be chic. Some members take this to heart and always appear turned out in natty ensembles. Others, like Marco, grab the nearest clean blue jeans, which match just about any shirt in his closet. I wear black and tonight it is the black sleeveless shift dress with a flair skirt. My favorite red scarf from Hawaii, a long rectangle, would double as a shawl.

Freshly scrubbed, scarf on my arm, bowl of popcorn in hand, we headed out to Supper Club at Alys Beach.

"Do you want to show the gang your newfound coin?" Marco opened the car door.

"Not yet. It's my secret. Maybe next month."

"Ah, yes. You like your secrets."

Marco pulled the top of the Thrillmobile up and latched it closed. I curled into it with the bowl resting on my lap. We zoomed onto 30-A close to a small nursery selling flowers, pots and patio furniture. The speed limit is maddeningly low at 35 mph but Marco has cop eye. He sees them before they see him. He brakes before they can register his speed. A visual radar. So he sped along undetected.

Soon we see the faint lights of the butteries in the settling dusk. The Alys Beach sidewalks are made with pavers that look like cobblestones. We swerve onto the main street, south of 30-A in a new section to their home. Hand-crafted copper lanterns framed the front door with warm, dusky light. The loose rays were meant only to locate the door but not highlight it. Eliza and Wilson were like that. They showed enough for you to recognize them but not enough to know them well. Some in Supper Club have told me how odd it was for Eliza, given her pedigree, to strike up such a visible friendship with me, a Yankee of mixed origin. It's our fate, I tell them.

Marco helped me unwind out of the Thrillmobile. The salty air curled my unruly ringlets tighter. A gust of wind from the gulf picked off a handful of popcorn from the bowl. It floated on the wind for scant seconds like snowflakes before crashing to the street without a sound.

Imagine cobalt blue tiles flecked with specks of orange lit up with flashes of fire from the flames of floating water candles. There, in the middle of an oblong pool, a green little boy perched on a stone, with gold streamers tied to his head that danced in the breeze as if for Mardi Gras. Huge cracked ceramic pots stood like sentinels in the four corners of the piazza, filled with trailing licorice and coral-colored verbena hugging the bases of feathery windmill palms.

An iron bar-height table and chairs were unoccupied but bottles of wine were set up in formation at the ready on the outdoor bar counter top nearby. As we passed by on the way to the living room, I knew the bet was lost. A platoon of Argentinean Malbec. Not a Cabernet in sight. I owed Marco twenty bucks. He leaned over to me, whispering in victory, "I'll take it out in trade."

Just as Marco reached to open the door to the living room, the door opened itself.

"Good evening, y'all. I saw you coming with that popcorn and wondered if I missed something. Are we having a movie to-night?" Bobby Carlyle snorted at his own joke. He always laughed hard followed by a honking snort. Tonight he wore a bolo tie around the open neck of cowboy shirt tucked into patched blue jeans.

"No movie tonight, we are the show. And you are in it!" I stepped into the hallway. "The popcorn is according to Eliza's orders so you'll just have to wait and see when we eat it."

"That's so. Marco, what did you bring us tonight?" He slapped an arm around Marco then led him back out to the bar with our wine bottle, scuffing his cowboy boots across the tiles as if they were too heavy to lift.

I made a mental note to explain to the new members the Supper Club wine policy. All couples bring their own bottle of wine, thereby spreading the cost of wine amongst all. The host couple generally provides any extra. I wouldn't add that some couples are more generous than others. Or that we could always expect Wilson, the faux bum with Dom Perignon taste, to show off new finds or trendy blends which his close buddy Bobby could supply.

To Bobby's chagrin, Marco, as usual, had brought our current low budget household standby, an old vine red. For Bobby, anything less than twenty-five dollars a bottle was undrinkable. Wine was serious business for him, the owner of Bobby Carlyle Wine and Spirits. He had served many a fine wine during the years he worked at Highlands Restaurant, a white tablecloth restaurant in his hometown, Birmingham, Alabama, all the while studying the tastes and habits of the drinkers of fine wine. When Fern, his wife, inherited her family beach house in the old part of Grayton Beach, they decided to renovate it and settle beachside. Bobby opened the wine shop and promptly adopted the title of wine expert of 30-A.

Fern greeted me in the kitchen where she stirred a tall pot of thick tomato soup. Mounds of freshly chopped basil piled high on a plate filled the room with an earthy aroma. Long silver swirls hung from her earlobes like micro slinkys, bouncing up and down like the real thing when she spoke. The short spikes of her streaked hair matched the taupe in her cropped jacket perfectly. She was known to be very matchy matchy, so her cork wedge slides perfectly suited the ensemble. No doubt she found those at the Off 5th Saks outlet store.

Eliza waved and then turned back to lean over a baking tray of garlic and herb crusted lamb chops. She tested them with her thumb the way Emeril does, registering temperature without a thermometer. Her ultra modern Euro-style kitchen with lots of stainless steel and full overlay solid maple cabinets contained the perfect work triangle. The glass orbs that hung from slim silver wires over the island had been special ordered from Fusion, a glass art gallery in Seaside. From the polished Alessi teapot to the square plates, Eliza exhibited the elegance of ultra simplicity. Her layered sleek hair was pushed away from her face, softly colored with coral lipstick and blush. A white-polished cotton belted blouse rested casually on her silk navy blue pencil pants. Wearing only diamond studs in her ears she had opted for the quiet look of old money that night.

"Where is Wilson?" I set the popcorn on the counter top.

"On his way home from a client who wanted one more look at a property in Rosemary Beach. He won't be long." Eliza moved on to check the other tray of lamb chops. "We'll need to sprinkle a tablespoon full of popcorn on each bowl of soup just before we serve it, okay?"

"Okay, I'll be ready. Are the bowls in the dining room?"

"Yes. You can bring them in here now. It would be easier to prepare them here and serve them, don't you think?"

"Yes, good idea," I said and went to get them. The tables shimmered with crystal goblets, sterling silver and low votive candles scattered throughout. The main dining table and two additional ones set up just for this night each showed off sets of three square glass vases, thick and heavy like glass block, containing branches of scarlet orange bittersweet. It grows in the upper Midwestern countryside, where the autumn chill arrives early. Eliza must have had these flown in yesterday because bittersweet does not grow in warm coastal climates. She sets the bar high for the rest of us.

I glanced into their den, where a flat screen TV hung on the wall facing a tightly upholstered pale green chair with matching ottoman. An antique deck of tarot cards were displayed on an occasional table. Above hung a formal portrait of Eliza Blackmon's great great-grandmother, Eliza Powell, or so said the engraved nameplate on the frame. I stepped in to get a closer look. The colors had darkened with age so the black background no longer showed much contrast with the dark burgundy dress worn by the subject. The shreds of lace punctuated by dashes of red in tiny bows still outlined the contour of the small collar on the high neckline. The nubby knots of a gold chain were painted with pure yellow ochre capturing the light of that long ago day forever. A gold coin attached to the chain lay flat against her bosom.

As many times as I had been at Eliza and Wilson's previous home, this painting had escaped me. The looks of the two Eliza's were eerily close. The bright brown eyes with flecks of green, the turned-up nose, and the rosebud lips confirmed the lineage of my best friend.

Once, we had a coffee outside Modica Market in Seaside where Eliza told me stories of her great great-grandmother's campaign for hygiene. "There is water around here, use it. That was her motto," said Eliza. "It's practically our family mantra now."

But there was more. Eliza Powell, now peering at me through portrait eyes, had supported the Southern Cause by converting a barn on the plantation into a convalescent clinic for the scores of war wounded arriving weary and scarred from battle.

"She was enthralled with Florence Nightingale and her pioneering practice of sanitation, hygiene and fresh air during the Crimean War," Eliza explained. "She even bought her book. Then there was America's own Clara Barton on the Civil War battlefields. No matter Clara Barton, daughter of abolitionists, toiled for the Union. My great great-grandmother believed her to be a heroic woman because she responded to the pleas of the soldiers' families to find their sons missing in action. She started the first humanitarian program to locate both Union and Confederate missing soldiers. So my great great-grandmother Eliza declared the Powell Clinic open for any soldier with the promise to assist them home, North or South."

One day, Eliza promised, she would show me her grandmother's copy of Nightingale's *Notes on Nursing* but first she'd have to search for it. Having seen her attic in her previous home, stuffed with sealed boxes and antique trunks, I knew it would be later rather than sooner, if ever.

To me, great great-grandmother Eliza Powell, poised in time and paint, was not a stranger. Thanks to her great great-grand daughter, my best friend, I had admired her from far across time.

Gradually my eyes began to focus on the gold coin hanging from the knotted chain. The coin had a pattern. Carefully painted with shadow and highlights, a textured drawing of a turtle adorned the coin. If you could hold the coin you could feel the turtle with your fingertips. I knew this. I had a coin just like it. Slowly I began to feel a thumping pulse in the palm of my right hand, radiating into my fingers. The colors of the portrait's face brightened as if warm blood surged within it. I sensed raw energy, frustrated and urgent but not angry. Again, I felt compelled to attention, only this time it had a focus. Eliza Powell's portrait. Her face hailed me, using brilliant color to convey a silent salutation. A contact. A physical, real time contact. Eliza Powell? Is this really you? Why?

A door sprung open and I turned to see Wilson Garrett enter through a side screened door. When I looked back at the portrait, the colors were dull again. My hand released from the unnatural sensation. My senses quiet. I backed up into Wilson who had come up silently behind me. He caught me stumbling against him.

"Say, is this newest addition to our family heirlooms sweeping you off your feet?"

"She looks just like Eliza. It's uncanny."

"I'll take that as a yes," Wilson said.

"And the coin. I noticed the coin fashioned as a medallion."

"The coin?" He peered closely at it.

"I found one just like it on the beach a few weeks ago." I turned from the portrait to look at Wilson. His eyebrows arched out to the edge of his face and his jaw fell slack. "Are you ill, Wilson? You look white as a ghost."

"No, just low blood sugar. Think I'll get some wine." He pivoted on his heel and strode directly toward Bobby Carlyle.

I didn't tell him about the peculiar sensations of my hand, the presence of a consciousness not my own, or the heightened color in the portrait. I kept that a secret. My secret. My stuff. Anyway, Wilson considered me Eliza's zany friend and I always felt he resented me but I never knew why.

Bobby watched him approach, stepping out from beside the bar, and assumed a ballet dancer's third position, the heel of his right foot placed at the arch of his left foot, both pointing away at an angle. He then crossed his arms, right on top of left with his hands open, fingers pointed towards his shoulders. Wilson stopped in front of him and assumed the same position. Then they extended their hands as if to shake but only crossed their thumbs, keeping their palms flat and open to the ground. They let their grasp drop and spoke to each other, Bobby looked in my direction. I couldn't hear what they said. They turned toward the bar where Marco was pouring glasses of wine.

Their private choreography disturbed me, encroaching on my already unsettled thoughts about the ethereal connection to the portrait. Bobby signaled to Brantley Vernon, dressed as always in his signature golf shirt with the collar worn up and the tails out. He quietly joined Wilson and Bobby. The "Rebs" as Marco and I privately referred to them. They revered the Confederacy and this was no secret in Supper Club. Over the years Marco and I had listened to them rehash the Civil War glory days over and over, whether it was battle heroism or the doomed Confederate submarine Hunley.

Brantley did not disguise his distaste for Northerners who, to his way of thinking, only won on points. He maintained a cordial level of association with us because Marco was a physician and as Brantley, the golf pro at Crooked Creek Golf Course would point out, "It's in my interest to be friendly to tourists with money and with doctors at the ER."

I watched the three men drift away from Marco and close ranks. Bobby and Brantley leaned in to Wilson. Bobby looked my way and I caught his eye for an instant, a cold stare that bore right through me. I didn't flinch. I had nothing to hide. Did he? I wondered.

Reluctantly I took my tray of bowls to the kitchen. A few minutes later, Marco met me with a glass of wine and urged me to leave the kitchen and mingle with the rest of the gang. So we did, even as I vaguely sensed the coin in my empty palm. Before I could say anything to Marco, Consuela Martinez broke my concentration. She strolled in clutching an enormous wooden bowl filled with mixed green lettuces and foil tents containing fried squash pieces and fried okra. "Buenas noches, y'all." She adjusted the purple and yellow silk scarf draped across her shoulders which matched her halter dress. Eliza commanded her to set everything on the counter top and join us outside by the pool.

"Harley, are you okay?" Eliza paused with a serving spoon suspended in the air. "You look flushed."

"Yeah, I'm okay. I need to ask you something, but not here. Too much confusion."

"Sure you are okay?"

"Yeah, but we must talk soon."

Consuela joined me outside near the pool's edge as far from the little boy as I could manage. She leaned over and whispered, "I saw the Frida paintings last week."

"And?"

"Breathtaking. I believe the exhibit will come here next year. I'll keep you posted."

"But your own work, Consuela, is every bit as good as these big shots who somehow managed to get famous," I said.

"Well, most are famous after they are dead. I think that's how they manage it." Consuela winked at me. "Scarcity drives the market."

Before I could weigh in on art marketing, Marie Justine Junot tapped our shoulders. "Bon soir." Jean Louis stood behind her gripping a heavy cast iron pot with bright red hot pads.

I pointed toward the kitchen. "Put your pot on the stove and it will stay warm from the oven." Consuela took a step back to clear the path.

"D'accord," Jean Louis said. "This thing is getting heavy." He winced at me as he dutifully walked on.

I turned to Marie Justine, her Quebec chignon adorned with a wisp of wild rosemary, and we kissed each other's cheeks a deux. Runway perfect in a dusty green skirt topped with a sheer black sweater set she whispered to me, "Ah, looks like Adelaide managed to make something. I wonder if it will be edible?" I couldn't answer because Brantley's wife, Adelaide, had entered our perimeter, making it unsafe to be honest in English or secretive in French. While other supper club members didn't care, she felt intensely insulted if Marie Justine and I conversed in French even for a minute. Our shared French Canadian origin, she being the recent immigrant, and I, the daughter of an immigrant, annoyed her no end. But Adelaide's pride on general kitchen incompetence even while she sold home and dining accoutrements at Pizitz in Seaside annoyed us even more. She had made the persimmon tart, which would be interesting I thought, since she had called Eliza to ask just what was persimmon.

"Good evening y'all, isn't this place fabuloso?" Adelaide waved her hands around as if presenting a gift room from the Price is Right. Her highlighted blonde hair did not swish as she moved unlike the real TV models. Her white sleeveless turtleneck sweater over black and white toile capris matched her black and white glittery flip flops, the sleek uniform of a beauty queen.

"Très chic," Marie Justine chirped. "Where is Brantley?"

"My sporting husband is over there by Wilson and Bobby." She waved again this time as if on a float in a parade. "He couldn't wait to see them. You know they're quite taken aback that Supper Club is now officially integrated."

Marie Justine's eyes widened. "You mean he has a problem with Chantal and Darius? If I'm not mistaken this is America and the 21st century."

"Well, it's still the Deep South and this is something new. You see, men like Brantley and Bobby, or even Wilson, don't like change. They don't take to socializing with newcomers. It takes them time to get adjusted to new people as social peers, you know, given where they came from, what they do, that's all."

Marie Justine's eyes glowered. "What does 'new people' mean? Jean Louis and I were new just a few years ago. Did they have a problem with us?"

"Not in so many words. But let them have a few drinks and they'll say things that could never be said in public, you know

19

about foreigners or anyone whose great great-grand-daddies did not wear the Grey. At least you and Jean Louis aren't black or worse yet, Injuns," Adelaide said. "Don't y'all worry, they know how to handle themselves."

"Do you hear yourself, Adelaide? Is there some purity test going on? How dare they! If one ugly word is spoken." Marie Justine squared her jaw as if she might bite. "And by the way, the French Canadians were pretty tight with Native Canadians."

"I don't mean anything. You asked. I answered. You don't like the truth. Not everyone is into your 'all you need is love' world. But, don't worry and don't be so sensitive. Nothing is going to happen," said Adelaide. "Those old goofs are just worried they've become irrelevant."

"To what?" Marie Justine's voice slit the air.

"To the world. They are just middle-aged men and all they care about is football and keeping their jobs. Color only matters to them because they consider it makes for unfair competition. They are the last of a dying breed." Adelaide waved a hand to no one in particular.

"Racists should go extinct." My lips curled around the words.

"That's pretty harsh, Harley." Adelaide's eyes narrowed to slivers of blue on a face beginning to spot with red flush.

"Probably not too harsh, Adelaide, but then don't worry. We are not out to embarrass Brantley or Bobby. But I am on the alert." Marie Justine crossed her arms.

I glanced away only to have my attention snared by more choreography by Wilson, Bobby and Brantley, who crossed thumbs and flattened their palms with each other, this time with additional embellishments. All three spoke something in unison as if chanting a coded message. And they all turned toward me.

"So Adelaide, what gives with the little dance I see going between yours and a few others?" I watched the men disperse.

"Oh that. Brantley and the others want to go to a new Civil

War re-enactment battle somewhere up in Indiana or Ohio. But first they have to master the signs of some secret code if they want to be part of an inner circle of soldiers, something like that. They imagine they are descendents of some noble Confederate gang." Adelaide yawned. "Sorry, I am so over all that Civil War stuff."

As if out of nowhere, Reese McElwain waddled into my sight line. Tonight she wore her shoulder-length bottle auburn hair loose with fluffy bangs scraping against her small eyes. Her ruddy cheeks perspired with a sheen of moisture, glowing, as I had learned to say in the South. Southern women do not sweat.

"Hey girl, what are you staring at?" she said.

"Nothing, just looking to see who's here and if the new members are here yet. Do you know them?" It wouldn't do to say I couldn't believe she had poured herself into that knit top that barely met the waistline of her cargo pants. Thankfully she had tossed on a leopard print blouse that she wore open like a jacket.

"We know Meg and Colin Coffee and don't you know Chantal Carter and Darius Jawara?" Reese nodded to Marie Justine even as she scanned the room with her beady eyes and dabbed her forehead with a tissue.

Marie Justine looked at me then smoothed her hair with her hands. "Yes, Jean Louis has had business dealings with Darius. They are from Mobile. And they go to St. Rita's."

"I never saw them there." I said.

"That's because you only drop in on the occasional Mass when you feel guilty about something." Marie Justine cracked a smile.

"Don't worry about my soul, Chère Marie Justine, we home church."

Reese McElwain rolled her eyes. She never knew whether to take me seriously or not. For her, church is not a laughing matter. Even the homemade mint ice cream she made for tonight's menu had been whipped on a vintage ice cream maker she found during her volunteer shift at the Salvation Army. So to her, a blessed machine for righteous hands. To me it made no difference, because I don't eat ice cream.

Adelaide and Marie Justine abandoned me for the bar to refill their glasses with Wilson's special inky Malbec, from the sun drenched grapes of Argentina. Reese turned to greet Dana, another heathen like myself, who swirled a tray in front of us teasing with warm and gooey cranberry and sausage stuffed mushrooms. Mario Obstbaum, her splendid Brazilian husband, stood glass in hand next to Marco and Spencer Dell, pouring wine all around.

I scouted the room for Brenda and Glen Royal who always showed up at the last minute with the menu's bread. Brenda used to work for Sister Schubert's Bakery in Luverne, Alabama, and thus claims expertise on all things bread. Tonight it was cottage loaf bread, whatever that is. The clicks from her spike heels across the patio tile signaled their arrival. The black leggings under a sundress struck me as trying too hard, but then, I in basic black should know better than to cast judgment on fashion. The piazza hummed with chatter against the flickering light from stars and candles, and soft piano music drifting from speakers in the shapes of stones tucked into corners of the garden.

Across the pool, Consuela and Guillermo laughed with Meg and Colin Coffee. When Wilson walked by, Colin stepped away and caught him by the arm. There it was again, in a flash, seamlessly performed, the third position stance, the crossed arms and the odd handshake. Obviously they were in the same gang Adelaide mentioned since they flashed each other that same code. So another Civil War buff had joined the 30-A Supper Club. I felt conspicuous standing alone watching other Supper Club members gather like clouds before a storm. My thoughts flashed back to the portrait, my coin and Wilson's pallid reaction. I felt out of sync with the frivolous atmosphere so typical of Supper Club but I had to make my way toward Chantal Carter and Darius Jawara. I waved for Meg and Colin to join us so their official welcome could begin.

"Hi, welcome to 30-A Supper Club. I'm Harley McBride,

and this is my husband, Marco Polo. How does this all work? Just a few guidelines. Supper Club meets the second Thursday of the month. Each of us takes a turn at hosting duties. That means as host you provide the entrée and some extra wine to match the menu. All other couples should weigh in a week ahead to get their assignment. Every couple brings a bottle of wine. The meal is usually presented as a buffet with formally set tables and seating for everyone. If you decide you'd rather have a cocktail party style, with an hors d'oeuvres only menu, you can do that too."

"That's it?" Meg Coffee flicked her red pageboy and pursed her lips in sort of a grin. "If you don't mind, I am dying to ask you a question."

"Sure, anything." I knew what she would ask.

"Where did you get your name?"

"My father's motorcycle."

"Oh, I knew it," A wide grin overtook most of her face and she clapped her hands like a toddler.

"You'll discover all sorts of obscure fun facts to know and tell soon enough from all of us in Supper Club." I took an instant if unfair dislike to her.

"Well, fun is something we try to practice, like fitness. " Colin Coffee began rising up on the balls of his feet and then lowering himself.

"Fitness? Oh dear, supper club is the one night a month I don't count calories or worry about more than one glass of wine. Are you into fitness?"

"Absolutely. It is part of our daily routine. Our part of being strong," said Colin. His biceps sculpted curves into his polo shirt similar to the curve of his muscular smile. His even white teeth seemed like a personal testament to good dentistry but then again, he was a dentist.

"Our part? Strong? What do you mean?" asked Darius. He turned the wine in his glass to bring forth its nose. His starched oxford cloth ivory shirt folded smartly on his tall and slim frame. The long sleeves had been turned back to just below his elbows exposing a powerful right forearm, a tennis player's arm.

"Our part as good citizens. Strong for everything. If you are physically strong, you are mentally strong, ready for any natural disaster, any terrorist attacks, any war, anything that comes down the pike. I like to be prepared, and I like my family to be prepared." He paused then added, "History would have been different if we had been stronger." Meg Coffee nodded to her husband with a full smile and took a gulp of wine that left tiny red curves above her lips. Marco calls them Frito Bandito marks as a joke but he is being kind. To me it's the hallmark of a peasant. It means you don't know how to sip wine from a wine glass.

During the tiny but awkward silence, all eyes turned to me. I had to say something. So I went with Scarlet O'Hara's standby, "Well, fiddle dee dee. Supper Club is simply about good food and good company." I turned to Chantal quietly taking in the whole scene. "That's Patricia and Spencer Dell standing near the green little boy in the pool, do you know them?"

"The chiseled hairdo and the guy with the tattoos and pony tail? I know they own Cocoons Deli, where we get that fabulous smoked tuna dip," said Chantal, "Doesn't Patricia work at Roland's? A stylist or some such thing?" Chantal took a sip of wine then adjusted the elastic waistband of her skirt. "Thank goodness there is no strict dress code for this. Comfort is my fashion these days."

"None at all and never will be. Tell me about yourself, other than going to St. Rita's," I said.

She hesitated. Perhaps to choose just what story to tell. That night, she gave me a resume story, the one that identified her hometown (Mobile) where she grew up, where she went to college (Loyola of New Orleans) and law school (University of Alabama), maybe how many brothers or sisters she had (one of each), at least the location she met her spouse (Mardi Gras) and that she practiced family law. Not a hint of attitude, not a tinge of viewpoint, the story was innocuous and could belong to anyone. She did mention three grown children, scattered at the moment between Mobile, New York and Los Angeles. Although tempted, I did not press for more detail that night. That's the beauty of Supper Club. There is always next month. Each month is a new party with all the familiar faces, the continuity of community in action.

Meanwhile, Darius and the Coffees strolled over to meet Walter McElwain, resplendent in his pink and green madras golf shorts, black socks and wingtip leather shoes. His bald head matched his bowling ball belly in a way that struck me as unnatural. Loss of hair can be understood, but the belly? I have asked Marco a hundred times what causes that distinctive shape and he always answers, "Beer, darling, too much beer." Despite the hours of golf Walter played, the hours he drank beer simply must have been more. He never complained of golf maladies like sore forearms or twisted knees, but he did complain on occasion that the beer cart babes at certain courses did not make rounds often enough for his taste. Walter saw me and bellowed, "Harley, darling, where have you been all my life?"

"Here, Walter, but I have sworn to another."

"Well, I may not be the man you want, but I'm the man you need, little darlin.'" He grinned from ear to ear and raised his wine glass in a toast.

Secretly I wondered how Reese put up with this massive man who claimed to be recently retired from police undercover work. For years he had infiltrated white collar crime networks. Was he truly retired?

Eliza waved to me and pointed to her wristwatch. I pulled Chantal along through a door that led by mistake into the room with the portrait. I stole a glance at Eliza Powell's face and was relieved to see nothing, feel nothing.

In the kitchen, Fern and I began to ladle the soup into each cup, then sprinkle each with basil, topped with the white popcorn. They looked like exploded firecrackers. Once placed on the tables, they matched the bittersweet sprigs. Eliza's knack for presentation wins again. She plans with an architect's precision. And I barely want to plan at all.

Consuela scattered the fried okra and squash pieces over the green leaf salad with her steady painter's hand. She stood back to survey her masterpiece. Satisfied, she took the bowl to the dining room. Marie Justine fussed about an extra towel to put under her pot, worried that it might heat the table's antique wood. Brenda pulled the mound of cottage loaf bread apart into three pieces, arranging them like lettuce wedges in a silver breadbasket. Eliza scooped the lamb chops onto crispy leaves of romaine lettuce, and Wilson carried the platter to the sideboard sliding it next to the pot of carrots and peas.

Eliza tapped a few members and said, "Supper's ready. Get your plates and go ahead." That's all it takes to prompt the 30-A Supper Club into dining mode. Quickly a buffet line forms and just as quickly disappears.

"Bon appetit y'all." Wilson Garrett, the official host, lowered his spoon into the soup.

Walter McElwain leaned back in his chair and surveyed the dining room, "Now I've seen some sights and smelled some wonders. Popcorn on soup? Lordy, if my momma could see such a sight."

Seating is never the same but the Carlyles and Vernons always sit together. Tonight the Coffees joined them but the men sat at one end of the table, the women on the other. Wilson joined Colin, Bobby and Brantley, dragging Eliza along who was too polite to make a scene out of resistance. I couldn't tell if the others noted this unusual arrangement but Marco did nod toward me that he saw it too. I dreaded telling him about my strange encounter with the portrait and Wilson because I couldn't fully explain it to myself.

Meanwhile, Chantal and Darius sat with the Junots at a table for four. Dana and Mario picked up the plates at the adjacent table for four to sit with Marco and me. We hadn't seen them since their trip to visit Mario's family in Brazil so there would be an endless range of news and stories to tell.

Once we were seated, plates full, glasses refreshed, Darius leaned over to Mario and remarked, "Do we ever get to hear how names like Mario and Obstbaum got together?"

Mario grinned. "Oh that. I'll give you the five-minute version. You see, my grandfather grew up in Germany. When he was hauled on to a train headed toward some concentration camp, he decided he'd better not go. So he jumped from the train and made his way to a boat heading for Brazil. He married a local girl, they had a son, my father, a goalie in the Brazilian soccer league who married my mother, Angelica. Along came me, Mario, named for her father. Two great families equal one wild name. You couldn't think this stuff up if you tried."

"That is some epic saga," said Darius.

"You want a saga? Here's your saga." Mario nodded toward Marco.

"Let's move these tables together," said Jean Louis, urging us with his hands.

So we scooted tables and chairs closer and held onto the vases making the two into one. "Okay then Marco, let's have it." Jean Louis settled into his chair.

"I'll make it short and sweet." Marco took a healthy swallow of wine. "The first Marco Polo of my family grew up in Chicago's Little Italy, the son of Sergio Polo, a restaurant owner from the old country. It had red checked tablecloths, Chianti bottles, and reeked of hot Italian bread, garlic and olive oil. You know the type. Sergio's Cafe was off the beaten track, not like the famous Rosebud Café where Harley and I met. So Sergio's became a favorite of Al Capone and his gang."

"Al Capone? For real? You'd better know that I am a serious skeptic," said Chantal.

"One and the same," said Marco. "When Mr. Capone wanted to spend time away from Chicago, he'd trek to the Wisconsin Northwoods where broad bough evergreens and old growth hard wood trees grow."

"Hey, Canada is more north than Wisconsin," said Marie Justine, "How can you call it Northwoods?"

"Don't know. That's just what we call it. When you see the white trunks of the birch trees and hear their floppy leaves rustle just before dusk as the bald eagles whine, you know you are there and you love it," Marco said. "Couderay, where Mr. Capone built a hideaway on 400 acres surrounding a small lake, lacked a chef who could prepare Italian cuisine. He persuaded Marco Polo to settle nearby, start a restaurant and then work for him when he was in residence at the compound. It helped that Mr. Capone underwrote the costs of the tiny restaurant and sent his minions there to eat."

"Is it still there?" asked Darius.

I zoned out while Marco told about Al Capone's arrest, then his grandfather's move to Little Bohemia, the lodge used by John Dillinger and his gang until the FBI raided it. Then the part about opening the sporting goods store, and Lac du Flambeau reservation where he and his brother hung out with the native kids at Indian Beach. As olive skinned Italians, they could pass. The oft-told story bored me now. All I could think of was my coin. It matched the coin in Eliza's great great-grandmother's portrait. What could explain the physical transformation of the portrait's face? Something had to explain the pulsation in my hand. I believe in science. But do I believe in ghosts? A squeak in Chantal's voice interrupted my reverie.

"Passing? A white kid wanting to pass for colored? That's a new one on me." Her eyes locked onto Marco's.

"Well, we were kids and wanted to play with our friends. All the action back then was at Indian Beach on Big Crawling Stone Lake, a very deep lake especially around the big stone. That's where Capone's men dumped all his getaway cars, stolen cars, anything that could incriminate him. In wintertime, his stooges would cut holes in the ice and push the cars in. All those sunken cars made excellent reefs that collect all sorts of fish." Marco studied the faces around him and shrugged.

"You believe that?" asked Chantal, "About the cars being dumped?"

"Absolutely. You don't grow up around the mob without seeing things, knowing things. Heck, we are a family who worked for, cooked for, the mob. You see everything but learn to keep your mouth shut." Marco added, "As for the fishing, it's still one of the best fishing lakes in the area, especially around the big stone."

Darius leaned toward Jean Louis, "Do you believe all that?"

"I think I'm safer if I do," said Jean Louis, "but I think I'd like to try fishing in Big Crawling Stone Lake once to see if it is as good as Marco says. Say, I've heard that Al Capone used to come down here to Grayton Beach. Bobby, is that so?"

Bobby heard his name and turned his chair toward us. "Yeah, it's true alright. Capone had a bunker in Grayton Beach, the better to run his bootlegging operations in the South. And the grandson of his love child with a woman from Freeport about a half hour north of here, works at the hardware store up there."

"See, I knew it," said Jean Louis, nodding to everyone.

Marco poked me in the side. "Where are you?"

With a shrug I pointed toward the portrait in the adjacent room. "Eliza looks just like her great great-grandmother. I find that eerie." Everyone at the table turned to catch a look.

Eliza slid onto a side chair and pulled up at our table. "How's everyone over here? What are y'all talking about?"

"Your old family portrait," said Dana.

"Oh, you mean my great great-grandmother's portrait in there? That's Eliza Powell," she said. "Her people hailed from Kent, England, arriving in South Carolina in the late 1700s. They migrated to the area that became Bullock County, Alabama, at the dawn of the 1800s where my ancestral uncles and fathers are said to have brought the farm out of the state of nature. The town of Union Springs grew up in the middle of plantation country by the 1830s."

"What's it like there now?" Dana asked. "I travel in parts of Alabama; it's near my sales territory."

"It is still a sleepy town but now in the midst of corporate-owned farms instead of plantations. The same but different. It's an architect's heaven. The oldest existing home, the Hunter-Anderson home dates to 1843. It's a yellow, wood clapboard house, only two and a half rooms, with simple white filigree and a small porch."

"Are there any big houses?" asked Marie Justine.

"There's Alabama's finest surviving example of Moorish Revival style built by Sterling Foster also in 1843. It's a two story foursquare frame house with thick columns. It has onion-shaped arches built in between pillars forming a fixed shade in the second-story balcony, which were great fun to hide behind. Friends of our family lived there," Eliza explained.

"What about your family house?" asked Chantal.

"Looted and burned. The Moorish house escaped because it was closer to town. Most of the Powell family is buried in Oak Hill Cemetery, along with the Rainer clan, also original settlers of Union Springs. The Old City Cemetery just behind the Trinity Episcopal Church contains the graves of Union and Confederate soldiers, at the corner of Prairie and Blackmon Avenue," she added.

"So your father's family has a street named after them too? That's pretty impressive," said Mario, "But why?"

"The Blackmon claim to fame is from Colonel Homer Blackmon, famous from the Indian Wars of the 1830s. Union Springs has had a Blackmon Avenue for years but I don't know when it started," she said with a shrug.

As she spoke, it occurred to me that she more than anyone here in the room could claim the title, blueblood Southerner. With a street named for a plantation family's famous ancestor colonel who shooed the indigenous people off the land only to replace them with Negro slaves fresh off the boats, she belonged to the oldest Old South. I wondered what might run through Chantal or Darius' minds when they hear tales of antebellum times. Eliza told me once that her great great-grandmother never believed in paper money so she kept the family treasury in gold and silver, preferably British sovereigns. She added almost as an afterthought this quirk probably saved the family fortune. A fortune built on slave labor, I thought but never spoke out loud to her. What's the point?

The din of chitchat from the other tables grew louder and suddenly clashed with our own. It broke my reverie. I could hear Glen Royal clicking his hook on his wine glass, quite a feat a few glasses later when he gets a bit smiley as he always does. The hook is his resistance to convention, his statement of no regret that he blew off his own hand with cheap pyrotechnics one Fourth of July. He told me so once, when I asked him if he'd lost the hand in the Vietnam War or first Iraq war. "Naw," he snarled, "just stupid human tricks."

Although Brenda wants him to get a prosthetic hand, Glen prefers the notoriety that comes with the hook. "They all know me," he said, "The Realtor with the hook."

Before long, a few of us cleared the plates. Adelaide and Reese went to work distributing the evening's dessert. They served small square plates with a wedge of persimmon tart and a scoop of homemade mint ice cream. Each table received a tray of thimble cookies. I begged off dessert because of the ice cream and planned to take just a taste of Marco's tart. Jean Louis cringed at the sight of the persimmon but Marie Justine gave him the "stop it now" squint.

Once dessert is served, the evening closes quickly. I pulled Marco with me to look once more at Eliza Powell's portrait. I lightly touched the tarot cards on the table half expecting them to feel hot. They were, instead, fragile and cool. As we stood others began to collect around us.

Wilson joined us, explaining that only recently had they acquired the portrait from one of Eliza's relatives. Fern and Bobby stood behind them, and Brantley Vernon stood next to me. Consuela and Guillermo remarked that she looked burdened as matriarchs often were, but still had kind eyes. Before I could say anything, Marco saw it. He whispered to me, "It looks familiar." I nodded.

"I'll ask Eliza about it tomorrow."

"Ask me what? You two are in cahoots about something." Eliza leaned on me.

"That coin your grandmother is wearing. What is it? Does it mean anything?"

"I don't know really," said Eliza.

"I found one like it at the beach a few weeks ago. It has the same picture of a turtle and then some numbers on the back. It is amazing to see it in the portrait." I noted the faces surrounding me and immediately regretted my words. Wilson Garrett, Bobby Carlyle, Brantley Vernon and Colin Coffee, who had just slipped in, did not smile. They exchanged glances between themselves. "Why the looks? Why the silence?"

"No harm intended, Harley. It's that, these days people recover junk from the beach all the time so finding something that may be historically significant is highly unlikely," said Wilson.

"It's rare that Civil War treasures get loose because they are generally well protected by those who appreciate them," said Brantley, "Wouldn't you say so Bobby?"

"Yeah, the real thing is hard to come by these days. Take that skull those kids found on the beach a few weeks ago. You know right away that's not some unknown Rebel soldier. Been a long time since the war," said Bobby slapping Brantley on the back. He turned away from the portrait, "Wilson, didn't I tell you this Malbec's the best thing to come down the pike lately?" A snort escaped him.

"Yes, sir, it is," he agreed. The two men walked out onto the piazza toward the bar, joined by Colin and Brantley.

Marco tugged at my skirt and gave me the "let's go" look. I went to the kitchen to retrieve my bowl and Eliza grabbed my arm. "Don't let those old Civil War buffs scare you," she said. "They close ranks when any Yankee shows too much interest in their games." We said our good-byes and the Dells reminded us all that they were hosting the next month.

When we had locked our door for the night, I went to my

jewelry box where the gold coin now rested on a tiny red satin pillow. No doubt the turtle symbolized something, and the numbers had to be clues. I shut the box.

Marco turned off the lights and let moonbeams enter the room. In the shadows I slid under the covers to the warm chest and secure arms of my sweetheart and kissed him good night. I decided to launch a quest to identify the coin and to lay claim to it. It would begin the next morning. Curiously, I felt energized even though I was sleepy. Thankfully, no haunting images from my Cairo past visited me, but the bright face of Eliza Powell came to me as I drifted off to sleep. She almost seemed alive.

Menu

Smoked Tuna Dip served on Endive

Billini with Figs & Warm Brie drizzled with Raspberries

* * *

Baby Greens with Pine Nuts and Apple Shavings

Twice Baked Goat Cheese Potatoes

Autumnal Roasted Vegetables

* * *

Beef Tenderloin with mushrooms in Madera sauce

* * *

Chocolate Pecan Pie with Bourbon Whipped Cream

Buttermilk Lemon Cake with Pineapple-orange Glaze

* * *

Cabernet

October

Over the next few days I played and replayed Supper Club in my head. The portrait staring at me, alive with pink skin and rosy cheeks. The colors of vitality. Those same seconds my hand felt crowded with two pulses throbbing in a space only designed for one. Something weird had happened.

We left before I thought to ask Eliza if she had her great great-grandmother's coin necklace in her possession. If she did, surely, she would have said so that night. Or would she? Sometimes Southerners hoard family secrets even from each other, or so said Eliza to me once upon a time.

Even if coins can be lost over time, apparently peculiar greetings with secret codes can live on, alive and well in the Deep South. What would possess Bobby, Brantley, Wilson and Colin to flash long dead gang symbols to each other at Supper Club? Those middle-aged men looked silly making secret handshakes. Their indifference to my discovery of the coin only confirmed that even after all these years of Southern living we were still considered foreigners.

As much as Marco and I participated in our community, we would always be the couple from Chicago who moved to the Deep South where social layers remain obscure, networks inaccessible and actions alien to us. We think we live in the New South except when we are reminded that the Old South has not surrendered. Dixie is everywhere, from the food, which we love, to the Confederate flags, which we don't. Her admirers continue on and to find them in the 30-A Supper Club is no surprise. Their slamming me as a mere tourist with found junk made the affront personal. Ridicule only stokes the fires of anger. Always curious, now I was angry too. This was a scary combination.

With no time to waste, I forged ahead into the arcane world of historic coins. Bit by bit, various references indicated key attributes that were missing on the coin itself. It lacked the marks of currency for any sovereign nation. No state symbols, seals or royal profiles were visible on either side. No monetary values like 5 shillings, or 10 cents or 20 francs were present. No discrete border rimmed the edge. The coin's edges were buffed in a style more commonly found in decorative medallions used as jewelry. I suspected it had been minted privately for a specific purpose. The numbers engraved on the back could mean anything.

By any measure, my next online search was a flop. The symbolic meaning of a turtle brought up limitless articles and sites about feng shui. I did find a good bargain for a turtle sitting on top of gold coins, a funny looking thing on Ebay, but resisted buying it.

Surfing "American Civil War money" under various titles, ranging from the War of Northern Aggression to "the recent unpleasantness," improved my aim. After reading a few, I understood that Southern society was willing to support the cause but scared it could end up broke. Despite the nationalistic call for financial allegiance, some families secretly hoarded their gold, which made perfect sense, as the paper money issued by the Confederacy was merely an IOU. Trusting that you could one day cash the bills back in for gold or silver coins meant you also had to have a winning bet as to which government would win the war. You were either double lucky or double unlucky. The Confederate States of America never created its own coinage for mass circulation and no secret stash of gold bullion a la Fort Knox ever existed. As the war dragged on, any available metals were sent to the war effort and a coin shortage developed, not-withstanding Eliza Powell the great great-grandmother. This tidbit of information, made me rethink her personal stash of gold and silver. Perhaps the great great-grandmother's preference for keeping the family gold meant she could foresee the future. Maybe other families hoarded coins too. Maybe they knew each other.

I leaned back in my office chair and watched the white oaks sway in the breeze. The community college campus hugged the corner of two busy thoroughfares at the outskirts of Panama City. Cars sped by along the far side of the parking lot, past haggard trees and run-down, abandoned restaurants. The seedy motel next door always had a vacancy sign even when the parking lot was full. I could see everything and nothing. Without looking away, I grabbed a few M&M almonds from my stash and ate them one by one.

I imagined Southern belles and dashing beaus, kissing beneath a tree unaware that Daddy or Uncle had stashed gold beneath its gnarly roots. My mind filled with stereotyped images courtesy of *Gone With The Wind*, and I wondered about other wartime hoarders of gold or silver. What if they knew each other? Surely Eliza's great great-grandmother shared her doubts and fears about the war with like-minded friends. She could not have been the only one. There had to be others.

What were her networks? Nodes and ties, values and visions, likes and dislikes. I loved this kind of talk. If Sherlock Holmes could untangle the webs of Victorian social life to expose the villains, surely a sociologist could troll the Old South networks to identify a gold coin. But I couldn't do this alone. Eliza, Southerner and friend, would have to help. She had the access and belonged to the networks. She was the Old South.

On my way to class, a Confederate flag caught my eye in the corner of a poster on the hallway bulletin board. Ian Wilkes, the John C. Calhoun Professor of American History celebrated for his expertise on the Civil War, and infamous for his endless supply of Hawaiian shirts, would be presenting a public lecture the next day. This fifty-something professor, tall with youthful, wavy sun-bleached surfer hair, held the one endowed chair in the college. Our paths rarely crossed but we shared some committee work a while back. "Wrapping up the Confederacy," his entitled presentation, might just help my quest.

*

The next morning's sunlight arrived slowly, now a sign of autumn's reign. Marco swung the Thrillmobile into the driveway and parked.

"Hi darlin'." He kissed me on the lips, lingering a bit. "What a night."

"Busy, eh?"

"Yeah. Not many cases, but complicated ones." He gulped a glass of grapefruit juice.

"Will you be fishing later on?" I slid a plate with an English muffin across the countertop to him.

"Have to try the new reel. Death to fishes!"

"Remember, I'll be late tonight. The Ian Wilkes' lecture. About the Civil War era." I swung my computer bag over my shoulder, leaned over and gave Marco a quick peck on the cheek. "See you. Death to fishes!"

I sped along 30-A wondering about Ian Wilkes, long the target of speculation by faculty and students. He had no family or pet according to a colleague, played no discernible sports, and was very matter of fact with everyone. Some students found him distant, preoccupied, or even cold. Still, his classes were sought after because the students considered him fair.

Once, I saw him at a hardware store wearing hunters camouflage overalls, with deep lines scrunched into his forehead, lips pulled tight. He walked with a military quickstep gait and disappeared into an aisle of tools and gadgets. Around the college community, his focus remained squarely on teaching and scholarly work, the business of history, despite the frivolous shirts and sexy hair.

My morning was busy with student meetings and a seminar. I spent part of the afternoon working on an article, the rest of it immersed in the dilemma Starr Elliott had with her MI6 informant and lover. It was not going too well and I felt great empathy for her. You want things you can't have, and have things you don't want.

The alert alarm on my cell phone rang, reminding me of the time, fifteen minutes before Ian Wilkes' lecture. I marked my place and tucked Starr Elliott deep into my briefcase. Time to go. I arrived at the larger than needed lecture hall and noticed the students had spread out like sheep on a hillside. My favorite seat is on the center aisle, way up in the last row. Watching people enter a room and choose a seat amuses me for some reason. I almost fell out of mine when Meg Coffee walked in and took a seat in the first row, near the center of the room.

What was a late-forties frump originally from Kinston, Alabama, sporting dyed red hair, doing at a Civil War lecture at the community college? The local paper had hailed her as the best early education teacher in the Walton County school system for kids with special needs, but a Civil War enthusiast? What next?

She and Colin lived in the swanky Watercolor neighborhood one street off 30-A. In that one night at Supper Club she must have mentioned at least half a dozen times that hers was a Kinston, Alabama, family. It is a uniquely old Southern habit, all this ancestor worship. My people. From this town or that town, this region or that region, you'd think they were all Shintoists. I sat back to enjoy the show. Surely something would happen once the cool Professor Ian Wilkes walked in.

Something did happen. He stopped directly in front of her and performed the little dance, the same dance I saw at Supper Club. So swiftly executed you'd miss it if you hadn't been closely watching. He added a slight bow to the greeting, as if in extreme honor to Meg Coffee. She struggled to stand from the squishy theater seat. She shook his hand in the palms out and flat style with her right hand while hiking up the back of her jeans skirt with her left. Could they be in the same gang? What was this group? I lowered my head and sank into my seat to avoid detection.

"Hi, Dr. McBride," a student said. She crossed in front of me and sat down a couple seats away. So much for keeping a low profile. Then two more of her classmates arrived and climbed over me. Still, Meg had not seen me although Ian Wilkes no doubt did.

"Today's story deals with how each Confederate general or politician in charge reacted when they each came to the full realization that epic tragedy had descended upon them," said Ian Wilkes. He nodded towards me. "With maps and pictures, we will learn how the various Confederate leaders passed around the news that the last gasp of the glorious enterprise of secession had passed into eternity, and that they should save themselves. Some hid, some were arrested by Union troops, and some fled to Brazil."

Brazil? I leaned forward to focus on the map showing the route such a voyage might take. Professor Wilkes paced back and forth, weaving the themes of lost hope, lost dreams, and lost lives into a tapestry of despair. "The failure of the Confederacy occurred in its hapless execution of the war," he said, "not because the core belief in stronger local government bandied about under the rubric of 'states rights' was inauthentic. But to hide the atrocity of slavery under this slogan was immoral. Support for slavery became a fatal distraction to the secessionist aim of the Southern states. The Confederacy should have jettisoned slavery first. Get rid of it. Make it a non-issue. Then a clear agenda of states' rights might have led to the desired secession."

Potent stuff for an afternoon lecture at a community college. Why wasn't he teaching at some Ivy League school or some big Southern university? He stopped pacing and scanned the room with his bright blues eyes. The Hawaiian shirt moved like a cassock, flowing just enough that the pink flamingos waltzed with the palm trees. He tapped the slide on screen using an old-fashioned wooden pointer, a slim cane topped with an ax head, not a laser pointer in sight. The history professor using an antique struck me as quaint.

Meg Coffee sat still but her head followed him back and forth like a spectator at a tennis match. I knew we'd meet at Supper Club next week, but to avoid the risk of meeting her today, I left as soon as the final words were spoken. I had no doubt that Professor Wilkes saw me leave and if that left him wondering about my sudden interest in his specialized world of the 19th century American South, all the better. I had chummed the water. Marco, my fisherman, would be proud.

The next morning, I opened my email in the kitchen with one hand on my laptop, and the other petting Tulip. Marco had already left for the hospital and my first class started in late morning. First up, a message from Patricia Dell about Supper Club next week. Could I make autumnal roasted vegetables? Yes, I can, I answered right away. The best part of going to the Dell's house is the limitless supply of smoked tuna dip, best in the universe and only available at Cocoons, their very own deli store.

I scrolled down the list and spotted a message from Professor Wilkes. "Noticed you at the lecture yesterday, please stop by my office anytime. Best, Ian." Best to you. I closed the computer and went off to school.

Earlier that morning I had held the coin in my hand. I traced the back of the turtle with my finger and studied the numbers on the flip side. It felt warm and alive, not cool as expected. I put it back on the tiny satin pillow in my jewelry box. An errant breeze passed through the room, which unnerved me because the windows were not open. Even Daisy raised her head with ears pulled back in the alert position. Uneasiness had taken hold of me ever since I noticed the similar coin in the portrait. My coin had journeyed from land to sea and back again. What story could be told if only I could recover its identity? And recover it I would.

Professor Wilkes' e-mail raised hopes that my quest for answers might be a short one. My secretary, one of the school's gossip queens, had confided to me that, Hunkamonga, her pet name for him, was born and bred in the Deep South. His people came from very old families in Georgia. "He's a confident man," she said, "You know the type. Probably a Special Forces soldier."

It made no difference to me. Would he grant me access to the obscure world of the Old South where history had never died and its ghosts might still kill? I'd heard from Brantley Vernon that the South is haunted with vengeful, unreconciled spirits from the War. "There was a lot of hate in that War," he said.

I rapped on Professor Wilkes' closed office door. He did not answer, so I left. To pass the time before my lecture I surfed the Net for roasted vegetables recipes. A quest for the meaning of the coin could take a long time, but Supper Club was next week. The term "roasted" threw me off, as I did not have a clue how to roast a root vegetable. As much as I love to eat, I escaped the gourmet cooking spell but at the price of terrible insecurity when it comes to cookery.

A knock on the door startled me. The door, already opened a crack, swung slowly inward but the hem of a shirt with a 1950s sedan and a Route 66 sign gave him away.

"Please come in, Ian. Have a seat."

"Hi, Harley. I took the liberty of stopping by since I was in your neck of the woods." He used the same cane from his lecture to ease onto the chair. "I messed up my knee in a fall while rock climbing. It's better, but it catches now and then."

"Rock climbing?" I said. "Where are rock faces around here in the flatlands of the beach?"

"Oh, it wasn't here. It was at a military post in North Carolina. Not actually rocks, but that's what we call it," he said.

"Just in case you have to scale a building wall or tower, is that it?"

"Yes, actually. Something like that. Now, what brought you to my lecture? The Civil War is somewhat off the beaten track for a sociologist last I heard."

He scanned my office taking in the old Parti Quebequois posters from my mother and antique maps of Limerick, the

McBride ancestral home in Ireland. My bookshelves were jammed with the usual sociology canon of classic theorists and landmark works for the specialties taught at a community college. My bailiwick consisted of women's studies, work and occupations, medical sociology and the textbooks for the introductory classes of 101 and 102.

"Are you about to add historical sociology to all this?" He turned his intense eyes back to me.

"Don't worry, I am not stepping on your territory. To answer your question, I found a gold coin in the gulf back in August and then saw a similar coin in a portrait of a woman, dating to the Civil War era. I thought you might know something of coins or symbols on coins from the antebellum South."

"Oh, maybe I do, maybe I don't. What's it worth to you? I don't give away my secrets for free." He tapped the cane on the floor gripping the ax head between his thumb and forefinger.

"The sheer honor of working with me should be enough. I'm the hottest sociologist in these parts." Are we flirting, I wondered, aghast at the thought?

"Pretty hot, I must agree. Always wanted an excuse to work with the teacher whose classes run a waiting list."

"Oh yeah? Well, here's your chance. Now about the coin."

"The coin, okay, the meaning of the symbol and why it could have been either common or uncommon enough to be featured in a portrait." He ran a hand through his thick blonde hair. "Do you have it with you, the coin?" He turned slightly and the light landed on a shiny pin almost hidden in the Route 66 sign shaped into his shirt collar. The pin looked like a coin, a copper penny but it was slightly larger, more the size of an Indian Head nickel. It had a swirl on it. Like a snake.

"No, but I have a picture of it." I took out a four by six photo of the coin, highlighting the turtle shape embossed on one side and handed it to him. His fingers brushed against mine, firm and slightly calloused. Working hands. A delinquent rush of heat spread from my hand to my shoulders and startled me.

"A turtle, you have here. What is on the back?"

"Numbers, but I forgot to bring a photo of that side. The shape and size of the numbers are too deliberate in design to denote value such as a nickel or shilling. Perhaps the numbers have some other meaning?"

"Some other meaning?" His blue eyes took hold of mine.

"Yes, you know, like a membership button, a fraternity or sorority pin, where everyone in the group has the same button, badge, or in this case, a coin. If it meant membership, then maybe you'd know of such groups and could suggest a direction for me." I leaned back in my chair. "I love a good mystery. Maybe it was a secret women's group during the Civil War."

"Only a sociologist would think of group membership, but in all honesty, I am not aware of any secret women's group active during the Civil War. That doesn't mean one didn't exist, you understand. The biggest secret group of Confederate men was the Masons. It wasn't particularly secret but its members used secret codes in their rules, meetings and in communications with each other. But, the turtle, as depicted on your coin, is not a Masonic symbol. I am afraid I am not much help." Ian Wilkes shrugged his broad shoulders and tapped the cane. "I am curious about the numbers. That might be a better clue. I'd be happy to take a look at them."

"I didn't know the Masons were involved in Confederate affairs. The nation's founding fathers, yeah, but the Confederacy?"

He gave me a sly smile. "Hey, we're here to learn. You and many others would be surprised to know that Freemasonry actually served as an important network among those who intended to lead the secession. Well-known guys of the Civil War era, Albert Pike and John C. Breckinridge, the vice president under Buchanan, held key positions within Confederate Circles and the elite inner circle of the Scottish Rite Masonry of Charleston. Together they, among others, orchestrated events to deliver a pre-war aim of electing Lincoln which would then serve as a justification for secession by the Southern states."

Much to my amusement, Ian Wilkes had revved up like the Supper Club civil war groupies, nostalgic for historic leaders they never met, who wallow in their legacies for a vicarious thrill. His performance of the ritualistic footwork and greeting to Meg Coffee, the same as performed by the Wilson Garrett, Brantley Vernon, Bobby Carlyle and Colin Coffee ensemble struck me as more than coincidental. It had all the makings of a pattern.

A sociologist's first clue that she might be onto something, particularly something she knows nothing about, occurs at that one pivotal moment she realizes that she's watching the same show over and over. Swap out the actors, but the actions are the same in similar settings. It begs the question why were these people greeting only each other like that and no one else? The short answer in my head was that they belonged to the same group. What group and for what purpose had yet to be discovered.

This was not sociological research, however, and I really only wanted to identify the gold coin for curiosity's sake. Still, you can't turn off how you think, and I already am on record as curious plus half. So I plunged on with one more question.

"Ian, how do you know Meg Coffee? You greeted her with the same, shall I say gang symbols, that her husband used at our Supper Club last month."

"Her husband, Colin, and I went to college together years ago. I've known Meg for years. She's a big Civil War buff. We go to battle re-enactments now and then. We've been practicing Confederate patriotic greetings that will be used in a new one in Ohio. You know Meg?"

"Just met Meg and Colin last month. They have recently joined our 30-A Supper Club, a little group that meets once a month for dinner and conversation. I'll see them next week for our October meeting." I glanced at my watch. "I have class soon."

"Sure. Say, if you'd bring me a photo of the numbers maybe I can decipher them. May I keep this photo? I might run across something now that you have intrigued me in your treasure hunt."

"Yes, of course. Thanks for stopping by. To be continued."
We smiled at each other. He shook my hand firmly and his eyes met mine with a half wink. We tried to size each other up, to anticipate our motives and our next moves. He was not sure of me. I did not believe for a minute that he didn't recognize the symbol on the coin. His copper coin pin pointed me to my next Internet search. He slid out to the hall, his black and white check Vans sneakers silent against the linoleum tile floor, the John C. Calhoun Professor of American history. Just who was John C. Calhoun anyway? Somehow it all mattered, but I couldn't say why. Getting to know the handsome, clever Ian Wilkes might not be half bad either.

I shifted mental gears during my slow commute home and conjured up a list of vegetables for supper club. Colorful, tasty, easy. New potatoes, red carrots, purple onions, turnips, golden beets, and garlic. When I pulled up to our driveway, Pigalle, our mechanical porch flamingo made of tiny pink lights was lit. His head and wings lifted and lowered in rhythm. That's our sign to the neighbors that we are receiving, but when Marco Polo is home alone, he lights Pigalle for me.

As I thought, Marco had spent the day fishing, but none were keepers. "You'll never guess who I saw at Seagrove Village Market huddling over their burgers like convicts so no one could hear them."

"Who?"

"Wilson Garrett and Bobby Carlyle."

"Could you hear them?" I sipped the generous glass of Zinfandel he poured for me.

"Of course. They didn't notice me in my fishing hat. They argued over gold coins that might match yours."

"Matched? What does that mean?"

"What I gathered is they were shocked to know about a second coin, the one you found. Whatever you said about Eliza's great great-grandmother has them undone." Marco stroked Tulip, who had jumped up on his lap, from her head to her tail.

"Well, if they could identify it from the turtle symbol alone, why didn't they say something? Why the silence?" I replayed Professor Wilkes' charming ignorance in my head and wondered about him too.

"Darling, I don't know why they wouldn't be excited about your coin since they obviously know something about its meaning or origin, but you'll just have to wait until they offer something, if ever. It wouldn't be cool to admit I eavesdropped."

"The coin is just a curiosity. Why the mystery?"

"Probably just two guys with too much money and too much time on their hands. They can afford to dabble in Civil War nostalgia while the rest of us do real work that takes up real time," Marco said.

"Which real work were you referring to, the fishing work or the medical work? Your October tan betrays the hours you spend on the windy surf, you know."

"Oh, don't trip me up on those definitions of work. You know what I mean."

"Do I? Maybe you should explain it to me." I smoothed the collar of his polo shirt and dusted off the sand stuck to his shirttail.

"It might take some time." Marco picked up my hand and kissed it. Then he walked out to the porch and unplugged the flamingo. Pigalle went dark. Clasping my waist, he pulled me out of the kitchen turning off the remaining lights one by one. I could hear Daisy's and Tulip's motors purr as they remained motionless on the couch watching our retreat. I turned my attention to Marco who had some explaining to do. It was a good explanation.

*

Thursday arrived, a perfect Panhandle October day. Supper club would assemble under a harvest moon. Vegetables were spread out before me as if ready for a cookbook photo shoot. The new potatoes were quartered but still in their reddish peel; the beets were chopped into squares, the red onions split into round purple rings, the turnips were cut into slim strips, and the red carrots I chopped like coins. I hesitated on the number of garlic cloves. Not everyone appreciates that pungent spice. Chopping had taken forever. No wonder I passed up television's cooking channel. Who's going to prep all my ingredients and put them neatly into little round glass bowls, ready to go? At five o'clock I started to cook. Marco strode in from work just as the first skillet met fire. After several skillets, first to parboil, then to brown in olive oil, I spread single layers of veggies on several cookie sheets and baked them for about 20 minutes.

When it was all said and done, the vegetables scattered on a broad shallow serving tray reminded me of flashy gingham print fabrics found in craft shops. I tucked some sprigs of parsley along the edge of one side, which fluttered when the tray moved. Marco picked out a couple of carrots and popped them into his mouth despite my protest. Off to Supper Club we went, Marco in a yellow linen guayabera shirt and me with a red blouse and black capris. At least we didn't clash with the roasted root vegetables.

Everyone showed up for Supper Club that night. The Dells' house has been a landmark in Seagrove for years. Patricia and Spencer grew up locally in Point Washington, five miles north. As Panhandle kids, they vaguely knew each other. Cupid's arrow struck later. Patricia groans when she tells the tale of meeting Spencer at a bar in Gainesville where he played with his band Five Mile Backup. "It's so lame," she said, "I was flirting with the guitar player, and he bought me a beer. I didn't recognize him at all. When I realized he was this kid on the track team in high school I barely remembered, well, just my luck. 'From jock to rock', I'd tease him. Anyway, here we are back home but at least on the beach."

Sitting squarely on County Road 30-A , their yellow clapboard box faces the beach and the one high rise condo on the other side of the road built before height limits were set. The two story building with the painted marquee "Cocoons" has a blue neon "open" sign hanging in the front window and an exterior staircase in back that leads to the second floor front door of their home.

If you walk in from the small parking lot out front to the

first level, deli delights waft through the air. Kegs of fresh green or Kalamata olives of all sizes floating in brine, exotic cheeses, racks of wine, a shelf with every hot sauce known to mankind, and their signature smoked tuna dip tempt you seven days a week, hours varying by the season. For the carnivorous inhabitants along the 30-A corridor, Cocoons is the place for ribs, slow cooked in the family's secret barbecue sauce. The black cylinder smoker sits out in back of the building which Spencer fires up with full or half slabs. Sometimes the wind carries the white smoke like incense to us locals living nearby, proclaiming that a new batch of ribs are at hand. It takes less than two minutes for us to drive to Cocoons from our house. I could already taste the smoked tuna dip and was grateful for our quick ride.

Marco tucked the car into a wedge of space near the cold smoker. Others already lined up at the staircase and began the climb single file like folks marching up the stairs toward church. Patricia Dell greeted us at the door, sporting a chiseled coif that was sheered in the back and bobbed in the front. It suited her high cheekbones and wide brown eyes. She was the hottest stylist at Roland, and lucky for me, knew how to cut curly hair. She could transform any ugly duckling into a swan and there were ducks aplenty around here, according to her. "I'll never be out of business as long as women use a 35-year-old mirror," she said. "You know what that is, don't you? When you look in the mirror you see yourself as 35, no matter if you are ten, fifteen, even twenty years older."

Patricia hums pop tunes in the salon. She listens to her clients, brush stroke after brush stroke, like a therapist. They hash and rehash their lives snug in the black leather hydraulic beauty shop chair. She offers no advice unless it has to do with hair. I have seen her stop and take a deep breath but then she shakes out her arms and begins again, comb and scissors, click, click, click. Chatter begins anew, or maybe a new tune. I could not do her job.

Tonight she wore an edgy black jacket over black and white checked trousers. Although tan, she rarely catches the sun, since skin care products are her passion and is always testing a new one.

Her new favorite bronzing gel with aloe gave her a golden glow. She waved me toward the sideboard where I placed my platter.

Eliza Blackmon whispered as she gave me with a hug. "Something is going on. Last night, the coin necklace from the portrait appeared in my dreams."

"How strange."

Eliza linked arms with me, "Any progress on your coin?"

"Not yet. You have any ideas?"

"We should talk, but not here." She squeezed my arm and hesitated as if troubled by a secret that she should not share. Before I could coax her to disclose any more, Brenda Royal scuffed over to us in four-inch espadrilles with ballerina bows tied at her ankles.

"Hey y'all," she said. "Isn't this place darling? As many times as I had passed by this building I had never imagined anyone lived here. I remember the first time I came. It blew me away, all the chintz slipcovers, the candles, the antique rocker, and the guitars. Did you see Spencer has a Gibson and a Fender Stratocaster?"

"Haven't you heard him play? He's brilliant," I said.

"No, does he play around here?"

"At the Red Bar, with his band Five Mile Backup." Eliza and I stared at each other in disbelief. Brenda stood there utterly clueless but her fail-safe automatic pilot kicked in and rescued her. She gave us a demure, "How did I miss that?" She glanced around the room to find a path for a quick exit.

Her aerobics job demanded hours of physical workouts to which her dedication was legendary in the exercise crowd. She lived for the endorphin rush, or so she told me once. "I only feel good when I am sweaty." Tonight she did not sweat a drop even while admitting she never made the connection between Spencer and the popular local rock band. She found her getaway with the excuse of getting more wine and teetered away with tiny geisha steps because her skintight blue jean mini skirt encased her thighs like a paper towel tube. Her chestnut hair, tipped by Patricia, glittered in the light. I studied Glen's puppy dog eyes as they followed every jaunty move of her tight derriere. He slouched half on a bar stool, steel hook pinched around the stem of a wine glass. His face looked full of story as he vogued the good old boy Talladega attitude, wearing buzzed hair, stone washed jeans and his shirttails out. On other occasions he'd ask me about a stock car race the way us Chicagoans speak of baseball as in, "How 'bout those Cubbies?" But for him it was "How 'bout that Junior?" NASCAR did not impress me, being a Formula girl myself, but we got on famously. It is so much more fun to be adversaries than to agree on all that stuff. Still, that night Glen had left his light heart at home, bringing instead the heavy aura of discontent.

Before I could speak to him, Meg Coffee put her fleshy arm around me. "I understand we know someone in common."

"Ah, let's see, Professor Wilkes."

"Yes, he's almost kin. Colin, Ian and I go way back to college days at the University of Georgia when we were young and beautiful." Meg touched the back of her hair with her hand and put a hand on her thick waist, attempting a fashion model's pose.

"Oh you're still beautiful." I awarded her the compliment she sought. "And Ian is quite charming too, by the way." Immediately I regretted the offhand compliment to him. She didn't need to know what I thought of him.

"Oh, I'll be sure and tell Ian you said that. He tells me you are interested in Civil War coins," she said.

"Well, one coin, actually. I found it on the beach."

"What is the Civil War connection?" She peered at me with a beauty queen stare.

"I am not sure if there is one. I only noticed it to be similar to a coin worn as a medallion in a portrait of Eliza Blackmon's great great-grandmother that dates to the Civil War era. It's purely a guess."

"Missed that last month. I suppose I was distracted with all the other fuss of Supper Club. Did you know many loyal Southern women offered up their most treasured gold and silver jewelry to the war effort?"

I suddenly noticed she wore a copper pin which had caught the ray from a track light pointed in her direction.

"Yes, but gold and jewelry sacrifices pale in comparison to the sacrifice of beloved sons, husbands or brothers to the whims of civil war. Gold seems to be the least of it, don't you think?" I said.

Meg recoiled as if she was suddenly allergic to something. "So you don't believe in defending yourself, to preserve your own way of life?" A puzzled look covered her face, the unnerved expression of a true believer confronting a pagan.

During this exchange of combative pleasantries, Eliza had stood by in attentive silence soaking in our conversation like sand in a rainstorm. Then she could absorb no more. "What way of life, Meg? A white man's lifestyle built on the backs of Negro slaves? That's no lifestyle to defend. That's one to condemn. And, don't give me any of that states' rights crap either, Meg." Her vehemence surprised Meg who drew her face back into her neck with eyebrows arched, mouth open.

"Excuse me, but is there a war going on around here that I have missed? I thought we were talking about a coin found at the beach." Now that I had managed to stir things up, I was compelled to calm things down. "Come on you two, this war has been over for a long time or so I thought."

Meg shrugged. "We know better than to expose our dirty laundry to newcomers to the South. Arguments over the War are endless among true Southerners and I apologize for this momentary lapse of etiquette on our part to you, a Yankee no less." Meg flashed a patronizing smile towards me. "Now back to the coin, can you make out the symbol on it? Ian said it was not official currency of any type."

"I make out what looks like a turtle, but to date I don't know what a turtle might symbolize." I wished a glass of Zinfandel would suddenly appear. Lady Luck must have heard for Colin Coffee appeared beside me with a glass of red luster courtesy of Marco standing across the room with his glass raised to me.

"A turtle?" said Meg. "A turtle is a symbol of money."

"Money? Who uses a turtle for a symbol of money? That's the first break I've had on this. Meg, you are a gift." I squeezed her soft shoulders. Just as my curiosity reached hyperdrive, all hopes for more information were cruelly dashed. Meg opened her mouth to speak but Colin brusquely interrupted. "Honey, are you boring Miss Harley here with more of that Civil War trivia? Not everyone is as enthralled as you are with antebellum lore and the loss of the Tara lifestyle." We got the message. She was to shut up. I was not to benefit from any disclosure of old Southern secrets.

Colin had assumed a general's posture when he spoke to her. He tensed his cut muscled arms and clenched his jaw over a neck taut with ligaments latched to an erect spine. His physique spoke volumes about his fitness zeal which might have worked for him but clearly was not working for Meg. The steady pull on the buttons of her blouse gave her away. Strangely, I felt sorry for her being tethered to this overbearing prig. I felt fortunate that Marco never calls me on anything I say. He just calls me "his babe."

Meg glanced at Eliza, the silent witness to it all. She pulled Meg toward the kitchen to help salvage what self-respect she still had. "Let's see what our jobs are here tonight. What did you bring?" asked Eliza.

"The wild rice."

"Good, Harley brought the root vegetables that go with it."

Entering the kitchen, we found Adelaide modeling her latest bargain from the Talbot's outlet, a black eyelet tennis skirt trimmed in lime green that goes from court to dinner party. "Of course, you'd never play in this. It's too pretty for that," she said.

"A sporty look without the sport, how clever," I said to the women assembled in the kitchen.

Meg grinned now that she was in safe territory. Dana laughed with gusto, tossing her feathery brown hair to one side. Brenda, holding a serrated knife in her hand, paused in her attack of the sourdough bread to add, "I like your outfit. It's better to look good than to feel good. Of course, that's me, the spike heels girl."

Leaning on the countertop, Adelaide chugged from a glass of wine then peered down at her chest making sure no drops landed on it. She fluffed her skirt and took a deep breath before leaving the kitchen to model elsewhere. Chantal backed in the other doorway carrying a tray with two chocolate pecan pies. Marie Justine followed with a bowl of whipping cream yet to be whipped in one hand, a bottle of bourbon in the other. "Step aside we have work to do." She commanded like a general and occupied the small butcher block table in the corner. Chantal plugged in a mixer. Marie Justine pulled a shot glass out of her pocket, poured a shot of bourbon and handed it to Chantal who tossed it back like a pro.

"That was for the whipped cream," Marie Justine said.

"One for the cook, one for the cream. Hey, that's how we do it in Mobile," said Chantal.

"Are you sure you are not French?"

While the kitchen comedy continued, I heard Consuela call to me. She and Reese McElwain had perched like mourning doves on the ends of a love seat and were surveying the tables. If Alys Beach was one end of the 30-A dwelling continuum, the Dells' home represented the opposite end. Their simple cottage wore close to fifty years of beach front age, humidity, salt, heat and wind, all kept at bay by layers of paint, re-roofing and storm windows. Its iconic Panhandle character keeps loyal customers coming to Cocoons, family after family, generation after generation. Patricia designed the upstairs flat to encourage flopping down into squishy sofas, where you put your feet up on padded ottomans and relax. For tonight's gala, Patricia and Spencer set up two card tables of four, set four places at a coffee table, put four places at the bar, and squeezed the rest at a dining table better suited for six.

Dana found me and said, "Look at this. Patricia can make something out of nothing. Burlap!" She touched the tablecloths. "Then she covers them with a couple of offset red bandanas, tosses in a few white votive candles sitting on sprigs of rosemary and voila! It's fabulous."

"Where are the men?" demanded Consuela. "We cook something nice, put on some sexy clothes, some bling and parfum, and look, they abandon us for each other." Her golden chandelier earrings shimmered in rhythm to the singsong melody of her lament. "I bothered to pull on a Spanx for tonight just so this sheath dress would fit like a kid glove. Harley, go call them in. Your Marco will listen to you."

"Oh, I don't think we should do that," said Reese. "I am sure they have important things to talk about. Men do, you know." The alarm on her face puzzled me. Consuela's eyes opened wide and she waved her hand as if shaking off water.

Now was not the time to launch into a women's empowerment lecture, although several lectures from my spring elective course on feminist theory could have come in handy here. Reese had always been the hesitant type, generally fearful and timid to act without an okay from her husband. In truth we were only acquaintances despite the years of contact in Supper Club. I gave up trying to socialize with her outside of Supper Club long ago. Her litany of do's and don'ts advice sends me running for cover. We could never be close friends because I'm not much for following rules just for the sake of rules. I'm not that insecure.

Dana confronted Reese's fear as she plied us with scoops of smoked tuna dip on endive wedges from the crystal platter on the nearby coffee table. "Sorry Reese, no can do. Those boys out there are talking football or golf, neither of which affects climate change, the damn security of the world, nor Wall Street. So relax, it's not the end of the world. I say we lock the door to the balcony and make them beg to come back." Fierce eyes and smirked lips lit up Dana's girl-next-door face. Her long dancer's neck, the square shoulders, and her plunging neckline could turn heads. I've seen many a head turn her way. In private, Marco calls her the "Siren of Seashell Lane," invoking the name of her street. With a hand on one hip, wine glass in the other, Dana asked, "Where's Patricia? I think this calls for some drastic action."

"Right here," she said, coming from the kitchen. "Those boys out there again? We're just a few minutes from supper. Let's reintroduce ourselves to them. Shall we?"

Dana pulled the sliding screen door back and stepped into the huddle. She called back to us that, yes, both golf and football were the culprits. Then she plowed into the middle of one group where Mario stood and demanded a refill. As if stung by bees, the men stepped back and suddenly looked around in vacant stares to see faces of hostile, abandoned women. As they sought us out, solicitous voices groveling "honey, would you like some more wine?" made them seem sticky.

Marco signaled for me to join him on the balcony. The cool breeze off the gulf smelled lightly of wet salt. The blades of the palms clacked together sounding like a baby's rattle. He asked me if I'd seen anything tonight, and I said no, forgetting for an instant the copper pin on Meg's blouse. We conferred together in the soft tones only lovers' use, trying to surmise some semblance of meaning from the glaring absence of fancy footwork and kooky handshakes between some of the members tonight. We rejoined the crowd who had begun to pick up plates from the table marking the seating arrangement for that night.

Two wine bottles, a Cabernet Sauvignon and a Pinot Grigio, were open on each table amidst the votive lights. Spencer's wine supplier recommended these for the beef tenderloin. The mushrooms and Madera sauce challenged the wine gurus of 30-A Supper Club, according to Bobby Carlyle who concurred with Spencer's apt choices. "This menu needs a wine strong enough to compete but not overwhelm it," he said to Brenda who stood in front of him in the buffet queue.

Perhaps it's my background, growing up in South Side Chicago at my Dad's Irish saloon, but after a couple of glasses most wine tastes the same to me. Of course, I can detect "belly wash" to quote my father, either as beer or wine, but I am a better connoisseuse of beer than wine. Marco is my sommelier.

Meg Coffee scooted in next to me at the table. She leaned toward me and said, "Our vegetables and rice are a hit." She launched into a lengthy diatribe about the community college, asking what was sociology really about since she had heard it was usually subversive and most sociologists were on watch lists. Was I on a watch list? It gave me a headache. Suddenly I felt less sorry for her. Where do you start when you begin to suspect someone is courting you with an ulterior motive? Could she also just be a simpleton trying to act friendly? Although her compliments were a fraction too many, the awe factor a bit too emphatic, I decided to play along and see where it all went. Her knowledge of the turtle symbol had intrigued me, as did Colin's surly rebuke of her. While we engaged in "getting to know you" chatter, I did learn about her career teaching special needs kids, which really requires extraordinary talent. For the time being, I reconsidered my first impression that she was just a clumsy social climber searching for attention.

Soon enough Patricia and Spencer began to pick up finished plates while Chantal delivered plates of lemon cake or the chocolate pecan pie with bourbon whipped cream to the tables. When she placed a plate in front of Darius, he grabbed her hand and squeezed it. She pulled it away and hissed, "Honestly, Darius." Marie Justine stood in the doorway with the bourbon bottle and took requests for an extra splash of bourbon straight to the pie. "Over here, s'il vous plaît." Jean Louis held his plate up for her and said, "A big pour, Chérie." A tendril of hair had fallen out of her chignon. Framed by indirect light she could have stepped out of a John Singer Sargent painting.

Such is the world of 30-A Supper Club. Members reveal and conceal, and sometimes these are the same thing. We all share acquaintance, many of us share friendship. A few of us are close friends. Marco and I bid our thanks and goodbyes and left trooping down the stairs, perplexed by the absence of the ritualized behavior so obvious only the month before. Meg Coffee and Reese McElwain bothered me for their willingness to fold in the presence of their spouses like Angel Trumpets that can only bloom in the scant minutes of special moonlight. Into the shadows they disappeared to survive. Aren't they 21st century women? Don't they have that famous Southern grit?

And, I realized Supper Club alone would not help me find answers to the questions about my coin. Instead, there was something furtive, even obstructive about a few of the members. It was just a coin after all. Did it matter that it might be a Southern coin? I began to feel silly at my own stubborn interest in it. Marco still believed it was worth more investigation and urged me not to give up. I knew he could imagine extraordinary probabilities since he grew up in a land where myths of the gangsters, thugs and hidden loot ran rampant. His trusty reassurance steadied my resolve to dig further.

Tulip and Daisy jumped onto the bed as Marco set his alarm clock. They found their favorite spots along a hip, aside a knee, mine or his, no matter to the cats. I pulled a tiny reading light from my night stand drawer and the paperback from under the mattress. I clipped them together and opened to the last chapter and snuggled in. What would Starr Elliott, FBI agent, do in a case like this?

Menu

Salmon Mousse in Cucumber Boats

Butternut Squash Soup with Garlic Croutons

* * *

Orange and Red Peppers with Toasted Brazil Nuts and Feta

Broiled New Potatoes with Rosemary and Parmesan

Phyllo-Wrapped Asparagus and Camembert

* * *

Buttermilk and Sunflower Seed Bread

Sage Roasted Game Hen with Orange Cranberry Sauce

* * *

Brown Sugar-Glazed Pumpkin Pie with Vanilla Bean Gelato

***

Rhône or Pinot Noir

November

November mornings are brisk affairs. Tulip snuggled deeper into the down comforter. "Lucky you," I grumbled to the warm cat and rolled out of bed.

Suddenly a crash came from the other side of the bedroom. The pewter dish bounced on the cement floor with a twang, spilling coins in a heap. A few coins rolled away like a starburst. Daisy froze for a few seconds, horrified, then forsook her prey and scampered under the bed.

Our huntress had been chasing a baby salamander that slithered in during the night. Such Panhandle creatures are welcome since they know their way back out and hopefully eat a few bugs along the way. However, if you had a long-haired, fluffy monster with golden eyes chasing you, you'd seek shelter in a crevice somewhere too. So I don't blame the salamander or Daisy for the commotion, but thank them. For the pennies.

Pennies and more pennies, I scooped them up and put them back into Marco's pewter dish. He saves those one cent copper coins in this dish. Copper and more copper. Like Meg Coffee's copper pin. How could I have missed it? There had been a sign. Not only Meg, but Wilson, Bobby, and Colin. I couldn't remember one on Brantley Vernon but I didn't see much of him that night either. They each wore a copper lapel pin with a swirl on it like the one I saw on Professor Wilkes. The swirl could be a snake. There was a connection between them and it had to do with my coin. I could feel it. Just like the soft pulse that has started to fill my palm without warning, then vanishes.

Marco had worked the overnight shift, followed by a staff meeting. It always seemed strange to leave for the college without seeing him, but this was one of those days. While sitting in a long line of traffic, Maria's number lit my cell phone.

"Hey Mom, no one was at home," she said.

"Your dad's not home yet from an overnight shift and I left early because of traffic in which I am currently stuck. Hasn't moved for ten minutes," I replied.

"And you don't like to wait. Well, nothing new here. Your Gamal sent me an e-mail recently about smuggling and INTER-POL. He added how he enjoyed meeting me and sends his regards to you."

"He's not my Gamal. Okay? Anyway, he was always extremely well mannered and a master of protocol. So don't confuse business with friendship here." I smacked the steering wheel with my hand.

"Don't be so sensitive, Mom. I know the culture here. I'm a political anthropologist, fluent in three languages including Arabic. You are not the only social scientist here."

"This is not a competition, sweetie." The traffic began to move.

"Then quit with the attitude. Gamal is highly regarded and his interest in my work is genuine. Is this a problem?"

"For who?" I shifted into third gear and instantly wished I could take back my defensive tone.

"For you. You don't sound like yourself whenever I mention his name," said Maria.

"Don't be silly. There is no issue, no problem. I just want you to be careful. It would kill me if anything happened to you. I'm your mother. I'm supposed to worry about you."

"It's not about you being my mother. Gamal will be working with me in the months ahead. He promised more stories about you and the time when …"

"What stories, what time? Stop poking around in this, or creating something where there isn't anything."

"Mom, I wish you'd be honest with me. What's the deal with Gamal? " said Maria.

"Nothing. Nothing to tell. That's all the honesty you are going to get. Listen, sweetie, the traffic is finally rolling, I've got to go. Call me soon. Sorry about my temper."

"Bye." Maria's number darkened as I closed the phone.

Somehow, I'd have to ratchet down my reaction whenever Maria mentions Gamal. How could it still hurt so much after all these years? A lifetime ago. My fieldwork in Cairo felt prehistoric in today's terms; pre-fax machine, no e-mail, a rare photocopy and then on thermal paper which would fade in time. Back then, we thought a telex was cool. Kids today don't even know what that means. I reached for my iPod sitting on the adapter and turned up Lynyrd Skynyrd's *Free Bird* full blast and escaped to a safe zone.

I stayed there until I reached my office and noticed an envelope taped to the door. I grabbed it off the door and lugged my briefcase onto the desk. I slit open the blank white envelope and unfolded a piece of paper. The words "beware of snakes" was scrawled below a primitive drawing of four snakes twisting around each other. For a moment I smiled because this line is one of several Marco uses when he's feeling frisky. But this creepy note had nothing to do with him.

Who would want to warn or threaten me with an old fashioned handwritten note with a simplistic ink drawn sketch, delivered by foot? The medium is the message, thank you Marshall McLuhan. That's how a sociologist would read it.

After all, a sociologist is a detective and like any good private eye, must procure clues from the margins, the fringes, the very fault lines of society. C.Wright Mills, a sociology rock star, gave us the basic tools of the trade. First, check into the history. Second, scope out the back-stories of the people involved. Third, dissect the institutions like an anatomist. Which parts dominate, which don't, and why.

With Mills and McLuhan in mind plus, the limited clues I had to date, the strange greeting rituals, copper pins, and now a warning about snakes, I understood that the 30-A Supper Club was no longer safe. Any answers about my coin lay beyond it.

So being a 21st century detective, I returned to the Internet, where fact and fiction converge in an endless tussle for hits. Starr Elliott used the Internet like a dagger, cutting away all the fluff to get to all sorts of shadowy places, so why couldn't I? Knowledge is power and for that you risk it all. Even your heart. That's what got her into the predicament with the MI6 agent. I would keep that in mind and be careful of Ian Wilkes. He would not be my MI6 agent.

I trolled Civil War Web sites, link after link, pairing copper coins and snakes, which eventually led to sites about the Copperheads. They were Northerners living in border areas opposed to war against the South, mostly found in today's Midwest and Ohio Valley regions. Identified only by wearing the copper pins embossed with a snake, these localized cells of "copperheads" sought to undermine the stability of Northern society, toward opening up a new front for the South.

Various references suggested they took orders via underground communications from a secret order known as the Knights of the Golden Circle. These ragtag traitors or patriots, depending on your North/South allegiance, disrupted elections, smuggled contraband and even assassinated U.S. military and government officials. Said to be poorly organized in their time, it was thought that the members disbanded and activities ceased by the end of the Civil War. Copperheads today were nothing more than the stuff of legends or had to do with questionable old copper pins scattered about in antique dealers displays. Anyone wearing a copper snake pin today was just nostalgic.

In all fairness, detailed American Civil War history had never reached my top five list. Until now, it hadn't occurred to me that the War's legacy as lived by generations might actually be observable in private customs. Members of my own Supper Club practice them. The War's inheritance had wrapped around descendants of the Old South unevenly in myriad forms of prejudicial laws and customs. Is it pride or pain from the war that still lingers in the deep recesses of wounded psyches that pass unhealed through the generations? Did the uncountable number of Web hyper links to every conceivable fact of the Civil War, from women's work to pirates, from battlefield analysis to Confederate Gatling guns, mean there was still some score to settle?

The phone rang. "It's Eliza." Her voice faded in and out.

"Are you at your office? There's so much interference."

"Oh, it's all this medical equipment and the thick walls. Anyway, could you meet me at Fonville Press at 5 o'clock?"

"Yeah, what's up?"

"Want to talk to you about something, but not at home."

"Everything okay?"

"Oh, yes. See you then. And thanks."

The facts about Civil War Copperheads, Eliza's strange call, and the warning about snakes bothered me. Who but Professor Wilkes and the members of Supper Club knew about my coin? How could this coin be worth a warning about snakes? None of these folks were the type to send me such a silly looking document. Or were they? Should I widen the zone of suspects? What if one of them told someone else who told someone else? If I diagramed Supper Club as the center point, placing Professor Wilkes close by, then a potential suspect could be one, two or even three degrees of separation away. There was no place to start but at the center. But who was the true center?

By mid afternoon, I went to see Professor Wilkes. Copperheads were his bailiwick and he had a copper pin with a snaky swirl on it to boot. He'd likely be a sympathizer, being a Civil War expert from the Old South. What if he was just an eccentric who wore memorabilia? A very cute eccentric at that, but if he didn't know what a turtle meant, surely he would know what a snake meant. Or would he feign ignorance?

My quest for copperhead history would have to wait. The secretary for the history department said Professor Wilkes had failed to show up that day. She didn't know why.

It took expert weaving through the rush hour traffic to meet Eliza at five o'clock. From Highway 98 to County Road 30-A passing through Rosemary Beach and Seacrest, finally zipping by the butterie towers of Alys Beach, I squealed to a stop in front of Fonville Press. There she sat. A corner table, a travel magazine in hand, steamy coffee in her mug. I ordered a coffee, black, and joined her. The indirect lighting bathed the large room in a foggy glow.

"Thanks for meeting me on such short notice," Eliza said.

"What's going on? You look worried."

"It's about Wilson. Ever since you mentioned finding that coin he has been obsessed with my great great-grandmother."

"That's odd. Did he show any interest before? He is a Civil War buff," I said.

"Oh, he was indifferent about the portrait. It has no value other than sentimental for me. Now he asks about the coin all the time." She took a sip of coffee.

I studied her face, her downcast eyes, rolling the edge of the magazine with her fingertips. "Eliza, you have the coin, don't you?"

She nodded, "But I haven't told him. It is with private family papers entrusted from my great great-grandmother to my great grandmother, to my grandmother, to my mother, and ultimately to me."

"So Wilson doesn't know about this?"

"There were conditions handed down with the coin. It must be kept in the maternal line, never spoken of to any husband or husbands. There are papers too. They are to be passed unopened only to a daughter. If no daughter exists, it goes to the closest female descendent -- a niece, for example -- but always the maternal line. That's what I can't tell Wilson," she said.

"Where is this bundle of secrets?" I leaned back in my chair.

"It's at the house, but Wilson will never find it. Don't worry. It is safe. I'll just keep denying any knowledge. That is the truth. I know absolutely nothing about it, but if you pursue the hunt for your coin's identity, maybe you could throw him a bone. Give him a clue or update now and then. It will take the pressure off me, unless you have already given up on your hunt. It's up to you completely." She whispered although we were alone in the coffee shop.

"My quest is on now more than ever." I pulled "the beware of snakes" warning out of my briefcase and showed it to her. She paled at my description of the copper coin pins engraved with snakes worn by our friends. "What else do you know, Eliza? You are the Southerner here. This is your heritage, not mine."

"You must believe me: I don't know what that means. All my life these Civil War devotees find ways to keep the secessionist flags waving and harp on the inglorious end to the Southern way of life. Like that Meg Coffee we heard at Supper Club. You must believe me. There are fanatics. Wilson is just a dabbler, but now I'm thinking he may be more deeply involved," she said.

"Deeply involved in what?"

"There are still secessionist movements in existence, active but in deep cover. They never accepted Lee's surrender and have never forgiven the North for the occupation that followed. This must sound crazy to you but to us, it is very real." Eliza looked around, "God, I could use a drink."

"Nothing but the soft stuff here. Sorry," I said.

"How about a double espresso with a twist of orange peel. I'll be up all night anyway obsessing about all this."

I procured two more cups of double espresso. "Eliza, if you have papers and the coin, then why not open them and then we'd know what both coins mean. Surely no harm could come almost a hundred and fifty years later. It's not a state secret any more, even if it was a Confederate state secret in its day."

"No, it's not that easy. We are told the papers can be opened only when three like coins are gathered in the presence of the female descendants to whom they had been respectively entrusted. I'd be afraid to open the papers. There could be a curse." She glanced around the room.

"Three? There are three coins? How are these coins supposed to find each other? When, where? It is rather farfetched, don't you think?"

"Is it? You saw the old tarot cards at my house. Eliza Powell read those cards. My grandmother said Eliza Powell could see."

"See what?"

"Not see what. See. Just see. As in a sixth sense. See beyond the obvious." Eliza said.

"Well then, we still have a practical issue. How do we get three coins together?" I spun my espresso cup slowly in the saucer.

"You don't get it. We don't get them together." Eliza sighed.

"Who does? What does?"

"Fate. Fate will assemble the women and only then should my papers, their papers be opened. I believe this, Harley. Eliza Powell had the touch. And the tarot cards. She was known for her readings. If she left orders to follow, I am going to follow them."

"Are you serious?"

"Absolutely. By virtue of my birth, I am part of a covert enterprise," she said. "I won't disrupt or compromise this by opening the letters before the designated time."

"Eliza, what makes you think this is an enterprise, or operation?"

"Because what else could it be? Why keep a lookout for the occasion of two other women with like coins. What would be in the papers other than instructions to do something? And, my grandmother always told me not to worry; I would know what to do when the time came. She used 'to do.' Not 'to know.' Not 'to understand.' To do."

"Does your daughter Rainer know about this?"

"She's in. We can trust her," said Eliza.

"Okay. Guess it would be bad luck to open your packet." I stirred the espresso with the orange peel. "And I am not a descendant. The coin does not belong to me although I possess it now. There are no papers either. If you are unwilling to open yours, then we must identify mine by other techniques."

"I can't open it. It violates Eliza Powell's trust. Her legacy. Please understand. I am truly sorry it will make things more difficult for you. Just look at us, deciphering a Civil War secret while sitting in a coffee shop at Alys Beach. Hardly believe it myself," Eliza said. She glanced around the room, sinking back in her chair.

"Who besides you, Rainer, and I know about this?"

"No one. I have an aunt with a daughter, my cousin, but they know nothing about this. So far there has been a direct line through daughters. Guess you could call it 'a need to know' sort of thing," she said.

I pondered her role as a time spanning sentry, much like the ancient crusader soldier still guarding the Holy Grail in a hidden cave. Was it a Monty Python movie, or Indiana Jones? Either way, my best friend was hell bent on playing that role. Real or not, it was real to her.

"I'll help as much as I can." Eliza leaned in toward me. "We can't involve Wilson. I know that now."

I needed her as my partner in this quest and with this new information, a new front opened. The benign Internet searches would have to give way to the rougher patches of investigative work, where I would systematically categorize words and behaviors of Supper Club members for clues. Ian Wilkes needed scrutiny too. Instead of lightening the load, Eliza only pulled me in deeper toward things I knew nothing about.

Before we left, Eliza gave me Rainer's phone number in Birmingham. She hopped into her sleek black Jaguar XF and sped off toward home. I raced home in a red Mini Cooper with a black and white check roof and lugged a stack of essays into the house. I ignored them for the mysteries surrounding Eliza, her heritage and my gold coin. They filled my mind and troubled me.

The next week, Marco and I went to Birmingham, for his seminar on pediatric emergencies at Children's Hospital. I visited Reed Books and The Museum of Fond Memories, my favorite rare books and curiosities shop. Well-worn books were squeezed into long walls of shelves. Tables held stacks of once cherished scrap-books, and out of print magazines. Scratchy LPs played Mitch Miller or Jelly Roll Morton on an old turntable. Inside the door, an old department store mannequin with demure 1950s eyes and sensuous full red lips greeted me.

I found Jim Reed, perched on a chair, behind a counter heaped with sheet music and old Life magazines. The store windows are jammed with stuff: books, old posters, and political buttons. Original art nouveau stained glass above the door and windows give rise to the rough bricks of the building, constructed in decorative times before steel and glass became de rigeur in urban landscapes. Jim matches the building. His elegantly trimmed grey beard and gentle eyes may bewitch you, like the building, into thinking this is a soft ride down memory lane. It is not. You find everything in his shop. Even things you'd rather not see, like a rusted "whites only" sign. He was the right man to ask about my coin.

We wound our way through rows of freestanding book-shelves. "Never had much interest in the Civil War. I don't have much interest in wars of any sort." He stopped and turned around. "Peace is much more interesting and harder to do."

Jim left me and I began to peruse the dusty old volumes stuffed into the Civil War section. I found a two volume pictorial record of the war. Later, he brought over a few old coin books to check. "Can't you give me any more hints about this coin? How do you know it is Civil War era?" An Ella Fitzgerald LP played in the background. He stood with arms crossed like an old time professor with one hand stroking the chin of his beard in deep concentration.

"It might be linked to a special group."

"Groups, you say. There were groups a plenty back in those days," he said. "If the turtle really means money, as you've been told, then I'd start with the groups who stashed away gold."

"There were groups that hid gold? Why would you hide gold? I'd think if anyone had money they'd need it, especially during Reconstruction."

"Yes, but what if you wanted to do something with it later?"

"Later? Like what?"

"Like fund a new Civil War. I do know that the dream of secession did not die with the surrender of Lee at Appomattox." He stood back and scanned the shelf of books. "Mind you, there are stories about secret societies sworn to uphold Southern honor, but to my knowledge they don't exist today."

"Maybe we don't know about them precisely because they are secret," I said. "They could be alive and well, existing off the grid."

"Yes, you are right, of course. You might find a lead on the Internet in Southern secessionist sites. One of their links might lead you to an answer. My inventory is probably too quaint for what you're after."

He left me to scan the works while he went to see another customer. I found a slim book wedged between two paperbacks, which told the story of Freemasonry and the South. The name John C. Calhoun caught my eye in the table of contents. Copyrighted in the 1930s, the book featured old tintype photos and words printed in a font no longer used. I bought it on a hunch. Jim Reed began to dial his phone while he waved goodbye to me as I stepped past the window of the shop toward our car. Coincidence? I didn't think so. Careful, I thought to myself, "paranoia will destroy ya."

Marco told me to forget it. He'd known Jim for years and a peacenik of his ilk could never be part of anything other than a peace group. "It would be against his nature."

"I hope you are right." My uncertainty persisted. Halfway

back to our beloved Seagrove home, I longed for the gusty wind of the beach. "How about a walk at sunset?"

"Good idea."

Stretching back in my seat, the Thrillmobile advanced through the countryside toward home.

*

The host of November Supper Club always faced a menu challenge. The traditional turkey dinner, loved by many, abhorred by more, never made the short list. Too common and too much of it. Bobby Carlyle, former chef at Highland's Bar and Grill, known for its French cuisine, antique wine posters and elite patrons in Birmingham, usually designed something spectacular. Often it bordered on the impossible for us regular folk. Fern e-mailed an easy menu for a change. She asked me to prepare the butternut squash soup using her mother's cast iron soup pot. "Not a problem." I clicked the reply button. "I'll pick up the pot tomorrow."

Grayton Beach, once a remote seaside village south of County Road 30-A, grew at random from 1885 when Army Major Charles T. Gray built a homestead here, five miles south of Point Washington, the nearest settlement at that time. By the turn of the nineteenth century, Grayton Beach attracted families from inland towns of Florida and Alabama for vacation retreats. The early inhabitants and the regular visiting families were fiercely committed to Grayton Beach's faded clapboard cottages with low sloping roofs green with moss, where you could stroll out to the squeaky, sugary sand and turquoise water from your front door. The historic dwellings are smothered in short scrub oaks, palmetto shrubs, wild rosemary and indigenous grasses, known collectively as Florida scrub. They are tucked among new multi-bedroom, brightly-colored boxes hoisted up on stilts which rent to crowds of vacationers. There are still quiet streets untouched by modern growth, but you have to drive past short strip malls offering the typical beach fare of T-shirts, flip flops, and plastic pail sets. A few sell snorkeling gear, surfboards or kayaks and even wet suits.

Fern and Bobby Carlyle's house sits off the main road, down a dead end single lane dirt path. It is within walking distance of an old grocery store and dance hall built in 1939. About twenty years ago it was transformed into a bar/restaurant, famously known as the Red Bar. Spencer Dell and Five Mile Back Up play there the fourth weekend each month. The band's name is painted onto a weathered piece of plywood leaning against a filmy window in the grizzled wood structure. Marco swears they have the best crab cakes around.

Just past the speed bump on the left, is Bobby's wine shop, a freestanding old house squarely nestled among oleander bushes and fall blooming gardenias. A few cars were parked on the crushed oyster shells out in front. He left the exterior of the beach shack intact, but the interior was covered with latticework bins that held wines from everywhere. The small green neon "open" sign was lit and I could see him through the window standing at the register on the phone.

I arrived at their house a few minutes later, leaving a small trail of dust from the road behind me. Fern stood on the wrap around porch. She saw me and waved. "Thanks for coming by. I couldn't care less about the pot, but Bobby, you know, his chef reputation is on the line so he insists on perfection."

"I don't mind. My mother believed in using the proper pot for specific recipes. I am not so picky but if Bobby wants butternut soup made in that pot, he'll get it."

We walked into the heirloom beach house, decorated with snug slip covered chairs and sofas, awash in calm beige damask. Color came from her prized art collection.

"You've seen my John Lonergan collection, haven't you?" she said.

"He's the one from Pell City, Alabama?" I stopped to admire a still life with red onions.

"That's right. Instead of scattering them throughout the house, I decided to hang them together. Think they show off better as a group. Don't you?"

"Guess so. Like a gallery in a museum. His landscapes from the South are phenomenal."

"I think it would be smart to collect the works of painters in his atelier. No doubt their value will only increase in time. But no one is better than John. He's a genius," said Fern.

"You really are a fan." We walked into their commercial kitchen. "And this must be the biggest black pot I have ever seen. What's this?" A recipe card for butternut squash soup was propped up in front.

"Bobby favors this recipe if you don't mind."

I had not seen Fern in a while, other than at Supper Club. The dark circles under her eyes matched her listless manner. Something was wrong.

"You look tired, Fern, are you all right?" I tapped the black pot.

"Oh, yes, nothing is wrong, physically that is. Oh Harley, it's Bobby." She stared at me eyes wide, stunned at the words she blurted out.

"What's wrong with Bobby?"

"Something is going on with him. He is never home. He's late for dinner." She put her hands on her face as if hiding from those very words.

"Is it work? Too much golf?" They had been married a long time. Their kids Ivy and Bobby, Jr., also known as Deuce, were busy high school students. Fern and Bobby were a perfectly oiled, seemingly indestructible team, embedded into the viscera of 30-A high society and in their hometown, Birmingham. A split would set tongues wagging forever. Neither would invite a scandal but you never know the ways of the heart. Or other parts, as Marco says.

"It's not work or golf. He's either on the Internet or out with Wilson. He's just out." Fern led me toward the office, and we stopped. "Look in here, where he spends his time at home."

The office contained bookshelves, floor to ceiling, and a headless, padded tailor's dummy, wearing a Knight's Templar uniform. A curvy metal helmet with an adjustable visor balanced on pole above a high necked collar of chain mesh placed over a white linen, thigh-length dress with red crosses appliquéd to the chest and back. Hammered metal gloves poked out from the loose bell sleeves and shiny disc knee pads on top of shin guards covered the poles used as legs. Polished tin shaped into silvery spats covered rough leather moccasins.

It stood next to a large map of 14th century Europe. A large Masonic symbol consisting of the compass and the big "G" hung over a glass curio case filled with antique ribbons, coins, spectacles, opera glasses, and porcelain figurines. A few lead soldiers, dark with age, were lined up in battle formation. The sunlight cast streaky rays through the windows across the room. Fern walked toward the desk and picked up a book. "Another civil war book. You'd think he could let it go."

"Let what go?" We had stepped through a time warp to a place filled with the tools and artifacts of another age, another life. Even the loveseat and chairs reupholstered in the gold and silver brocades of antebellum colors evoked the sensibility of a past era. "I didn't know Bobby was such a serious Civil War buff."

"It has never ended for him. He is committed to keeping the cause alive as if it is his family honor at stake. You see, although the people of the South suffered after the war, his family managed to piggyback onto the carpetbaggers from the North. His grandmother married into one of those families of northern industrialists, the ones who built the Birmingham steel industry. His great great-granddaddy never forgave her. Of course, the wealth poured in. Railcars packed full of coal, limestone, and iron ore rolled in one end of the mills and rolled out as steel at the other end. Bobby grew up in great wealth but felt guilty about its dubious source. He endowed the history faculty position over at the college to honor his great great-granddaddy and the Southern side of his family."

"So what if he's entrenched as ever in his Civil War activities? It's all rather benign isn't it? Sort of like Star Wars groupies that dress up as storm troopers and go to sci fi conventions? They don't actually do anything," I said.

"That's where you are wrong. It isn't benign. It costs money. These people have meetings and talk and talk and talk. They collect memorabilia, which isn't cheap. Bobby had to have this Knights Templar uniform. I won't tell you how much it cost." She picked up the hem of the skirt then dropped it quickly as if burned her fingers.

"A lot I'd bet." I scanned the room and took it all in.

"Let me see if I can say this sequence correctly. I've listened to it from Bobby for years. The Knights Templar were routed by a conspiracy between King Philip IV of France and the French Pope Clement V who excommunicated them in 1312. Some of the Knights fled to Scotland taking refuge with the stonemason guilds. These early Freemasons guilds or as Bobby calls them, the Neo-Templars, defenders of individualism and civil liberties under the banner of free thinking, found themselves constantly at odds with the Vatican. They managed to spread back into the European continent and eventually to the new colonies. Charleston, Bobby's ancestral home, became the headquarters for the Scottish Rite Freemasonry in the South. The other base was in New York."

"He still belongs?"

"He's a very high degree. That's what the levels are called. Degrees." She looked at the computer. "Something has happened in the last couple months. He's obsessed with something. He won't even talk to me."

"Do you want me to talk to him? Or Marco?"

"No, nothing would help. I almost wish he had a girlfriend. That's something I could fight. I can't fight ghosts." She ran her hands through her hair.

I didn't want to get in the middle of their personal crisis, but I did want to talk to Bobby about my coin. I felt a bit guilty about using their problems to try to solve my mystery, but sometimes my curiosity can win out over good sense. He must know Ian Wilkes, given the John C. Calhoun Professorship endowed by his family. I didn't know what to make of the Masonic connection, but I had a feeling the answer might be in the book from Jim Reed's store, as yet unread. The students' essays had to come first.

I made my way back to the car with cast iron pot in hand. My red Mini rounded the dips in the dusty road. No matter what was going on with them, a Knights Templar outfit in Grayton Beach bordered on the ludicrous. I saw Marco's car in the driveway and hoped there weren't any fish in the sink waiting for me. He could clean his own fish for once.

*

The next day Marco and I strolled along the beach. November Gulf water can be calm or churn with a crashing surf. That day the sea rolled onto the sand with long curves and halfhearted effort. My feet crashed through the foamy chilled water. Sturdy grey pelicans dive-bombed into a bubbling swirl of fish.

"So Fern doesn't know where Bobby goes? Is that it?" said Marco.

"Yeah. She's lonely. He won't talk. He's never there. Stalemate."

"I saw Bobby, Wilson, Vernon and Colin playing golf the other day. They were loading their bags onto the carts. All of the bags had the same skull and cross bone insignia printed on one side and a star over a crescent shape on the other," he said. "Made me think of Shriners, but they acted more like frat boys who can't give up the brotherhood."

"Why didn't you mention this before? This is something."

"Well, I forgot. Anyway, I couldn't hear what they were saying, for all I know they were talking about golf, which is what you do when you play golf."

"I'm missing something here?"

"Think like a sociologist instead of a girlfriend."

"Girlfriend?"

"Yeah, don't think about Fern as a poor soul you know who

is unhappy. Think, why did she show you the office? Was that deliberate or accidental? Does it matter? Either way it gave you a view into Bobby's world you didn't know about, and it might relate to your coin. Have you read that book about Calhoun and the Masons yet? Maybe Bobby's family played a part in the story. And, lastly, I found this in the mailbox." He pulled out a copper pin embossed with a snake from his pocket.

"Was there a note with it?" I peered closely at it, feeling with my fingers to decide if it was new or antique. No tarnish, no gouges, with a modern pin apparatus. This new coin meant something to someone.

"No, but its message is clear."

"It is?"

"Yeah, you wear it, you're in. You're one of them. You don't, it means you choose not to join yet." Marco kicked up the sand as he walked.

"How do you know that?"

"Don't forget, I grew up in the shadow of the mob. Just because you are not in it, doesn't mean you don't know the way it works. This is a test."

"To see if I know anything." The detective becomes the subject. "What would you do, Mr. Mobster?"

"Supper Club is tomorrow. Play it close for now. Cool. Play it cool. Someone might ask about your coin. What we may hear tomorrow should give us a hint." Marco put his arm around me, and we walked a little while longer.

This was no longer about simply identifying a coin. My head swirled with the images of Eliza's great great-grandmother, a Knights Templar uniform, and Copperhead snakes and pins. My quest had grown to identify not one but possibly three coins. I no longer regarded some members of Supper Club as innocent and unrelated to each other or my coin. Instead they were organized potential adversaries who send threatening notes and wear silly copper pins.

The next evening, at half past six, Marco placed a piping hot cast iron cauldron of butternut squash soup in a padded cardboard box in the back of my red Mini. The traffic moved quickly. This was the off-season for the sun-worshiping masses. The snowbirds had hunkered in for the evening by now. We zipped past Seaside, past Watercolor to Highway 283 and a four way stop, where we turned left towards Grayton Beach. Just past Pandora's and next door to Hibiscus, two restaurants beloved by locals, a flashing red light warned of speed bumps and another stop sign. I crept over the speed bumps to keep the soup from spilling and then cruised by Red Bar to the dusty road of our hosts.

Early bird Eliza parked her Jaguar in the driveway. Adelaide and Brantley's car stuck out from the side yard next to Brenda and Glen's SUV. I tucked my little vehicle close in behind the Jaguar and the Junots flashed their headlights behind us. The fall gardenias bordering the base of the screened porch filled the air with their sweet scent. Lanterns lit the path to the door; the dusk resolving quickly into night at this time of year. I held the door for Marco and the rest of the assembly with trays and pots in tow.

After we unloaded our heavy pot in the kitchen, Marie Justine, Brenda and I found the men at the wine table already tasting Bobby's recommended Rhone or Pinot Noir. The wine bottles we brought per Supper Club rules were set aside on a nearby table. Fern's family beach house had been a modest retreat when they remodeled it for year round use. A few new rooms were attached so skillfully you'd swear they were original. Bobby added a built in wooden bar with a brass footrail and leather bar stools just off the dining room. It had Tiffany glass and beveled mirrors, all the fixings of old saloons found in big cities with long histories.

The bar in my Dad's saloon was built from mahogany and Brazilian cherry, dark with age, heavy on the brass, light on the decorative stuff. Now run by my brother, it is a workingman's bar with most of the glassware stored in the freezer. Every mug filled by tap and slid onto the counter top was a frosty mug. This was the McBride signature. Beer on tap iced up in our mugs, the sign of heaven on Earth.

Bobby's bar had too much glitz for my taste. Just like Bobby. He reeked of money but never showed any contentment. I wondered if his Knights Templar outfit brought him happiness or remorse, reminding him of lingering wrongs, battles still to be fought, honor still to be restored. It must be exhausting to dwell in the past. Even Fern said so.

I took a glass of wine from Bobby, the Rhone definitely dry but wondered why he didn't serve a Chardonnay, the other choice often paired with game hens. I scanned his shirt for a copper pin. Nothing. Marco pulled me along towards the screen porch door and whispered that his reconnaissance had revealed no copper pins in sight. "I knew it. No pins tonight. Cool, that's the way to play this."

"But, what does it mean. What if the pin came from someone outside of Supper Club?" I said.

"No way. They are all connected. We just don't know how or why. And, we don't have to be in a hurry anyway. There's no urgency on our part. The coin is an incidental curiosity to you. Slow down, my hot headed babe." He kissed me squarely on the lips. "Just have fun."

Patricia Dell caught my eye and came over.

"New highlights?" I pointed to her sharp bob.

"Trying out some new product. It washes out fairly quick, so you don't get a root line. What are you up to, besides kissing Marco?"

"Same old. Nothing really." I shrugged.

"Still looking into that coin's origin?" she said.

"Yes, but not as a full-time job. I'll figure it out sooner or later. Or never."

"Well, just be careful."

"Careful?"

"Hey, I grew up around here, and these Civil War buffs take

their mission seriously. You know, to restore honor and all that. They never take kindly to a Yankee mixing in their turf. Drives them crazy for Southern memorabilia to fall into all y'all's hands. It's like fighting the war all over again."

"How can this level of sensitivity exist all these generations later? I don't get it."

"That's because you are the victor. You folks from the North don't have to be sensitive. Meanwhile, what's poor Johnny Reb going to do now but lick his wounds and wait for revenge? There's no end to waiting for revenge. He'll endure it with pain and honor. That's to say, even in this day and age, be alert. Personally, I can't wait for you to identify the coin. To think you found it right here along 30-A." She took a gulp of wine and we wandered over towards the gang in Bobby's office.

Jean Louis hunched over Mario to catch a better view of the lead soldiers in the curio case. Adelaide and Chantal stood near the Knight's Templar costume chatting about something. Reese McElwain stared at the Mason's symbols on the wall, while Walter's eyes glazed over as he looked at the expanse of books on the Confederate government. The retired cop shook his head saying to himself, "All this law and no justice."

Eliza and Wilson stood close to Bobby who kept smiling at Brenda. Glen scowled at the old maps in a dusty scuffed ledger and Darius stood apart, glass of wine in hand. I sauntered up, curious about his take on all this paraphernalia . "How strange to be a slave, just property to someone else." Darius took a sip. "I believe in the equality of all people. Rule of law can institutionalize equality, but the law has to be just and applied fairly at all times, for all people."

"Are you running for office?"

"Forgive me, no drama intended." His lush baritone voice slid over my ears. The angled face of smooth espresso skin lit up with inquisitive eyes as he spoke. He dressed with the marks of high pedigree, neatly rolled up sleeves, a pressed pleat in the back of his cotton shirt tucked into pleated cuffed khakis, sockless feet in polished penny-loafers.

"Hey, you are talking to me, the Supper Club's resident sociologist. And though cultural contexts are my bag, even I find the altar of adoration to all things Confederate a little much to take."

"What about that coin you found. Any idea about its origin yet?"

"Not yet. I'll figure it out someday."

"You should talk to Chantal about it. She comes from a family of formidable women and can trace her ancestral tree back before the Civil War. Her kin were house slaves. Her great great-grandmother could read," he said.

"And your family?"

"Mine came much later, during the fifties, from Senegal. My grandfather and grandmother came to New York City after World War II. Most of my family still live in the New York City area, but my father, an English professor, took a faculty position in Mobile in the seventies. I am not the typical black man in America since I am not a descendent of slaves but relatively recent émigrés. Publicly I share the same color and therefore endure the stereotypes, heroic or vilified," he said, "as the wind blows."

"Thank you for telling me this. It explains why I thought you understood Marie Justine and me last month when we spoke French," I said.

"Bien sur. Of course, I am fluent in French, it's our family language. Senegal is, as you know, a former French colony. I must use it with my very old grandparents."

"Mine too. But back to the coin, thanks for the heads up about Chantal."

"She'd love to discuss it with you. She knows a great deal about obscure things that went on back then. Oral history, letters, and diaries. The documentary evidence that you sociologists like if I am not mistaken."

"Just the thing."

Before I could say another word, Meg Coffee accosted me

out of nowhere, with a "where have you been?"

Darius gave a half smile. "Not to worry, I'll get another glass of wine."

Left to Meg's devices, I was snared into a syrupy greeting that didn't match the low level of our acquaintance. I hate to get hugs from people with eager, fleshy arms. As she wrapped them around me her hot breath smelled of Jack Daniel's.

"Don't you look cute tonight?" Meg said.

"Hi Meg."

"No, really, where'd you get that flippy little skirt? It's so cute with that jacket." With a fully loaded glass of pinot noir in one hand, she stumbled against me and grabbed my arm.

"Steady there. Are you okay, Meg?"

"Fine as frog hair. You have heard of that before haven't you? Because y'all are a Yankee after all," she said. Her Southern accent thickened with each sip of wine.

"Yes, I am a Yankee. Can't hide it. But, actually only half."

"Half? How can you be only half Yankee?"

"My mother's family is French Canadian. Never got around to citizenship. They were permanent expats," I said.

"Well, then, you're half forgiven." She put her warm arm around me again.

"For what?" I glanced around the room for someone to come to my rescue.

"For being nosy in our affairs." She whispered hot breath into my ear.

I pulled away. Suddenly Walter let out a holler. "You don't say. Confederates in Brazil?"

"Man, what's the big deal?" Mario leaned back, his hand raised in mock fear at Walter's outburst. "All I said is, there is a town in Brazil, named Americana, that Confederate losers started, led by some guy from Alabama." The tips of his thick curls, backlit by the light from an antique sconce, formed a halo behind him like angel.

"That Confederate loser from Alabama you are referring

to would be Colonel William Hutchinson Norris, an Alabama State Senator from Perry County and a Mason Grand Master," Brantley Vernon said. He strode up to Mario and stopped in front of him, nose to nose.

"Man, you can take a step back. Did I say something?" Mario raised both hands in the air ready to push Brantley back. "I'm just saying how it is. I grew up in Sao Paulo. Americana is southeast. You just take the train."

Brantley relaxed only when he noticed the stares of the Supper Club members in the office. Tonight, he looked very trim and bronzed from the sun. His slithery righteousness reminded me of a middle-aged version of George Hamilton in the classic movie *Where the Boys Are*. Smooth, cool, and collegiate, without a hair out of place. Just like George in the movie, he had a line for everything.

"So you've been there?" Brantley's voice cracked.

"Many times. It's a weird place, though. They got this big statue to the Masons, you know, the square and compass, and the big G in the middle. They have their own Confederate cemetery too, because as Protestants they could not be buried in the Catholic cemetery way back then."

"The plaque to the Masons is there because Dom Pedro II, the last Emperor of Brazil, was himself a Mason. He invited the Confederates to resettle there with the goal to build a new cotton industry in Brazil with their plantation expertise." Brantley pronounced his words as if reading from a holy book.

"Well, there are monuments to fools all over the world," said Walter as he scanned the Masonic plaque on the wall where Reese stood.

"Hey, the story goes like this," Mario said. "Many ships left from ports along the Gulf Coast at the end of the war, full of Confederate soldiers, with women and children. The majority made it to Americana, but some ships sank on the way to Brazil. They never made it out of the Gulf, past the Yucatan Peninsula. As kids we heard all the ships were full of gold so no wonder the pirates robbed them and sank the ships too. We loved all the pirate stories."

"Well, thankfully Colonel Norris' own vault of family gold remained in his safe possession in Perry County after the war because a widow friend of his greeted a Union officer with a secret Masonic handshake before he carried out an order to pillage his estate. The Union officer, also a Mason, ordered his men to depart, leaving everything untouched. Being a Mason transcended the rivalries of the war," Brantley said. "Providentially, his fortune survived the perilous journey to Brazil, where he eventually fulfilled his destiny."

"What's with Brantley's holier than thou thing?" Walter leaned toward me and continued to whisper. "This strikes me as pretty stupid, all this reverence. But you know what I say about such people."

"What?"

"You can help ugly but you can't help dumb." He poked me in the ribs and laughed to himself.

Brantley's mini lecture revealed more to me than he realized. I had the impression that the great families of the Confederacy surrendered their gold to the cause. This meant Eliza's great great-grandmother's choice to retain, rather than squander possession of the family fortune on an ill-fated war was not an exception. Colonel Norris had hedged his bet on the war, too.

Meg interrupted my thoughts when she moved closer to my side. Dana waited at the doorway watching the show. Eliza stood behind her and nodded toward me. She had picked up on his words too. Darius draped his arm around Chantal who had sipped most of her wine with tight lips in front of narrowed eyes.

"And there's just one little detail you left out, Brantley." Chantal called him out in the momentary lull of silence. "At that time, slavery was still legal in Brazil, so what a deal for these ex-plantation owners. Even after a bloody war, they believed they could own another human being. They were no heroes. They were losers on the run. And the gold the Masons' protected, it's blood money. Sorry if I don't cheer."

Adelaide grew sickly green at the exchange between Chantal and her husband. She attempted to smile, but stood motionless until Chantal gently led her out of the library. "Come on, let's go help Fern in the kitchen." They passed by Brantley who remained silent.

"This is all bull any way you look at it." Glen held up a scrapbook. "Yeah, okay, it is history and all that, but damn, we white folks just can't give it up. We should have lost. Slavery sucks. End of story."

"Easy Glen," said Colin. He had watched from the doorway this whole time. "No need to insult anyone."

"Who's insulting anyone? I am just saying let's not go ga ga over some guy who hid his money and left town like a sore loser. My man, Robert E. Lee, didn't run away. Damn." He clicked his hook securely around his wine glass and chugged it. "I need some fresh air." He walked out of the room past Brenda without looking at her, who had perched on a chair's edge next to Bobby.

"Supper is ready, y'all," Fern said.

We paired up with our mates and straggled out of the office. Darius joined up with Chantal in front of Marco and me. Walking alone, Brenda reached the hall and paused. Bobby placed his open palm on her jaunty bottom, encased tonight in red spandex capris and deftly caressed it. Marco saw it too. Perhaps Fern did have a live body to fight after all.

The dour mood that hovered over us in Bobby's office subsided when we reached the tables. Cafe tables for four were placed around the living room and draped in brown, gold and red squares, all tied together with a center knot. Small gourds surrounded the center knot in the middle, and a tiny orange pumpkin balanced on top. The ends of the squares fell like an open handkerchief over the edges of the tables, mimicking fall leaves. Dark chocolate and caramel kisses wrapped in gold and brown foil were tossed between the plates and captured the flicker of candlelight from the wall sconces. Fern's family heirloom dishes, deep burgundy rimmed in gold were surrounded by ornate sterling flatware, an antique pattern no longer made. Red and white wine glasses overwhelmed the tables because Bobby insisted both are needed on his tables.

Croutons floated on top of delicate cups of steaming butternut squash soup. Fern disliked buffets so she commandeered Eliza, Marie Justine, and Consuela to help her in the kitchen. We sat with Dana and Mario, and I noticed Glen and Brenda sat with Fern and Bobby. The earlier tempest had mellowed and by dinner's end, the brown sugar glazed pumpkin pie with vanilla bean gelato managed to put everyone in a good mood.

Marco reminded me about his early morning meeting, so we set about giving a quick goodbye, thanks and wave to everyone en masse. Fern walked us to the door and said, "I must talk to you."

"Call me anytime. You have my mobile." I gave her a hug.

"Good night Marco." She hugged him too.

On the way to our car we breathed in the dry crackly November air against shimmering stars and glowing planets in a sky so vast they appeared to dangle low over us. Marco remarked that only Darius and Patricia asked about my coin even with all the Civil War chatter and memorabilia around us. I noticed that too and the absence of secret handshakes although I overheard Brantley describe one used by the Masons to Walter.

Once in the car, rumbling past the silent side streets onto County Road 30-A, Marco remarked, "Speaking of secrets, I'll bet that was a secret move Bobby gave to Brenda. What's going on there?"

"Don't know but I am about to find out. Fern wants to talk."

"I'll bet she does. By the way, I liked your soup but the game hens were dry," added Marco.

"Yeah. Me too. But Supper Club has never been just about the food." We rounded the corner to our street and sped for home.

"Chantal is sure spunky." He parked in our driveway.

"Yes, she is."

He pushed Tulip and Daisy away from the front door. As

I stroked them both, I realized that I never did connect with Meg again during the evening. No doubt she'd call me soon. For that matter, I didn't catch a minute with Marie Justine or Consuela and husbands either. That's Supper Club. Next month always comes around soon enough.

After crawling into bed, I began to think about Maria and a world I once lived in a long time ago. I could hear the clink and clank of metal as the silver merchant in the old Cairo market dove his hands into pots of old worthless coins. The sound faded when Daisy jumped in bed between Marco and me. As I stroked her fur, I drifted off this time with sights of soldiers from a long ago war marching toward a ship, as Eliza's great great-grandmother stands on the shore calling out a haunting story of coins and fate. Troubled by these images, I tossed and turned, unable to shake them away. How do coins assemble? If they call to us in dreams, whose voices do they use? Would I hear them?

Menu

Bite-sized Crab Cakes with Lime Garlic Sauce
Roasted Brussels Sprouts with Parmesan Cheese
Manchego Squares with Sage Wheat Pita Bread crisps

* * *

Venetian Spinach with Pinenuts and Golden Raisins
Mixed Greens with Green Goddess Dressing

* * *

Garlic Cheese Grits
Halibut Wedges with Citrus Walnut Tapenade
Wild Yeast Pan de Sol Rolls

* * *

Orange Ricotta Cookies
Caramelized Apple and Pear Pie with
Mascarpone Cream

* * *

Spanish Rojo, Pinot Noir or Prosecco

December

My mobile phone rang just as I saw the college up ahead. Eliza Blackmon's number lit up the screen. The faculty car park came into view. Ian Wilkes turned in two cars ahead, unaware of me. Parked, I redialed Eliza from the car as the Hawaiian shirt rolled out of the car, briefcase in hand and marched into the building.

"Hi, what's up so early?" I asked.

"What did you think about supper club last night? Different, wouldn't you say?"

"That exchange between Mario and Brantley hit some nerves. Guess Mario's opinion of this Confederate adoration business is on the low side. No surprise there. Like he says, countries have civil wars all the time. What makes this one such a big deal?"

"Wilson barely tolerates even the slightest criticism. For him it's a Southern blasphemy at the Church of the Holy Confederacy. Now, Brantley goes for the jugular especially when there is an audience. You should see him at Civil War re-enactments. Glen surprised me. Didn't think a guy from the sticks outside Talledega would be the sympathetic type."

"I am stunned that he, of all people, would be such a softy underneath all that gruffness. And other than Patricia or Darius, no one asked about my coin search, and I didn't see any clues or messages or secret stuff, did you?"

"Harley, you were the butt of their joke last night."

"Me? What are you talking about?"

"You made the butternut squash soup, for God's sake," she said.

"So? Fern asked me to make it and use their special cast iron pot. I agreed. What are you saying: the soup had a meaning?"

"You don't know what butternut means, do you? Okay, listen, trivia 101. If you were a Union sympathizer you were like butternut wood, a useless soft wood. You'd be soft in your support of the South and therefore useless, too. You were being told that you are not one of us Southerners, and are useless, something like that. Anyway, it was a private joke."

"A joke? Doubt that. Rather a put-down. If this amuses them, they are small caliber men," I said. "And women if Meg was involved."

"For sure."

"It'd take more than that to deter me from my quest. And speaking of quest, I meant to tell you something last night but never got the chance. Someone sent me a copper coin pin with a snake on it. What does this mean to you? Marco thinks it's a test," I added.

"In what way?"

"If I wear it, means I'm in, that I will play their game. If not, it means I either don't get it and/or won't play their game. I didn't wear it last night because Marco wanted to see if anyone else wore one. Nothing. So I don't know what is going on."

"Me either. What are you going to do now?"

"Dig deeper into the Copperhead scene. Check into the Confederate city of Americana. You should check into the whereabouts of your great great-grandmother's gold, her wealth. Do you have any of it? Was there a chest of gold and silver coins? This Norris fellow apparently had a vault full of it and I bet other families did too."

"Hmm. Now that you mention it, I never have seen any coins or bullion. Our family could gag on centuries of heritage, especially on the Powell side. But we were not a family of trust funds. It's not like the second or third generations of wealth you find now, like Wilson and his trust fund. We're such an old family that the money's been spent. We are on our own now. Hey, maybe that's what the papers will tell us, that there's a stash of gold somewhere. If ever we open them."

"Eliza, maybe you are onto something there."

"What do you mean?"

"What if your great great-grandmother's coin and my coin are clues?"

"Clues to what?"

"To what men fight over. Gold and its power. Maybe you've never seen your own family's heirloom gold because it is hidden. To find it requires the three coins you've been told about. My guess is that our Civil War buffs know this too. Eliza, let's not talk on the phone. What's your schedule for today?"

"I have patients until two this afternoon. After that I am free. We can meet anywhere."

"Let's walk on the beach. Meet me at three at the beach access of Bramble Court in Seagrove. You can park there off the street. Okay?"

"Perfect. Don't forget sunscreen even if it is almost December," she added.

"Yes, doctor. See you then." I hung up and sat motionless in the red Mini. My morning class with tired students at the end of the semester didn't begin for another hour. The newest Starr Elliott book was stuffed out of sight in my briefcase. I had planned to start it before class, to find out if the MI6 agent she loved had been killed off between books so she could have a new love affair in this one. However, after Eliza's explanation of the soup, my priorities changed. I could use this time to cull a fresh set of leads off the Web before the walk with Eliza.

My phone rang again. The call I expected lit up the screen. Fern Carlyle. I sat back in the car and left the door ajar. "Hi Fern."

"That no good, son of a bitch." Fern held nothing back. "I saw his hand on her ass."

"You did?"

"I guess all of Supper Club could see him ogle her. I am a complete fool. The stupid wife who is the last to know." She spewed on a familiar tale. Indifference had replaced passion. And, yes, her daughter Ivy, vivacious and prone to long cheerleader workouts and son Deuce, who does improv with his buddies when he's not running or pumping iron, do give her plenty of distraction. But, that doesn't help when the dark hours arrive where loneliness and worthlessness collide into nothingness. She sputtered between strangling tears, finding little relief.

I wanted to ask her if she knew what butternut meant. She might have been involved in the scam. But such a conspiracy required more communication than the two of them had going at the moment. Besides, she was over the war even if Bobby was not.

When her voice no longer quivered and an occasional half laugh escaped through her litany of sorrows, I signed off. I was sympathetic to her plight, but couldn't fix it. It's not easy to lose one's relevance in a relationship. I still possess the sadness that comes with defeat. I hate it after all these years. It never goes away, but just loses its immediacy. All I could do is point her forward, if that's what she wanted. That's all I knew to do.

Now with only ten minutes before class, I hurried to the lecture hall. The students were sprawled out across the seats, backpacks strewn everywhere, glassy eyed from staying up all night to finish papers or study for exams. None of us wanted to be there that morning, but there we were. I closed my eyes and watched my hands throttle up the way my Dad showed me as a kid on my own Harley-Davidson, squealed the tires, and pealed away, back on the sociology road again.

By the time class ended there was just enough time to get out to the beach to meet Eliza. I crossed through the building lobby toward the door. The Hawaiian shirt strode into my line of sight.

"Professor McBride, trying to get a jump on the weekend?" asked Ian Wilkes. He smiled as he held the door for me. I couldn't help but notice his taut biceps and broad shoulders.

"Oh, hi. Yeah, that, plus I have a meeting in an hour elsewhere. You know how traffic can be. You'll excuse me if I don't stop." I tried to squeeze by him.

"Of course. By the way, I hear you make an excellent soup," he grinned with a twinkle in his eye.

"Soup? Oh, the butternut squash soup. Meg or Colin must have told you," I tried to act casual but was shocked.

"Yes, Meg called me this morning and told me she'd seen you at the Supper Club. She's quite taken with you and your husband, Marco Polo? Now that's a name, the sort that would attract an intellectual type like you. Wonder how 'Ian Wilkes' would rate on the 'names that attract intellectual women scale?'"

"Oh, it would be top of the scale. You must have all sorts of smart women after you. I can barely resist you myself."

"My door's always open. Ah, but don't let me keep you." His eyes met mine and he slightly bowed. "Have a good weekend."

"You too. See you around." I skipped down the front steps and quickly stepped to my car. What the hell was going on? He's positively flirting with me. But why? Now even soup is more than soup and 30-A Supper Club is fully infiltrated by eccentrics. No way running into Ian Wilkes was a chance encounter. It weighed on my mind the whole way home.

*

"Eliza, he wanted to let me know he knew about the butternut soup." I shouted over the roar of the surf. We began to walk toward Seaside and had reached a beach house with a flagpole flying a Jolly Roger.

"Calm down. I want to listen for a sign," she explained.

"A sign? A sign of what? From who? Don't go off the deep end on me. It's bad enough Fern has decompensated. Then there's

Meg Coffee who wants to be my best friend forever. What gives? About here is where I found that silly coin anyway." I pointed out to the sea.

"Here." Eliza stared out toward the Gulf, the thick wintry waves pushing foamy crests into the shore, the undertow dragging sand away from it. "Here is where you found it? You mean my great great-grandmother's coin found you. That's how it goes, the story, the coins come together."

"Yes, but you said in the presence of the descendants of the women to whom they were entrusted. Coins do not seek out people either. You are a scientist, a physician. Get a grip." The chilly wind cut across my face. We scuffed the sand with our steps. I dug into my pocket for some M&M almonds and handed a few to Eliza.

"My grandmother told me that her grand-aunt Maggie, that's my great great-grandmother's sister, drowned in a shipwreck, but she never said where," Eliza said suddenly. "She'd say a bright star took her away to the dark ocean. It sounded creepy so I never pushed for more explanation. Looking back, I think my grandmother wanted to tell me more than she did. My mother would tell her to quit scaring me."

"Was she married? Aunt Maggie, I mean," I asked, stopping for a moment.

"No. Her beau was killed in the war, or so the story goes. She was Maggie Rainer. That's all I really know about her, unless there is something in those papers."

"What if "Bright Star" was the name of the ship? If we could trace that, then we might find out what happened to her, the ship, the cargo! And, I still can't believe Ian Wilkes knew about the butternut soup, from Meg Coffee in less than 24 hours." I kicked the sand.

"Doesn't this feel like some sort of race, a weird sort of game?" she asked.

"In a way. For what prize? Why all the childish secrecy?"

"Prize, I don't know. Money, maybe prestige. Say, do you

think Guillermo Martinez could help us? He taught at Annapolis before he retired from the Navy and started his fishing business," Eliza said.

"That's a good idea. He would know about ship manifests and that sort of thing. At least point us in the right direction. Someone has probably got a Web site about shipwrecks after the war. Wouldn't it be something if she was heading to Americana, Brazil?"

"It would explain things. You see, my family left Union Springs for a while to avoid the Union troops just after the war, but they all made their way back. Rainers, Powells, and Blackmons filled the Oak Hill Cemetery over time," she replied, "except for Maggie."

We turned to go back, now a mile out from our starting point in Seagrove Beach. The pale sun hid behind grey clouds, the humidity stuck to us as did the damp hard sand under our shoes. Eliza and I trekked across a winter's beach back to her car. The pounding surf and spray from the waves lulled us into momentary silence.

"Hey, I need to ask you something," I said.

"Anything, what's up?"

"There's this history professor at work, who is a Civil War expert. I asked him about my coin."

"Ian? Is he hitting on you?" Eliza blurted out, pulling me along to walk.

"You know him? Really cute? Very sexy?"

"And you like him! He's part of the Civil War community. Big flirt, lots of women. You'd be his type. He likes them smart. And you have two other things he'd like. One of them is the coin and the other is you, a pretty married chick. He loves the challenge of forbidden fruit. So, you are his newest love object." She laughed and slapped me on the back.

"You are no help. Not a word to Marco. Swear it."

"I swear."

I didn't quite believe her. "Can we get back to the issue of the coin, now?"

"Harley, you know, it's funny. I have worked as a

dermatologist since my residency. I know where my money comes from. Wilson sells real estate, but he's a trust fund baby, forever managing his family wealth. I didn't grow up in great wealth. My father was a successful businessman who supported his family. We always heard stories about the prominent Powells, Rainers and Blackmons of Union Springs, respected for their philanthropy but nothing about actual money. For heaven sakes, no one dared discuss such a private matter. Certainly not my mother and definitely not to us. Until you asked me where the family gold was, I never thought about it," she said as her brow tightened almost into a squint.

"Can you talk to her now?"

"Absolutely not. Hell would freeze. 'How déclassé,' she would reply, 'we don't discuss the family money.' Anyway, it was probably spent to survive those years after the war. With menfolk killed or crippled, the women must have used it up, then sold anything of value that they had. Always thought the most accurate moment of *Gone With the Wind* was when Scarlett used the curtains to make a dress. I hope great great-grandmother Eliza spent all her money and the rest of them too. So, what next? Do you really think this is so secret we can't talk on a phone?"

"No, but I think better out here where there are less distractions. As for what's next, I'll check with Guillermo. That way you don't have a thing to say to Wilson," I said.

Eliza sped off toward Alys Beach, and I walked along 30-A toward my street a few blocks away. The "open" neon sign on the door at Cocoons still lit the window. Spencer waved to me from behind the counter. He reminded me that Five Mile Back Up was playing that night at Red Bar and urged Marco and me to come. Patricia would be there as well as others from the neighborhood. I bought a pint of smoked tuna dip and agreed that we'd see him there.

From a distance I saw Marco standing in our driveway. He greeted me with a hug and an envelope addressed to me that had been dropped without postage in the mailbox. It was nothing but an invitation to a Christmas Fair at the Indian Museum at Fort Walton

Beach with a handwritten note from Meg Coffee asking if I'd like to go with her. For a moment, I had imagined, even hoped for something more exotic and even sinister, a secret message, perhaps. How quickly we take ourselves too seriously. A little music at Red Bar was what we needed.

*

By the second week of December, final exams were finished, grades were submitted. Free at last, I immersed myself in the shadowy world of butternuts, and copperheads. I flopped down on the sofa near Daisy and began with Civil War saboteurs. There were plenty to go around, some loyal to the North, some to the South. These super patriots of the North and the South blew up railroad tracks, burned down barns, and disrupted food and support lines but none of them struck me as meaningful to my search because, for the most part, they were not widespread networks or organizations. Small, autonomous guerrilla cells engaging in localized actions in specific regions did not fit the bill. For an organization to last over time, it would have to have an overpowering mission to defend, a comprehensive strategy for the long term, and a coded language for clandestine communication. It had to be big enough to span regions like the Underground Railroad. Now that was a network.

By mistake I had used fifty dollar search words like "financial improprieties," "secessionist strategy," or "military resource allocation." I started over with simple five dollar words. "Gold" plus "Copperheads" pulled up the Knights of the Golden Circle. I clicked on the link and was whisked back in time to an era of conspiracy, violence, and fanatical support for the Confederacy. Said to be disbanded by the1870s in official records, others wrote to the contrary, arguing that it lived on in the shadowy eaves of Southern networks.

This search nudged me away from the familiar, glitzy Hollywood portrayals of the South, to the veiled origins of a private Old South that still exists. In this inner amorphous sanctum, distant cousins still marry, "where are your people from" is a serious question, and tiny kingdoms persist thanks to trust funds amassed in unmentionable ways. The New South, in contrast, is a public enterprise where the mixing up of global capital and people from distant places with all types of homegrown Southerners produces mainly jobs, some anxiety and new but superficial friendships.

Marco and I live contentedly in the public New South. The coin I found is a key to the private Old South if only I can find the lock. I printed some pages about the Knights of the Golden Circle to show Marco and ordered a 1864 report by Felix G. Stidger, an undercover agent of the US government who infiltrated this organization. Where was that Ian Wilkes, now? He had never replied to my e-mail, sent a while back, with the images of the numbered side of the coin. No matter. I was pumped up to read an official historical record. Maybe Ian didn't like me messing around in his turf, but too bad. No one owns the market on curiosity.

A few days passed before I could devote any more time to my quest. The chance came on a sunshiny day from a cloudless blue sky over the East Pass channel of Choctawhatchee Bay that narrows into the Gulf of Mexico. I didn't mind the light breeze off the water, glad for my windbreaker jacket. I sat outside on a weather worn picnic bench, hugging the rail of a long wooden pier anchored on shore by Dewey Destin Seafood. Here at number 9 Calhoun Avenue, a couple blocks off Destin's main thoroughfare, Highway 98, is a grey wooden shack attached to a faded yellow trailer home. A huge deep fryer and a black barrel smoker stand outside. From the street you see old-fashioned Coca Cola signs on the walls and the Dewey Destin Seafood sign on top. The ice packed coolers inside hold the freshest fish around. The Destin family specialties are served right to your picnic table in red plastic baskets lined with wax paper. The clam chowder is decadent, the oyster po boys pure wickedness. The sweet tea will wash all sins away. I waited for Guillermo, having tempted him with lunch in exchange for information. I felt like a spy.

A shiny black Mercedes-Benz sedan pulled into the car park, the type a government official or drug dealer would drive. I adored them even as a little girl when one would pull up in front of our saloon. One day a special passenger stepped gracefully out of the car. I expected a fedora perched askew on a real gangster but instead it was just the skull cap on our bald local bishop. Well, perhaps he was a gangster of sorts, but I loved those cars anyway. Guillermo stepped with the unhurried gait of someone accustomed to power and authority, who never ran after anyone but was rather the one others would run after. The dark wrap-around glasses against his tanned face and silvery waves of thick hair gave him a movie star look. His baseball jacket embroidered with a Navy emblem made him look official.

"Hello, Harley. How did you know this is my favorite place? Did Consuela tell you?" He slid onto the bench.

"No, she didn't. It is one of my favorites and close to the harbor for you. How can anyone not love this place?"

"Well, that is true. Outdoors, great food, and still operated by the family of Mr. Leonard Destin, the man who started Destin in 1835. His home stood only 100 yards from here, just there to the north along the shore." He pointed towards the shore.

"You seem to know quite a bit about Destin history."

"I grew up in Pensacola and so this whole coastal area was my playground. I loved the sea, so my father suggested I make it a career, but I had to go to college. So off to Annapolis, the Naval Academy and presto, a career at sea. I developed a special interest in the Gulf Coast history because it is home. But, I came to help you, not to talk about me. What can I do for you?"

"How or where could I find records of ships that might have sailed from this area at the time of the Civil War to Brazil?" I began.

"Ah, you are thinking of the city Americana that Mario spoke of at Supper Club. Between you and me, that evening was a revelation. I had not registered the depth of sensitivity about Confederate heritage among our friends before. Perhaps until you found your coin, there had been no reason to reveal it."

"Guillermo, what was your work in the Navy?"

"Ah, spoken like a sociologist. You did not ask me my job, but rather my work. I can tell you this, my work often did not match the job. Is that enough to satisfy you?"

"Hm. Why am I not surprised?" I silently pumped my fist against my leg under the table. He was a spy!

"You know, I grew up with English and Spanish both as native languages, so learning other languages just came easily. You could say I spent lots of time fishing. I mean with a rod and reel too, but again you have managed to turn the conversation to me when it is I who came to help you."

"Yes, of course. Here it is. Eliza Blackmon's great great-grandmother's sister, Maggie Rainer, we think, left her home in Union Springs, after the Civil War, on a ship bound for Americana. She was never heard from again, presumed dead at sea. Eliza has no record of the ship's name or if a Maggie ever boarded. Her grandmother would say that a bright star took her to the deep ocean. I thought "bright star" might be the name of the ship. Is this too long ago for us to track down now?"

"Not at all. Records can be accessed. I can access them. Do you believe the coin you found belongs to this Maggie? Because her sister's portrait includes the same coin? Because there might be more to this than just a found relic?" He crossed his knees and leaned across the table.

"You're quick. Is it that obvious? "

"Only to me if you and Eliza have told no one else. You must play your cards close. Does Wilson know? If he does not, why is Wilson out of your loop, or am I prying?"

The wind blew some curls across my face. I paused while a waitress poured more sweet tea into tall glasses filled with crushed ice. She set bowls of steaming clam chowder in front of us along with a basket of hush puppies and a plate of fried oysters for us to share. If I expected Guillermo to help us, we'd have to let him in. "You are not prying, not at all. Wilson is outside our loop, as you call it, because he became obsessive about the coin in the portrait ever since I found mine. He's a secretive guy, and he would not share any historical information with me because I'm a Yankee. He doesn't share much of it with Eliza according to her. It's as if there is an unspoken race going on and he wants to win."

"Okay, then. I will research the names of ships that sailed to Brazil at that time and check passenger manifests such as they were then. Where do you think Maggie went aboard?"

"She's from Union Springs, Alabama, about forty miles west of the Chatahootchee River on the Alabama, Georgia border."

"That helps. She'd most likely travel down the river, to Florida, where it becomes the Apalachicola River flowing into the East Bay at the town of Apalachicola. She could have easily booked a passage from there to most anywhere."

"Eliza and I appreciate your help."

"It is a pleasure to help friends. Now, tell me, when will we get to see you and Marco alone? Without the mob of Supper Club?"

"Soon, I hope. I'll check Marco's schedule and give Consuela a call. When is her next show?"

"She has a show in the spring, but I don't remember where. Don't tell her I forgot where, okay?"

"Your secret is safe with me." We spooks know how to keep our mouths shut, I thought.

We switched our discussion to the state of fishing in Destin. Guillermo remarked how tourists arrive expecting unlimited catches only to find new regulations in force because of the latest oil disaster. We parted ways to his Mercedes and my Mini. He sped off.

I lingered back to have a look at the neighborhood, turning left down Calhoun Avenue into a forgotten neighborhood where crusty boats sat up on blocks by trailer homes or cottages built with cinderblock. Overgrown scrub oaks and uncut grass lined the dirt road. Hardy people settled Destin a long time ago. Their families still live here on the banks of the East Pass of the Choctawhatchee Bay.

I turned the Mini around and slowly navigated the dirt road back toward Dewey Destin Seafood because I had forgotten to buy some shrimp for supper that night. Inside the shop, a chubby woman with red cheeks and even redder lipstick, her hair held back with a blue do rag, scooped up shrimp.

"Hi, I need a pound of large shrimp, please. And , by chance, are you a member of the family?"

"Yeah. One of the last around. The younger generation doesn't stick around here. Only by the grace of God and the Masons, are the Destins here at all." She grabbed a towel from the counter and wiped her hands.

"What do you mean? What do Masons have to do with it?"

"It all started with Leonard Destin. He came from New London, Connecticut after a perilous journey with his father and brother who were lost at sea near Cape Canaveral in a hurricane. In 1845 he married Martha McCullom and settled down here. The War came and because he was a Yankee, they thought he was a spy. The Confederates threw him in jail in Freeport to be hung later on. But, the circuit judge spared Leonard's life because they were fellow Masons."

"Wow. That's a story."

"Yes, ma'am, and it is all true." She handed me the bag of shrimp on ice. "Make some grits for these babies."

"That's what's for dinner tonight."

"Do you have the Destin family recipe?"

"No."

"Here." She handed me a photocopy of a recipe card. "You'll never use any other."

Leonard Destin was a Mason. I sat in my car digesting this fact. Masons in Destin, Masons in Brazil, Masons in Fern and Bobby's house. Suddenly they were everywhere. I sped home, dodging cars, shifting gears like a formula racer, weaving back and forth between lanes. I opened the front door to see a grey book propped up on the kitchen table. A star floating above a crescent moon was embossed on its cover.

"Your book arrived," Marco said. "Say, you want to go for a

run? Might do us both some good."

I put the shrimp in the fridge, changed and we were off. Later that evening, with dishes done, Marco dug into his stack of medical journals, Tulip curled on his lap. I snuggled into the corner of our couch with Daisy lounging against my hip and opened the 1864 US Secret Service Report. My bag of M&M almonds was safely tucked between two cushions nearby.

*

Saturday morning came and we sat on the screened porch with our coffee. It was too warm and muggy for December, a sure sign of oncoming storms. The lush Florida scrub had turned winter brown and thin like old age. Even the palms drooped from their lattice pillars with limp blades tipped with rusty curls. The pine trees had shed bushels of long wide cones over the past weeks. The mockingbirds sang winter tunes while the grey squirrels rummaged for the nuts they buried a season ago. This was when I missed Chicago the most.

I pictured the frosty air, the bare trees webbed with sparkling white lights lining north Michigan Avenue from the white Wrigley Building on the Chicago River to Oak Street Beach in front of the Drake Hotel. Each store window would be crammed full of Christmas props, figures and merchandise. Carols drifted in and out as you strolled along the avenue, riding on the wind from tinny speakers on buildings or from live choirs from schools or churches. The Salvation Army red buckets and bell ringers occupied every corner adding to the street bustle of shoppers and sightseers. Seasonal, but charming, chaos.

An SUV turned into our driveway, Reese McElwain at the helm. I kissed Marco good-bye and asked him one more time if he'd care to join us on a pilgrimage to the Christmas Festival sponsored by the Indian Temple Mound Museum at Fort Walton Beach. He declined and promised to stay out of trouble until I returned whereupon he proposed that we should stay home this evening and get into some trouble of our own. I shook free from his grasp and grabbed my jacket and purse.

"Babe, come home early if the weather starts to change. Bad storms are predicted." Marco waved to me.

Reese drove the SUV like a tortoise, sure and steady toward Watercolor and the Coffee home, a little more than a mile away on 30-A. We waited outside their dark brown two story clapboard house, with taupe trim and copper screened porches. A matching coach house stood in the rear. Watercolor homes are strictly designed in an updated version of the Florida vernacular, houses recognized by corrugated roofs, wood clapboard and screened porches. Watercolor embraces the New Urbanism philosophy, with a down-home style, where living close to nature means streets of majestic houses built on narrow lots next to parks with swimming pools and tennis courts. Western Lake is on the edge of the city limit, a small fishing, canoeing fiord attached to the Gulf waters on the border of Grayton Beach. "So what's it going to be," I'd ask my students when we studied urban development. "Can New Urbanism be both urban and close to nature? Does a park constitute nature? If the people who work there cannot live there is it really urban?"

"What are you staring at, Harley? Your face is set like stone," asked Chantal.

"Oh, sorry, I was thinking. It's a bad habit." I said.

"Since when is thinking a bad habit?"

"Harley thinks all the time about everything too much," said Reese from the front seat. "I think sociologists are troubled souls."

"Why thank you, Reese. From you that's a compliment."

"What's with you two?" asked Chantal.

"Nothing. Reese thinks I am a heathen, and I think it's none of her business."

"I'll keep praying for you, Harley." Reese folded her hands in prayer.

"You do that. Don't worry Chantal, this has been going on for a long time," I said. "Anyway, to answer your earlier question, since I was a kid I'd wonder about houses. Who lives there, and what do they do? That led me down the path of perdition, the path to sociology, where I now get paid to ask that and an assortment of other questions."

"Doesn't sound too bad to me. Getting paid to do what you love? That's what I do." Chantal replied.

"Family law, isn't it?"

"Yes, there you see it all. It's just working in a giant laundry, where all the dirty linen of various families gets sorted, hosed down and hung out to dry. Guess I come from a family of washer women."

"What do you mean? I'll take the bait."

"Genealogy is a hobby of mine. I traced my maternal line way back several generations. They took care of things as wives, mothers and house slaves. Washing clothes, dishes, houses, people, it's all about keep everything clean and tidy. With this as my heritage, it's no wonder I found my niche trying to clean up the messes people make in their lives."

"Hm, that's a poetic way of putting it. So genealogy is your thing," I said.

"Ok, finally, here comes Miss Meg, our own Southern belle," said Reese who closed her cell phone after dialing a call.

"Hi y'all," Meg said and jumped in next to me, my new best friend forever. Truthfully, she gave me the heebie-jeebies. This road trip was her idea, and I agreed only because Eliza and I thought she might inadvertently tell us something in her effort to be friendly. I warned Eliza that she might be doing the same thing, cuddling up to me so that I would tell her something. We also thought it better for just one of us to go, and I drew the short straw. Still, I welcomed the chance to chat with Chantal since I still didn't run into her at church. Of course, maybe I should go more often, but that is another story altogether.

"How long have you been living in Watercolor?" asked Chantal.

"Oh, let's see, a couple years. We've been in the area since we moved here for Colin to set up his practice about twenty years ago. I still love Kinston, where I'm from, but you know how it is, once you get out it is never quite the same going back. I love the old Southern down home feeling you have right here," she said.

I knew that the "down home feeling" in this modern planned empire of multimillion dollar homes did not truly represent the authentic Southern rural aesthetic typified by Kinston, engulfed as it still is with cotton fields, a peanut factory, and cattle pastures served by winding two lane roads. A quick sojourn to lower Alabama took me to Kinston once, to visit the genteel Southern Girls Formal Wear, the local source for unique party dresses. But, Meg Coffee internalized the brochure of the neighborhood development and she ultimately constructed the world of her ambition to which she had obviously become accustomed. Only for cruelty's sake should it be shattered, and I was not cruel.

30-A Supper Club works over the years because it is a mix of personalities but Meg's friendliness felt too scripted for me. Therein lies the problem. Perhaps I read her wrong or sometimes a person just bugs you. As Reese turned right onto 30-A toward the west, I tried to hyperdown. We passed Blue Mountain and the Martinez home where we would gather next Thursday. Reese asked us all something about the menu and cooking chatter broke out in the car.

The SUV rambled along Highway 98 past Baytowne, Sandestin, to Destin. Outlet malls to sporting goods emporiums, art galleries, fast food. If you wanted quick and easy, miles of it lay in wait for you. Rows of holiday resort edifices, four to forty stories tall, with more under construction, lined each side of the highway on our westerly journey to the Indian Temple Mound Museum.

I peered out at the strip mall on the north side of Highway 98. McGuire's Irish Pub where Marco and I go for pub fare. The corned beef makes me nostalgic for my Dad's saloon, however, I am always disappointed that I have to ask for a frosty mug.

Calhoun Avenue, site of Dewey Seafood and my rendezvous with Guillermo passed by. All this plus the discussion of recipes made me hungry and homesick again for Christmas time in Chicago. When I was a little girl, all French Canadian and Irish relatives of my mixed American parentage began to gather for a yearly Christmas party at the saloon, once they realized what they had in common besides respective claim on my parents. They both hated the English. Whatever it takes. Southerners have no corner on the "lost the war" market of colorful characters, lost fortunes, or heroic lost battles. I could tell stories of war, brutal defeat and oppression in the Canadian North that predate this Civil War business by a hundred years. But, those stories, equally haunting, with just as much blood and honor, are also for another time.

I stared out at the East Pass, and watched a few tugboats pulling barges heavy with freight. The East Pass Bridge rises steeply and I could see the winter grey Gulf open wide to the south, the points of Destin harbor poking toward it. We descended into white sugary masses of the undeveloped sand dunes of Okaloosa Island on a road that cuts through land and air space controlled by Eglin Air Force Base. The bare sparse plant life tucked in around the pristine dunes gives you a snapshot of the look of the whole area before the encroachment of people and their buildings took hold. The only hints that man has been around are the occasional lookout towers and the miles of barbed wire fences that crisscross across the area.

But quickly we returned to civilization where colors, lights, resorts and attractions for the citizens densely crowded the landscape. The car climbed the Miracle Strip Parkway bridge, and took us over a waterway, grinding to a stop on the other side. We parked on the street in front of a steep grassy mound. Thick bushes and wide bladed palm trees surround a wooden thatch roof temple.

"Here we are, ladies," said Reese, "our own little bit of ancient history."

"I never knew this was here," said Chantal.

"Oh, I used to bring my son and visiting relatives here, when they were small. We always had lots of fun at the heritage festivals," said Meg.

"Where is the Christmas part?" I said.

"In the old school house next door and then in a tent they set up out back. I'll show you," said Reese.

We slid out of the car and filed up the narrow path that led to the upper area of the mound. The path cut away leading to the school. The other direction led to the temple and museum. Chantal and I took the path leading to the historic temple and promised to catch up with the rest after we toured the museum. There would be plenty of time to peruse the booths and tables of the Christmas Fair afterwards.

We climbed the steep path to the top of the temple mound. It contained rails and partitions that de-marked how the early inhabitants might have organized the interior for the various rituals of their day. A park's department sign told the story of the people who built the mound and worshiped in the temple in the 600's. Some theories say they are related to the Incas. They were not related to the native tribes that migrated here over centuries from the North that were called Indians by European settlers. I couldn't grasp the amount of time that passed between the building of the mound and our standing on it as something concrete any more than I could grasp the passage of time in my own life.

After a few minutes we strolled down the path toward the museum. Here, various rooms housed three-dimensional scenes with costumed mannequins and taxidermy animals portraying different epochs of man and nature's development. One room served as a library, packed with books and old fashioned vertical files crammed with manila folders bulging with newspaper and magazine clippings on many subjects from many sources.

"You know, the Indians of the Southeast owned slaves," Chantal said.

"I never really thought about that." I scanned the book titles.

"Most of the Five Civilized Tribes did. Especially Cherokee, who were very involved with the Civil War," she said.

"I had no idea."

"Yes, Chief Stand Watie, a famous Cherokee chief, allied with the Confederacy. He also reached the thirty-third degree of Masons. It was only in the 1830s that the US government forced the tribes by official treaties, to leave for the newly designated official Indian territory in Oklahoma. This was supposed to take care of the Indian problem, you know, send them to reservations so the white settlers could take the land. However, the many Indians on the land who wouldn't abandon their homeland subverted that big lie. The tribes had to hide their culture, their very existence just to survive."

"It's their right to resist," I said.

"The sad thing is that the US government reneged on many an Indian treaty, by failing to disperse funds and confiscating more land."

"Are you particularly interested in Native American history?" We walked into the adjacent museum store.

"Oh, as it relates to researching the paths of my own relatives. What interests me is the Muscogee nation right here in Bruce not far from 30-A. They are part of the loose confederation known as Creeks and they have been in this Panhandle area a long time. At the time of the Civil War this town, Fort Walton Beach, was just Camp Walton. The Walton guards posted here protected the narrows, which is the water we just crossed over on the bridge. No particular tribe dominated this area back then," she said.

"What happened to them?" I studied a CD of tribal music.

"They survived by keeping a very low profile, blending in but not to the point of assimilation. Now they are trying to get long-delayed, official recognition from the government."

"Do you think that could happen?"

"There is a bill working its way through the system now. I hope the government sees the light and decides for justice."

"You are more than just interested, Chantal, if you don't mind me saying it. You are actively following this story. What's does it mean for you?" I pulled some M&M almonds out of a bag and offered some to Chantal.

"How can you eat those?" She took a few.

"Don't worry, it's health food. Now what's with this tribe?"

"I am tracking a lead about my great great-grandmother Kate Carter. She came from Union Springs and after the war traveled south to Mobile. She settled in an area established by escaped and freed slaves back then called "the Plateau," now since the 1980s known as Africatown. I actually grew up in Mobile just off Davis Avenue, in what use to be the Black "downtown." But anyway, the story is that Kate Carter traveled by water instead of land to the Plateau. That meant she and her company came through here, Camp Walton."

"Traveled by water from Union Springs? She'd have had to sail down the Chattahoochee River," I said.

"How would you know that? You are not from here." Chantal gripped my arm and her face grew taut.

"Okay, but first why did you say to Reese and Meg that you didn't know the Indian mound existed?" It suddenly dawned on me that Chantal's great great-grandmother might be part of my puzzle.

"I do not want to become entangled with Meg with her obvious Confederate sympathies. Unlike you who expressed interest, so are now in her crosshairs, I intended to play dumb. Now tell me, how do you know the closest navigable river to Union Springs in those old days was the Chattahoochee River?" She released my arm and picked up a beaded keychain, spinning it on her finger.

"Okay, Eliza Blackmon's family is from Union Springs, and we have been doing a little homework on her great great-grandmother's family about their movements after the war. We think they left by water, down the river to Apalachicola. That's how I know."

"It fits. Apalachicola." She shook her head.

"What fits?"

"My grandmother always told a tale about her grandmother and the first time she ever saw the Gulf of Mexico, the ocean. She'd call it the Apalachicola moment."

"Well, that's all very interesting but I am still at 'what fits.'"

"Apalachicola is no mistake. It is confirmation of identity, time and place."

"It is? Whose identity?"

"My great great-grandmother was the head housekeeper at the Powell plantation; Eliza Powell was her mistress. Eliza owned my great great-grandmother Kate. They left together after the war. Kate Carter continued west probably sailing until she got here. The story is she and companions, now freed slaves from the Powell plantation, lost most of their meager possessions here at Camp Walton in a robbery by a gang of white or Indian thugs, who knows? Newly freed slaves were easy prey. Anyway, a small metal box went missing and Kate Carter grieved its loss until she died. I like to imagine that the box fell into Indian hands and ended up in a museum like this. Waiting for me to find it."

"How could you identify it?"

"It had her initials engraved on it. And a cross."

While Chantal and I shared secrets, a willowy young woman with dense black hair woven into a single braid stood patiently behind the counter of souvenirs. She asked if we needed anything and gave us brochures about the museum and the mound to take with us. She did not know the date of the next festival of area tribes, so I gave her my business card and asked her to call me when she knew.

We walked over to the Christmas sale.

"Does Eliza know about your families' connections?"

"Not at all. One day it will come up. I'll tell her."

Over by the tall Christmas tree, decorated with bows and beads, balls and clip on birds, Reese was bent over a table strewn with angels made of shells. She saw us and waved. "Hey there! Glad you decided to join us. Look at these. They are beautiful."

"Yes, they are. Going to get one?" I asked.

"Heavens, no. They are overpriced. Besides I've got one with me all the time."

"Ah, your guardian angel," I said.

"I'd never expect you to come up with that."

"You'd be surprised Reese. Say, where's Meg?"

"Over by the old school house, at the Civil War booth."

I wandered over to her as she picked up a pamphlet that read Order of the Sons of Liberty with a snake underneath the words. "Looks old and interesting," I said stealing a closer look at it.

"Oh, I didn't see you. Yes, it's curious. I think Colin may like it. I looked for anything close to your coin but didn't see a thing."

"That's nice of you to scope out the goods. I doubt I'll ever find anything about it, but that's fine."

"You never know."

I wandered over to the crèche scenes made out of cornhusks but didn't buy one. We had one made of olive wood, a gift from a former student of mine, whose father carves them in a forgotten shop below their flat deep in Bethlehem.

Reese rounded us up like wayward sheep pointing to her watch. The four of us collected at the top of the stairs that led to the street below. Across the street the shops glittered with Christmas lights and finery draped along their window's edges. Artificial evergreen garland wrapped around the streetlamps, a bundle of fresh holly tied to the top with a red ribbon. A two-story grey office building looked out of place with the quaint stores on either side. Smooth and nondescript at first glance, the narrow windows made it difficult to calculate the building's age. Then I saw it. The symbol of the Masons, the compass, the square and the big G converged together dead center above the top row of windows. The words "Temple Building" had been inlaid into the brickwork. It could never fade or be painted over, embedded into its very structure. It would last as long as the building itself.

While making my way down the steps behind my sister shoppers, I saw Bobby Carlyle, Brantley Vernon and Wilson Garrett, emerge from the front door. They stood waiting and within seconds, a car driven by Colin Coffee pulled up. They signaled him with their right hands, what looked like a circle - thumb to forefinger, at least from my vantage. They piled into the car and sped off to the East, toward Destin. Meg had to have seen them too. She said nothing which I found only the more curious.

Our drive back passed quickly under a sky shuttered with swollen clouds casting a sickly green pall across us. Delayed rumbling followed distant lightning strikes as Reese drove just ahead of a storm beginning to bear down behind us. Chantal sat in the back with me. We vowed to arrange a coffee with Eliza in the next few weeks. Safely returned to the land of 30-A, with Supper Club only a week away, we bid adieu until then.

Marco met me at the door with his latest creation, a round chickadee house topped with a copper roof in the shape of an upside down ice cream cone.

"How do you like it?"

"Looks like a bird castle." I gave him a quick kiss.

"Where's your Christmas haul?"

"Nothing to buy, but do I have a story to tell you."

"Then, come out to the workshop and tell me."

We walked around back to the small building tucked into the corner of the backyard. I flopped down on the old futon inside. The choppy rain began to hit the tin roof. Marco set the birdhouse down and slid onto the futon laying his head in my lap. "Talk to me, babe, talk to me."

*

During the excursion to the Christmas bazaar in Fort Walton, we managed to divvy up parts of the menu for Supper Club. Hors d'oeuvres appeal to me so I volunteered to make the tiny crab cakes. Still, crab cakes are tricky, so I called Oliver, who owns the Red Bar, to beg for his recipe, the best ever.

Chantal claimed the Brussels sprouts. Reese wanted the mixed greens, and Meg settled for the spinach. Consuela always served fish cooked in brown paper bags or wrapped in banana leaves tinged with spice combinations, something only an artist could create. Sometimes she'd stuff a whole salmon, presented with head and tail, on a long narrow platter garnished with cilantro sprigs and grape tomatoes. None of us could guess how she'd cook the halibut for this month's Supper Club.

The oil sputtered as I dropped the crab cakes into shallow hot oil in my cast iron skillet. Marco hovered over the wine cupboard searching for the bottle of Rojo he had picked up from Bobby Carlyle's wine store last week. Half an hour later, we sped toward Blue Mountain on the western half of County Road 30-A. Legend has it Blue Mountain got its name from the early 19th century sailors who would watch for the rolling hills, densely covered in blue lupines and greenery. When the flowers were in bloom, it served as a reliable landmark for navigating the tricky coastline on the way to Mobile or New Orleans.

We passed Cafe Tango, our favorite Blue Mountain restaurant, a little house tucked into the trees. Further on, we passed Goatfeathers Restaurant and Blue Mountain Beach Coffee and Tea Company and finally came to the narrow unpaved driveway of the Martinez family. It was not as far as Miss Lucille's Gossip Parlor, which was in the next town of Dune Allen. Marco wound the car along a curvy path up a hill.

The Martinez home is approached on a path of crushed oyster shells lined by gardens filled with winter time pansies, bright hues of red, blue, yellow and purple surrounded by creeping evergreen rosemary. They lead you to the nautical blue front door, trimmed in gold. The doorknocker is shaped like an anchor. The two-story submarine grey clapboard house with grand stacked bay windows, reminiscent of the Queen Anne style, faced the Gulf. The house also boasted a "consumption porch" once the rage for TB therapy in Victorian times, where TB patients would sit and soak in the sunshine, breathing the fresh air presumed essential to their recovery. The porch caught tonight's dusk and breeze, extending like an inverted dormer from the roof. A widow's watchtower, topped with cresting, shot up square in the middle of the roof. You could see a telescope on a stand through the window of the tower and a door that led to a platform that encircled it.

I couldn't wait to see their recently acquired painting by Frida Khalo, a close friend to Consuela's great-aunt. It was a rare landscape with a clear yellow sun and bright green trees. Consuela said it looked at home against the ivory Spanish plaster walls. "Not even my sets of red, orange, and yellow pillows or the viridian green rug on the terra cotta tiles can distract you from Frida's painting."

She cringed the day I asked her where she met Guillermo. It was too embarrassing she'd say, but told the story anyway. On vacation with her family one summer in Pensacola, she dove into the clear Gulf waters and lost the top of her bikini. Guillermo heard her scream and swam out to her to save her, thinking she couldn't swim, only to find her standing hands across her breasts.

"I shouted go away, but he kept coming closer," she said. "He figured out the situation then dove to find my top. Once he had it, he tossed it to me and swam away. By the time I got to shore, he had rejoined his family. My father thanked him as a gentleman. Later that night I saw him at the pool of our hotel where he worked waiting the tables. He told me he was going to Annapolis to join the Navy. I told him I was in art school in Mexico. We snuck out to meet later that night and walked along the shore in the moonlight. He kissed me and said he'd write. I believed him. The rest is history: school, marriage, the Navy and twin boys."

Consuela greets you with kisses, handshakes, or hugs and she used her whole arsenal that night. She stood in the doorway like a traffic cop, directing us to the kitchen or dining room with the night's goods. Tables covered in either red or green cloths with white napkins filled the salon adjacent to those in the dining room. A miniature pinata swayed from a table hook, the type used to hang bunches of bananas. Tiny pots of cactus with pink and red flowers encircled it like a wreath. White votive candles flickered at each place setting. The Christmas napkin rings of flat multicolored tin were embossed with a star. Spanish classical guitar music drifted by our ears, and Rojo wine from Spain tasted light on our tongues.

The dispenser of the wine, Bobby Carlyle, pontificated about the resurgence in popularity of Spanish wine. He lectured us about Rojo as compared to Pinot Grigio or Pinot Noir, either of which he'd have also suggested for tonight's menu. Whatever, I thought, scanning his clothes for a copper pin or any symbol. Nothing. Wilson Garrett, also devoid of a pin, arrived with Eliza. They were all there, the usual suspects. "It doesn't matter," Marco whispered to me. "You must not be too eager." Anyway, it was Christmas. I told myself to let it go until next month.

I mulled over my next move. Watch and listen would be my game. Jean Louis and Mario stood inside the doorway of Guillermo's office where he pointed at something on the table. I motioned to Marco, bringing me a glass of wine, to join me in the office.

The walls were covered with built in shelves and cabinets of highly polished teak and brass trimmed mahogany inspired by an elegant Dutch clipper ship, the Stad Amsterdam, Guillermo's current favorite. He filled the captain's quarters with books, maps, an African mask, here, an Arabic backgammon board inlaid with mother of pearl, there. These paled against a vast collection of ships in bottles placed around the room on shelves, cabinets and tables. Maybe a hundred old ships, tall ships, new ships, and pirate ships rested on the barest of platforms in crystal-clear glass bottles of square, round, even oval contours. His latest creation sat on a lacquered tray in the middle of his desk. Inside a quart-sized round glass bottle, a pirate ship, and vintage 1790s, complete with sails and flag, balanced on a wooden platform. "This is my interpretation of the ship sailed by the pirate Billy Bowlegs," said Guillermo.

"And who is he?" asked Jean Louis. "Another American hero from days gone by?"

"No, not at all. He was a British loyalist who fought against the Americans during the Revolutionary War and later became the most famous buccaneer from this area. He got his infamous start in Pensacola where he went AWOL from his British regiment and hid with the Creek Indians. His life of piracy led him several times to Spanish jails where at last he met his dubious end. It is said that he buried his loot in the Destin area, desolate of course in the 1700s. Some folks still search for it using old maps."

"Are you one of those folks searching for pirate gold?" asked Jean Louis.

"No, not me. All I need are my boats. I'll leave searches for lost gold to others." He winked at me.

"Yes, of course, Harley, how is your search going?" Jean Louis clinked his wine glass against mine.

"It's not going. No news. With the Christmas rush, who has time? Say, are you heading north for the holidays?"

"No, the crowd wants to come here. My sister and her family will descend on us a few days before Christmas. I'd love to escape from them. Say, Guillermo, is it possible to book a trip on the Stad Amsterdam? Does it sail from Amsterdam to US ports of call and back?"

"Yes. Probably not in time to escape your relatives this month. Are you interested in other times?"

"Yeah, you see, when I was a young man, I worked for a couple years in the shipping industry in Rotterdam and later Amsterdam. I still speak a little Dutch."

"Oh, now you'll get him started." Marie Justine entered the office. "He'll tell you all about his favorite drink, Genever, a gin, the Dutch national drink, or at least Jean Louis says it is."

"Yeah, you cannot believe it. In Amsterdam there are bars full of a hundred brands of the stuff. It's paradise," he said. "We should have a Genever tasting at our Supper Club."

While others arrived and filtered into the office to see the ships in the bottles, Marie Justine pulled me aside. "You know I am a voracious reader, and well, while combing through some old books about the War of 1812... you remember, when America invaded Canada, I found a small volume about the Confederacy in Canada." She pulled the postcard-sized antique book out of her safari jacket pocket and opened to a page marked with a bobby pin. "Here, there's a guy named Clement Clay, an ex-senator from Alabama who held the title Commissioner of the North. I don't know if there is any connection to your investigation, but it struck me as interesting ever since you told me the other day that the coin might date from the 1860s. Thought that you might like to read it. So here." She shoved it into my jacket pocket. "Oh, here comes Wilson and Bobby, they probably want to know your progress with the coin mystery. I like their wives, but these guys put on their slick Southerner act too thick for my taste. But, hey, we are the foreigners," she laughed.

She was so right. In their haste to appear slightly disinterested, they stumbled over their words asking me if I found anything about the coin. Nothing, I answered.

Meanwhile, the evening progressed. Consuela presented a tray of tiny crab cakes, circulating the room. Adelaide and Brenda stood next to the roasted Brussels sprouts on the coffee table in the salon, devouring them like potato chips. Brantley approached Jean Louis who intently studied the scale miniature of the Confederate submarine Hunley, the one vessel not encased in a bottle.

"Pretty, isn't she?" asked Brantley.

"Phenomenal attempt to marry technology with the science they knew at that time," said Jean Louis. "You really have to appreciate just how motivated those men were, to enter such a risky machine."

"Confederate soldiers were inspired, no doubt about that. They had the cause worth fighting for. They responded to the call where ever they were needed, even Canada," Brantley said.

Jean Louis stood up and rubbed his lower back. "Yeah, Confederates in Toronto, we learned that in our Canadian history classes. We let Confederate prisoners who escaped from Northern prison camps stay and relay information between England and the Confederate government. Oh, and the Toronto Operation."

"What do you know about the Toronto Operation?" asked Brantley after a swig of wine.

"Not much actually, just that there were plans to attack Maine by land and sea. They were foiled by the locals who reported unusual people and actions," said Jean Louis. "Maybe saying 'y'all' gave it away."

"Very funny." Brantley scowled as if personally hurt.

"Brantley, if I may add." Consuela offered the tray of crab cakes to the many hands grabbing at them. "That Toronto case is one I used in my art history course. The operation was compromised by artists, or more accurately Confederate topographers, sent to Maine to map the coastline."

"What do you mean?" He stood at rapt attention, hanging on her every word.

"To launch a land and sea attack you need to know the coves and inlets, rivers, cliffs, trails, that sort of thing. In those days, before satellite photography, artists worked as topographers to sketch the Earth for eventual maps. To send one or two under cover would take some time. The heads of this mission sent fifty at once, combing the coast of Maine. No wonder the locals figured out fifty men, all newcomers with Southern accents, all plein-air landscape artists drawing the coastline meant a military action was afoot. What were the Confederates thinking?" She laughed.

"I never understood what went wrong up there. It should have been so simple," Brantley said. "Who would have thought the artists gave it away? Consuela, that's a mighty insightful tidbit you just gave us. Sure you're not a spy yourself?"

"Oh, for heaven's sake." She flashed a half grin toward Guillermo. "What will you think of next?"

Brantley could not shake the revelation loose and turned to Wilson, "Vallandingham was a smart guy. He was going to create a Northwest Confederacy from his base in Toronto. This couldn't have been his error."

"More likely that Hines kid, who was in way over his head," said Wilson, swirling his wine in an etched wine glass. "He was supposed to have been a veteran spy, but he was too young."

Marco had quietly slipped into the room, standing next to me with his hand on the back of my neck. His thumb rubbed my tense neck and he whispered softly, "Let's get our plates." We picked up plates from a table and so did Mario and Dana. Jean Louis and Marie Justine grabbed the last two with Jean Louis announcing, "No Southerners allowed, please, oh except for Dana." When Marie Justine frowned he protested, "Everybody knows I'm kidding about us being foreigners."

I wasn't so sure.

We made our way through the array of platters, each containing colorful temptations of gustatory delight. How can you resist Venetian spinach with pine nuts and raisins? Or wild yeast pan de sol rolls? Or salad with homemade green goddess dressing? Or garlic cheese grits. The trick is to take enough for a good taste but not so much that you over eat. It is a delicate balance.

None of us could remember when we last ate halibut, a royal fish, pure white and mildly rich. The citrus walnut tapenade had Consuela's artist temperament, both tart and sweet at the same time.

Just as desserts were served, Fern left the table and went to the kitchen. She didn't return so I went to investigate. She sat in a chair by the sliding door to a patio, "I want to leave Bobby but don't see how. It's been coming for a few years. Just can't take it anymore. Even, here, tonight he is somewhere else. He's been gone for a long time."

"Whoa. This is serious."

"It would be my second divorce. Almost no one knows about my first marriage to a much older guy when I was only nineteen. Look at me. Trapped by another idiot. Trapped by family. Trapped by money. Trapped." Fern stared through the plate glass.

"We can't do anything here, now. Come over tomorrow. Let's come up with a plan." I turned to see Eliza enter the kitchen.

"Ah, ha! Man trouble. Can diagnose that across the room," said Eliza.

Chantal followed. Adelaide leaned in from the doorway, "Anyone sick?" She saw Fern's dejected face. "Oh, I get it."

We were ready to call it a night and began to gather our trays and spoons and bowls. All it takes to signal the close of the evening is for one couple to start rounding up their gear for departure. The rest follow suit and in no time, the host and hostess are left with the clean up. That is the one hardship of supper club. But, we only endure it once a year so the tradition persists. When I cued Consuela in on Fern's meltdown, she couldn't have been more gracious.

Marco and I rode quietly back to our house, his hand on my knee. "I ate too much. For sure I'll get heartburn tonight." We walked into our house to find Tulip and Daisy each curled in a ball at opposite ends of the couch. I saw the grey book on the table and remembered. "Marco, I forgot to tell you. Brantley mentioned a guy named Vallandingham tonight. He was the Grand Master of the Sons of Liberty. I read it only today in this book. I think that this group still exists in some form."

"Can you tell me about it in the morning?" said Marco, turning out the porch lights. "Let's go to bed."

I pulled the small book Marie Justine gave me from my pocket and debated whether to have a look at it now or in the morning. Marco yawned, rubbing his stomach and pulled me along. I decided for the morning and followed him toward the bedroom, not stopping to check our answering machine. Unnoticed, the red light flashed on through the night.

Menu

Baked Goat Cheese on Melba Rounds

Split Pea Soup garnished with Roasted Peppers

* * *

Baby Spinach with Apple Vinaigrette and Parmesan

* * *

Hoppin' John with Bacon

Collard Greens

Bone-In Ham with Cherry Sauce

* * *

Buttermilk Biscuits with Orange Blossom Honey

Texas Toast with Garlic Pesto

* * *

Chocolate Hazelnut Fudge with Praline Ice Cream

* * *

Riesling or Rosé

January

The flashing red light belonged to Jim Reed. His call anyway. The one I found late the next day. "Call me." Twenty-four hours later was too late to find him. His answering machine picked up only to ask me, the caller, to leave a message. I did not.

The image of Jim Reed speaking on the phone, waving goodbye last fall troubled me. Everything about my quest began to trouble me. It's slow pace, which was my own fault if I were honest with myself, but there was something more. Something creepy. The pulse that throbbed in my hand when I viewed Eliza Powell's portrait had started to beat when I read about the untied loose ends of the Civil War. Especially the Knights of the Golden Circle. Unless Jim Reed had a book about ghosts, I doubted he could help much.

A few days later, on a fresh, sunny morning, I left early for the new semester's first general faculty meeting. I wore my favorite leather jacket, driving gloves and a silk scarf wound around my neck to fend off the elements. To some Panhandle natives I was still overdressed. They didn't know I wore driving gloves all year round because the leather grip on the wheel and stick shift feels like speed. I see my father's hands through the cut outs on the gloves, working hands, steadfast, loyal. With a sharp turn, I squealed into a narrow parking space and got out.

125

When I looked up, a Hawaiian shirt, one filled with bright blue sailboats this time, stood before me. "Let's take a walk."

"Happy New Year. Why should I take a walk with you?"

"You didn't return Jim Reed's phone call," said Ian Wilkes.

"How do you know Jim Reed called me? Do you know him? What is this all about, Ian? I am not walking to the corner with you if you don't explain yourself."

"I'll explain, but let's walk. It is such a beautiful morning, I cannot stand being inside yet." He pointed toward a small grassy square with a few scattered benches. "We can sit there in front of everybody."

"Oh, I see, you are trying to protect my honor by sitting in public? Is there a rumor going around about us? All I did was attend one of your lectures."

"Hey, I know there is plenty of speculation about my private life around here. Wouldn't take much to start a rumor. Want to start one?" His eyes brightened while he watched for a reaction.

"Hmm. Not just now. Rather inconvenient. Happily married. You know the drill. But I promise you that if anything changes, you'll be first on my call list." I instantly regretted saying it. Because, it was a lie. Someone else was already first on that call list.

"Rejection! Seriously, though, we need to talk."

"Now what?" Demon curiosity took hold of me. I followed Ian to a bench. He sat closer to me than expected so I slid my briefcase between us to use as a weapon or shield depending on what went down. A saloonkeeper's daughter from Chicago's South Side could do no less. Ian's smooth talking made me vigilant. With one hand lightly laid over the other, I waited, thinking that my driving gloves would dull the sting on my fists if I had to slug him.

I did not peg him as a smoking man. Too physically fit, too neat. He lifted his head up to catch all the sun's rays and leaned back like a true surfer dude relaxing on the sand. He pulled a robusto cigar out of his shirt pocket, bit off one end, and spat it away like a pro. He lit it with a lighter encrusted with a star and crescent moon.

"Now, let me tell you a story." He took a long drag on the dark stogie.

"It began long ago, with empire, the quintessential ambition of strong men and women. A personal empire may be no more than, say for example, what resources you might amass to exude power over your own church choir. People. Networks. Raw materials. But it may also be envisioned as territory spanning north to Pennsylvania and Ohio; then down through all the Southern States of the Union and south to the Isthmus of Darien; from the West Indian and Caribbean Islands to Mexico and Central America. A perfect circle. 16 degrees latitude and 16 degrees longitude with Havana, Cuba, as the center, a golden circle of agricultural wealth derived from slave labor, governed by an elite cabal of white Protestant men. The vision of such an empire took root in the mind of John C. Calhoun of Charleston, S. C. early as 1835. The very John C. Calhoun named in the faculty chair in which I sit here at the college, thanks to the generosity of Bobby Carlyle and his family."

Ian took a deep cleansing breath, then a long drag from the cigar. He stretched his legs out in front, digging the heels of his black and white checked Vans into the sandy soil. "You see, Harley, even at that time, Mr. Calhoun thought globally of a region beyond the Southern states. Globalization is nothing new and his scheme was bigger than the conventional Confederacy. He needed the Southern states to anchor the plan that would create a new global empire. The networking began through small private groups known as Southern Rights Clubs whose purpose was to sow the seeds of disunion. States' rights, slavery, and the preservation of Southern culture from the onslaught of vulgar Northern industrialization and urbanization fueled the spirit of discontent. Alas, over twenty years, those who dreamed of an empire soon realized they must settle for the Confederate states alone. No less committed or ambitious, their energies turned to securing the South."

"Ian, this is such a lovely tale, and I do relish sitting outside in the sun on a chilly morning, but could you please tell me why we are here with you giving me a history lesson? Unless this is your way of working on your tan." I couldn't help but admire his broad shoulders and tried not to stare at the shape of his muscular thighs visible thanks to his tight fitting, well worn jeans. Truthfully, I didn't mind sitting so close. My hands relaxed inside my driving gloves.

"Ah, Harley, I love the sun." He stretched his arms out in front of him. "And it will all come clear in a moment, if I may continue." He flicked ash from his cigar. The hulls of the sailboats on his shirttail peeped out from below the hem of his green suede jacket, scrunched against the back of the bench.

"Try to wrap it up. Although I am a curious cat, don't toy with me or you might get scratched."

"A cat scratch? Duly noted. Okay, back to the story. One man, George W. L. Bickley, considered by some as an old humbug, a medical doctor with impressive fake credentials and forged degrees, began to organize the Knights of the Golden Circle. Some say he transformed the Southern Rights Clubs into the Knights of the Golden Circle, others say he was only inspired by them. It doesn't really matter. He created a structure for the stoked up belief in disunion and aspiration for a Southern nation. These groups now had a fancy name, a constitution, secret signs, symbols, rites of initiation and three levels of increasingly elite membership. He first began to set up "castles," as these Knights were to call their lodges, in Cincinnati. There is no doubt he borrowed the regalia of symbols, secret handshakes and the like from the Masons. It is said that many Masons, especially from the South, were secret leaders in the Knights of the Golden Circle. But, so what? Masons are hardly the issue here. If you ask who wrought the real damage to the Union troops and created instability in Illinois, Indiana, Kentucky, Ohio and on up the North, the answer is the Knights of the Golden Circle and their supporters known as Copperheads."

"And your point is?"

"My point is that by 1863, the Knights of the Golden Circle disbanded. Their leaders scattered, some were arrested and some went to Canada. They did rob a few banks and trains and hid the gold but little of it was ever accounted for or found. There is a legend that they began to blend into general society in order to protect stashes of buried Confederate gold, but that story is as dry as it is old. Nothing to it."

"Then they'd be known to each other only by secret handshakes and symbols on, say, a cigarette lighter?" I pointed toward his pocket.

"You are quick. Very observant, but of course, you are a sociologist. I like that." He shook the ash of his cigar. "You see, this folklore is sometimes invoked to assign value to artifacts from that era."

"So you are trying to help me with my coin. I'm glad to know this wasn't just a ruse to chat me up in the sun on this bench."

"Yes, of course I want to help. Friends, colleagues, that's what we do, help each other. And thanks for sending the photos showing the numbers on your coin. By the way, Meg Coffee told me you two had been at the market at the Indian Temple Mound last month. She bought a book for Colin, that intrepid Civil War buff, and said you were looking at coins. I wanted to save you from barking up the wrong tree. In fact, I know an antique coin dealer in Atlanta that you should meet."

"Ian, you are so sweet to worry about me. But why couldn't you have told me all this in my office instead of sitting out here?"

"There's no smoking inside." Ian stubbed the nub of his cigar out on the bench and tossed it into the shrubs.

I shook my head and walked toward the door. Ian trailed behind like a kid who doesn't want to go to school.

"Okay, then, Harley, I'll email you the name and address of that coin dealer."

"Thanks." I turned down my hallway. Once in my office I pulled Jim Reed's number up on my mobile.

"Jim? Harley McBride here. Happy New Year. Just returning your call. We missed you by a day," I said. It took only a minute to learn that he only wanted me to call Ian Wilkes because he knew a coin dealer in Atlanta. What took Jim half a minute to tell me, took Ian half an hour to unload. That entire minutia about the Knights of the Golden Circle implied my coin was not part of Civil War history and only led to a dead end. I didn't believe him for a minute. Why all the diversion? Ian's name rose to the top of my list of suspects who might have sent the warning about snakes and the copper pin. But why would he take such a personal interest in my silly gold coin? This played against his quiet man act. The guy who never mixes with faculty colleagues. Something wasn't right. His long speech was meant to discourage me. Why would he try to subvert my investigation? What did it matter to him? I now regretted sending him the additional images of the coin some weeks ago. It was a mistake to give away information.

There wasn't much time before the faculty meeting. I settled in at my desk, laptop open. I began to ruminate about big mouth Meg Coffee. Everything she saw of me, whether Supper Club or a Christmas Fair, she reported to Ian. I had to cut her out. Only Eliza and Chantal needed to know anything. Meg could only be serving as a conduit to something bigger and more sinister than we imagined. She might be slick but she underestimated me. Ian too, for that matter, read me all wrong.

I had been pouring over authentic expositions of the Knights of the Golden Circle and the 1864 Treason Report by United States Secret Service agent Felix G. Stidger. I knew far more than I let on about the affairs of the Knights of the Golden Circle. Yes, they disbanded in 1863, only to be reorganized as the Order of American Knights sometime during 1864 and a year later yet again as the Order of the Sons of Liberty. The Southern goal of disunion remained the same and the work carried on. Only the name had changed. Camouflage, decoys, red herrings, and distractions, the armaments of deception are the tools of saboteurs, deviants, revolutionaries, clergy, spies, criminals, politicians, technocrats, monarchists and anarchists. The list is endless.

To date, I had never found an official entry citing the dissolution of the Order of the Sons of Liberty. This weighed heavily on my mind, as did their practice of obtaining gold and silver either bequeathed by supporters or stolen from Union trains and from the homesteads of their enemies. Stealth governed the tactics of these foresighted gangs, so they cleverly buried their loot in quart-sized glass jars or book-sized tins, small caches easily spread out in the countryside, the frontiers of a nation they struggled to build. Sentinels defended the hiding places. Only they could decipher the symbols carved on trees and etched on rocks that pointed the way to more clues. A snake meant a river, a buried empty gun's barrel served as a compass pointing the direction of the stash, and a turtle meant money. With legends to decipher the panoply of symbols and scratchy withering maps drawn like spider webs, the Sons of Liberty could patiently wait, steadfast and ready, for the day when the South would rise again.

*

I, too, could be steadfast to my quest, even if the leads were vague. Supper Club was all about digging for clues, not recipes. Reese McElwain called me one Saturday afternoon, presumably about recipes.

"Harley, I need your advice."

"Mine?" I stroked Daisy lounging against a pillow.

"Yes. This is more in your area. You see, Walter and I were out doing errands. We stopped at the 30-A Nursery for a new copper sprinkler can. Next I made Walter stop at Cocoons for smoked tuna dip. Spencer told me Patricia was working overtime at Roland's because she's just back from being out of town on family business."

"Reese, is there a point to this?" I shifted the phone from one ear to the other.

"Yes. Okay. Next we stopped by Fusion to pick up a gift and we visited with Fern who, as you know, handles the jewelry."

"Reese."

"Patience, Harley. Fern did not look good. Distant, too.

Hardly talked. Next we dropped a bike off at Big Daddy's Bike Shop to have it repaired. As long as we were this far from Rosemary Beach, Walter suggested we get some coffee at Miss Lucille's Gossip Parlor, just down the road. I know it's his reward for the morning's errands. You don't have to suggest it. I'll say it for you."

"Wasn't going to say anything. Don't be so sensitive. Where is this leading?"

Reese paused and took a deep breath so loud that the phone almost shook. "Walter found a table near the front window and sat facing out toward the sea to people watch. That's the ex-cop in him, always wants to sit where he has a view of everybody. I brought our coffee and cookies to the table and took the seat opposite him. I could see everyone in the shop. That's when I choked on my iced latte."

"Is that what's wrong? You've hurt yourself and need Marco?" I sat up, alarmed that she was ill and I missed it.

"No, no. I'm fine. It's what I saw. Walter saw it too. Brenda and Bobby were huddled at a table in the corner. Walter said they must be very good friends. Maybe she is his personal trainer since they were holding hands. Make that kissing them. She let him kiss her hands. We both saw this. We snuck out a side door so they wouldn't know we caught them en flagrante."

"Are you kidding? No, I know you would never kid about something like this."

"Walter told me we should not get involved but keep them in our prayers. But, Fern seemed so sad when we saw her at Fusion." Reese said.

"She is sad."

"What should we do?"

"We?"

"Yes, you are much closer to her than me, but we are all in Supper Club together and see each other every month. I am out of my league here, Harley. I admit it, which is no small thing to say. You are more worldly than me."

"Oh, come on now, Reese. We really don't know what it was all about. We have no context. Before we jump to conclusions, we would need to see them behave in the same way in other places or at least at Miss Lucille's a few more times. Let's agree to keep this between ourselves until we have quite a bit more information. Reputations can be ruined by false accusation. Think of those poor women at the Salem witch trials."

"Witch trials? I hardly think we are on a witch hunt."

"No, but we need to be sensitive and accurate about this because if there is something to it, many people could be hurt. So shall we observe quietly a little while longer? I promise to talk to Fern if we decide there is something for her to know."

"Okay. Agreed. Oh, hey, on another note, Walter told me to pass along that if Marco ever wants some company for fishing to give him a holler. He loves to go on those party boats out of Destin Harbor."

"Alright then. I'll let Marco know. And, I do appreciate the call. We'll do what is right, don't worry," I said.

"I knew I could count on you." Reese's voice trailed off with a breathy goodbye.

Hanging up, the complicated aspects of friendship weighed on me. I sank like a marshmallow into the back of our ball chair, and spun around 360 degrees. I first saw these chairs in the British television show *The Prisoner* and vowed to own one someday. So there I remained with Daisy to sift and sort between what was known, unknown, what was seen, unseen, and what was said, unsaid. Sociology reminds us that sometimes a meeting in Miss Lucille's Gossip Parlor is just a meeting. Perhaps, after a little time, we would find there would be no message to deliver to Fern. In this case I wasn't sure.

The next week Brantley Vernon called to schedule a golf game with Marco. The night before their game, Adelaide called wondering if I ever played golf. "Not really," I said, "but I wore the outfit and pretended once for a fund-raiser golf tournament." She begged me to play the next day with the men since she persuaded Brantley to let her join him, that is, if I played. So I agreed.

The best perk of running the pro shop at Crooked Creek Golf Course is first choice of tee times. That day, Brantley chose a tee time at 11 am, safe enough given the January temperature of fifty. The bold blue sky and dazzling sunlight lit up the overseeded greens, so colorful they looked fake. Later I realized the green scuffs on my golf shoes at the end of the day were paint.

Teeing off first, Marco sent his ball sailing before it hit a tree and boomeranged back into some rough. The first of the day's swear words flamed out of his mouth. Brantley followed with a precise hit to perfect position. Adelaide hit next, then me. The order established, I concluded each hole with a laugh because what else do you do when you suffer at golf. It never occurs to me to practice; I'd rather do anything else. It was the chance to be with Adelaide that drew me out, especially since she begged. Inquiring minds want to know.

Our golf cart gave us a dedicated space without the chance of being overheard by our competitive alpha-male partners who sped along far ahead. Adelaide wasted no time getting to the point.

"Is Glen Royal seeing someone?"

"Not that I know of." I conjured up Brenda and Bobby at Miss Lucille's per Reese's description.

"Well, I saw Bobby Carlyle and Brenda Royal together in Watercolor. They were whispering about something over a glass of wine when I walked up to them." Adelaide leaned on her driver.

"So what? And I don't get the Glen question?"

"They looked pretty close. I never see Glen and Brenda together anywhere."

"Seems strange to think Glen has someone on the side. But I suppose his prickly persona and noisy hook could make him a hottie to someone." I swung my club pretending to practice my swing.

"She'd have to be into counterculture and heavy metal." Adelaide laughed at her own joke.

I couldn't tell if Adelaide's absolute certainty about the platonic nature of Bobby and Brenda's interactions meant she was covering for them or sincerely believed what she said. Adelaide, a cookie-cutter girl, perfectly coiffed and dressed as long as it was in the latest catalogue, never made waves or volunteered an opinion she hadn't heard first on Ellen or Oprah. Such women are to be handled gently for although they may not be as smart as they are beautiful, they do possess fangs. Wiliness powers them, and they cling to the sway of conformity. Their appearance is a decoy, so you imagine them smarter than they really are. What they lack in intelligence they make up for in guile. They are predatory social survivors, and the society columns are swamped with them.

"Glen is a Realtor anyway and the best are always showing houses or taking clients to lunch. It is a very social job."

"Yes, of course, but he's always gone. Brenda is so lonely, she cries herself to sleep," said Adelaide. "She said so."

"Is he gone all night?"

"No, but he stays up all night watching TV. I don't think Brenda's getting any."

"Before I'd jump to the conclusion there is someone else, maybe something else is going on. Is Brenda home every evening waiting for him?" I said.

"She has aerobic classes in the evening or yoga, something every night for the folks who work during the daytime," Adelaide said.

"So if Brenda is working evenings and Glen is home alone maybe the problem is their schedules. They are off track. They keep missing each other. Glen is tired and bored. When Brenda gets home she's too tired for another performance, if you get what I mean."

"Oh, I get it." said Adelaide.

"How do you know all this? Did Brenda say something."

"Yeah, after I ran into Bobby and her at Wineworld in Watercolor. She came into Pizitz the next day while I was at work. She explained they were planning a surprise party for Glen and not to tell anyone. They hadn't set a firm date because Glen is always away on weekends. Her eyes welled up with big tears." Adelaide suddenly sped up our cart to catch up to the other only to hold back while they took their shots.

"Don't most good Realtors work every weekend? That's when they show houses. Not mid week." I picked out a club.

"Yeah. So what is she talking about? NASCAR season is on break for a few more weeks and other races at Talladega don't start for a while. If anything, Glen would be home more right now." Adelaide pulled a ball out of her cargo pants pocket and walked toward the tee. "Do you think Brenda is playing me?"

"Who knows. They may be planning a party or not. Glen could be working or not. Is it really any of our business?" I followed, swinging my club like a baton twirler.

"No, I suppose not. For now, let's keep this between us."

"Okay." I did not believe she'd hold her tongue. For a 30-A socialite, what was the fun in that?

Marco loaded our clubs into the Mini. I hugged Adelaide and Brantley goodbye at the clubhouse. He insisted I should get Marco some different clubs, that he'd play better if he upgraded them. He probably would but Marco didn't love or play golf enough to buy a new set of clubs. As daylight dimmed, we drove home across long shadow stripes cast from the pine trees lining County Road 30-A.

On the way, Marco relayed a message for me from Brantley. He knew an antique coin collector in Atlanta named Han Li. Brantley knew him from the Civil War buffs that buy and sell collectables through him. He also said he could create a provenance for the coin so it would fetch a bigger price.

"Isn't creating provenance for found objects illegal? You legitimize a fake, tricking a collector into believing in its authenticity."

"You sure would think so. I didn't challenge him on it. Guys like Brantley wheel and deal. Better to keep distance from them."

"I wonder if Han Li is the same antique coin collector in

Atlanta that Ian Wilkes knows? Jim Reed couldn't remember the name but said Ian would know this collector. How many dealers could there be that cater to Civil War buffs?"

"Just ask Ian the name of his collector, don't give him anything else. If it is the same, then you'll know they are all part of the same network. What you do next, we'll think about that later."

A week later, Ian Wilkes e-mailed the name: Han Li. He provided the address and phone number but mentioned that he needed to make the referral first before I called Mr. Li. Although assumptions are risky, Ian must know Brantley Vernon. If he knew Meg and Colin Coffee and their crowd, he had to know Brantley.

With this additional twist fresh off the computer, I called Eliza Blackmon. There was much to discuss. We combed through our calendars to find some free time. She welcomed adding Chantal to our team since her family also hailed from Union Springs. We set a date at the Donut Hole on Highway 98, in two days.

Other than the yellow and turquoise neon sign spelling Donut Hole on the roadside, you could drive right by the white clapboard structure reminiscent of an old farm outbuilding. Once inside, you see old Formica top tables in wooden booths and you inhale the aroma of dark, fresh-brewed coffee, hot fried donuts, dusted, frosted or glazed, sizzling bacon, and cheesy omelets. You can order breakfast anytime, but the deli sandwiches and burgers made many a carpenter, banker, cop, family with kids, or church goer wait in line for a booth.

I parked my Mini with the black and white checkerboard top into a narrow space at the edge of the parking lot. Eliza's Jag, sleek and so money was parked a space away from Chantal's practical hybrid SUV. What did my car say about me, I wondered, walking to the door. I found them in a corner booth near the row of windows where you could watch the traffic and the blue cop lights flash by in hot pursuit of speeders. I slid in beside Chantal.

"How long have you known?" Eliza said, hands folded, peering directly into Chantal's brown eyes.

"Since December. Because my great great-grandmother lost her documents at Camp Walton, our evidence leading to her plantation home of Union Springs is gone. Oral histories can be colorful but flawed and failing memory tinges them with inaccuracy. When Harley mentioned your great great-grandaunt made it to Apalachicola, that's when I made the connection. It wasn't uncommon for newly freed domestic slaves to travel with their former masters for safety as both carved out new lives in post-war times. My great great-grandmother went from Union Springs to Apalachicola on her way to Mobile. My grandmother is named Eliza."

"I don't know what to say. Your great great-grandmother Kate Carter would be pleased to know, her great great-granddaughter is so accomplished. Who could have predicted our paths would connect in Supper Club from Harley's search over an old coin. It is not clear what happened to my Aunt Maggie there. My great great-grandmother returned to Union Springs and the homestead only with her children. My great great-grandfather died in the war. One family story said a group of special Soldiers of Liberty or something like that, came to hold a memorial service for him about a year later."

"Eliza, what group did you say?" I choked on the hot coffee.

"I don't know, something "liberty" is all I remember. Why?" replied Eliza.

"Why? The Order of the Sons of Liberty stashed gold and silver during and after the war for later use when they could resurrect their secessionist dream. Maybe your great great-grandfather belonged to this group before he died." For a moment my right hand throbbed hard and fast. Then it was gone. I struggled to refocus on my friends.

"Or, maybe they tried to woo Eliza's great great-grandmother into giving them her gold," said Chantal. "Ingratiate themselves and if that didn't work, intimidate her. A wealthy officer's widow alone, no matter how strong, could be perceived as vulnerable by such vultures back then."

"God knows the looting and treachery after the war is the stuff of legends we grew up with," said Eliza. "Where does that leave us now?"

"I wish they hadn't lost the box in the raid at Camp Walton, probably full of clues. Maybe even a coin. Eliza, you say there are three coins. They are to assemble. What does it mean?"

"I wish I knew. But don't ask me to peek at the papers yet. I'm not ready to break the tradition. I don't know what is unleashed if I do. Any broken rule has consequences. I'm scared of this." She crossed her arms and rubbed her shoulders as if chilled.

We stepped into a cool late afternoon breeze on our way out from the Donut Hole. Eliza embraced Chantal. "I am so sorry -- on their behalf I am so sorry. Would that I could change it."

Chantal nodded.

*

The new year officially arrives in the South when you eat Hoppin' John on New Year's Day. Black-eyed peas or, Hoppin' John, made with collard greens, ham or sausage, and rice are the basics that originated in the Carolinas, especially the Low Country. The tradition spread through the South with many permutations over the years. Chantal and Darius invoked the tradition with January's Supper Club at their home in Seacrest Beach.

Seacrest Beach is full of clapboard houses trimmed with fire engine red, cobalt blue or sap green stripes. A red brick swanky condo building anchors the east side. On the other end, a new orange brick condo with airy lime-colored, metal balconies that curled around the corners of wide windows looked like a fruit tart, lots of color and very sweet. Yet another Seacrest house is nothing more than a brown shack with a cedar shake roof impaled on stilts. It sits next door to a fancy stucco villa topped with scarlet tile and curly wrought iron designed with Spain in mind. There are many architectural juxtapositions on County Road 30-A. That's why we love it.

Supper Club arrived right on schedule, the second Thursday of the month. I baked the goat cheese until its aroma filled the air. Marco puttered around in the bedroom getting dressed. I sank into the ball chair and spun in half turns, second guessing myself. Should I have told Eliza and Chantal about what Reese and Walter had witnessed? Should I have told them about Adelaide's assumption about Glen? Just because it doesn't prove anything didn't mean it doesn't disprove anything. Back to square one. I would keep my mouth shut, but whether Reese or Adelaide broke ranks and set the rumor mill spinning remained to be seen. Supper Club, with its freely poured wine, loosens tongues. Let the wagging begin. Marco carried the cheese and Melba rounds on his mother's deep floral china platter to the car and placed it carefully in my lap.

Around the bend Marco drove, cop eye on full strength. We left at seven in the winter darkness, County Road 30-A deserted but for a few cars which turned in behind us. From the street light we could see the caravan of members' cars parked along the road like floats after a parade. The large porch across the front of the house was lit with tiny beams from the scattered pin holes of three hanging star-shaped metal lanterns. An iron basket of yellow and purple winter pansies suspended in a macramé hanger from a beam in the ceiling rocked to and fro in the occasional whiffs of sea air. I followed Marco into the house.

New members, Chantal and Darius, had to endure the first-time inspection. A definite perk of membership in the 30-A Supper Club is the chance to go inside the highly decorated homes of committed 30-A residents. After I put the platter of goat cheese in the kitchen on the paradiso granite countertop, Dana and Marie Justine signaled to me.

"Come on," said Marie Justine, "Chantal told us it's okay to take a tour. She expected it. What can I say? The girl is brilliant."

We found cozy bedrooms, beds covered with old-fashioned chenille bedspreads, dressers still dotted with their children's keepsakes and trophies. Shelves were packed tightly with textbooks and picture albums. Posters of Martin Luther King and Denzel Washington stared at each other in one room, while a map of Senegal hung in another. A third room had a slim shadow box filled with sepia tinged tintype pictures of Chantal's family, probably grandchildren of those who trekked from Union Springs to Mobile, long ago.

"It's quiet, without all those kids around," said Chantal, "Sabrina, our oldest, lives in Boston, working for Deloitte and now has a steady boyfriend. Michael is in his last year of law school. Emile, a musician, plays on Broadway. They share an apartment in New York and rarely get home."

"Good thing you have Supper Club, now." said Dana. She put her arm around Chantal's shoulders and squeezed.

Guillermo slid quietly by me saying, "Let's take a walk."

What is it with these men wanting to take walks? I watched him toss a glance at the porch. He had given me an unspoken order to follow. It wasn't the order that stunned me but his words. The exact words Ian had used and in the same way. Maybe Ian Wilkes wasn't just an innocent scholarly curmudgeon with a good body and oddball hobby of Civil War trivia. I stood under one of the star lights and listened to the spy I trusted.

"Harley, Eliza's sister Maggie. Her name is found on the register of passengers boarding a ship named Bright Star. She boarded on June 14, 1865. This ship's destination was the settlement of Colonel William Hutchinson Norris and his son Robert of Perry County, Alabama. Norris had purchased 500 acres from the undeveloped Machadinho Estate near Santa Barbara D'Oeste in Sao Paulo. It is now known as Americana, Brazil. The ship set sail from Pensacola but stopped at Apalachicola for more cargo, supplies, and additional passengers," he said.

"But it never made it?"

"No. It sank in the Yucatan Channel, between the peninsula and Cuba. Storms can erupt rapidly in this body of water because it links the warmer Gulf of Mexico with the cooler Atlantic Ocean. No survivors found. A total loss. Now you know Maggie's fate."

"Yes, but what of cargo or miscellaneous objects in the boat, what happens to them over time?"

"Of course anything heavy sinks, fish and sea creatures eat what they can. Some objects float back and forth, tossed in waves, swept up in currents but eventually disintegrate or settle somewhere. You wonder if your gold coin could be Maggie's since it matches Eliza's great great-grandmother's?"

"Yes, of course. What are the odds though?"

"Strange things happen. You've heard of synchronicity -- simultaneous occurrence of events that appear significantly related but have no discernible causal connection? That may be what you are enmeshed in -- a synchronistic event. Anyway, information requested, information delivered. Anything else I can do for you?"

"Have you ever heard of Ian Wilkes?"

"The professor? Yes. His research is first rate. He's known for scouring about libraries for primary sources in special collections that often require permission to use. I may have signed off on him to use one of the Navy's libraries, but I've never met him. Why do you ask?"

"Just wondered. He teaches at the college with me. I asked him about my coin because he's the resident Civil War guru but he thinks I am on a fool's errand. Anyway thank you so much for your help. This means so much to our crazy investigation. I know Eliza will be grateful for a truthful ending to the story of her aunt."

"I am at your service. Oh, as for Ian, ignore him and keep going on with this investigation."

We made our way back into the throng of guests. I saw Eliza but didn't tell her the news. I wanted to keep the secret for myself for a little while. My hand had throbbed steadily at Guillermo's words. I was sure my coin belonged to Maggie. I just couldn't say it out loud yet.

Marco, bottle of rosé in tow, refilled my wine glass. I took a deep breath and looked around the room. A mahogany grand piano stood along the wall near an antique needlepoint tapestry of bright peonies, lilies and roses. The needlepoint piano bench seat matched the tapestry but had worn thin from years of use. A stack of sheet music on a side table was held in place by a crystal trophy bearing Emile's name. A small framed photo of Darius as a teenager sitting at a piano on stage hung nearby on the wall.

Fern Carlyle set a silver platter of warm gooey goat cheese and melba rounds arranged on a doily on the coffee table.

Brenda picked up a book about James Bond movies. "Did you read all these or are they just for show?"

"You must be joking. Why would you have a book if not to read it?" Adelaide stared at Brenda with eyes wide as quarters.

"What's your problem? Lots of decorators insist on a few to make a room feel homey. But then, you've probably never worked with a decorator outside your own store."

Meg pulled Brenda to the kitchen for final preparations before Adelaide could return the volley. Brenda rolled her eyes at Reese who stood frozen for fear that she could read her mind. Thankfully, Patricia Dell walked over and gave us all a hug.

"Hey, y'all, we're just back in town, Spencer placed first in his age bracket at a triathlon in Naples. He rocked."

"That's great," said Reese, "Personally, exercise is not my thing. I never liked to sweat." A veneer of moisture shined along the edge and temples of her forehead

"Exercise is good for you, Reese. Find something to do," said Patricia, "for health's sake." She smoothed the skirt of her snug black and red dress of tiny geometrics which hung just above her lean black, over the knee, dominatrix boots.

Brenda rejoined the group. "Did someone say exercise? I am all about that. Sweating. That's my job. Aerobics, yoga, hot yoga, I must go through three sets of work out clothes a day. My washer and dryer are running all the time. But not tonight. Uh Uh. Tonight I'm going to get me some more wine." She sped off to fill her glass. Bobby Carlyle holding court at the wine bar quickly poured her a generous refill.

Spencer Dell called from the doorway to the kitchen. "The head cook, Chantal, says everything's ready. Y'all know the drill."

Darius reminded us how the tradition of Hoppin' John in the South is meant to celebrate the coming year as healthy, happy, and plentiful in the things we need. Marco handed me a yellow ochre plate that coordinated with his sage green one. I recognized Chantal's authentic Fiesta by its original colors.

"Why buy new dishes when mother's are perfectly good? Besides, I love to use family hand me downs. It is the practical thing to do."

Our plates were quickly loaded up with the salad, the Hoppin' John with bacon, succulent ham, and collard greens. We settled in, tonight with Spencer and Patricia and Reese and Walter at one of the muslin covered tables crowned in the center with sweet grass baskets filled with buttermilk biscuits. A single thick ivory beeswax candle resting on a pewter plate lit each table with a primitive glow. The tables had been set up close to each other creating the sense of a bistro. We could easily hear all conversations, which made for juicy listening.

"Did you bring these baskets from Charleston?" asked Consuela, "I believe that's where I have seen them."

"No." said Darius. "They are from Senegal, my ancestral home. The sweet grass baskets made by the Gullah women in Charleston are the same as the coil baskets made by the Wolof in Senegal. The baskets are a direct cultural link. Only these two groups weave them."

"So the people in Charleston came from Senegal?" Glen picked out a biscuit with his hook.

"Some yes, some no. The Gullah culture developed over time as an amalgam of various West African peoples brought as slaves to the low country because they knew how to cultivate rice. At that time, the low country farmers grew rice because it suited the climate, and the soil, but they needed rice growers. As you might have guessed, rice was also grown in West Africa. Slave traders, as they used to say, harvested slaves with those skills from there to sell in the Charleston region. The slaves skilled for rice growing held value and were rarely sold off to other farms, unlike in other areas. As a result, a stable community formed with a more or less common West African, including Senegalese, culture. The customs and language took root."

"So all that together is Gullah, I mean what we call them today," said Glen.

"That's right."

"Cool. These baskets are probably the first thing I've ever seen from Senegal," said Glen. "And probably the only thing I'll ever see from there too."

"Don't be such a hick," said Brenda, "If you want to go see Senegal, just go. Don't let me hold you back."

"Who said anything about holding back?" Glen squinted at her then looked away.

"Hey, not to change the subject, but really I want to change the subject. Has anyone noticed besides me that Colin and Meg here are flying a pirate flag?" Jean Louis turned toward Meg. "That's a nice flag, but it's not the sort of skull and cross bone I've ever seen. Is it something special, some pirate club?"

"Why, what does it look like?" said Spencer from our table. "You know lots of us rockers use skull and crossbones in logos or posters. Tattoo addicts love them." He pulled up the sleeve of his shirt and flexed the biceps of his right arm. The hollow eyes of a skull suspended above two crossed swords stared out at us. Below it, the words, Five Mile Backup, filled a waving banner with kite tails at each end. "I'm the real deal."

"So you rockers aren't pirates? Ah, gee, always thought they were! Just kidding," said Jean Louis. Marie Justine poked him to get on with his description. "Anyway, the skull sits right on top of the bones, with the ends of the bones sticking out in four corners. The traditional pirate skull sits above the crossed bones."

"If I may jump into this discussion," said Guillermo, "there are several pirate versions. Think of them as the pirate captain's signature, a skull above crossed swords, a skull profile above crossbones, and some had hearts and hour glasses on them. These symbols intimidated the merchant ships, scaring the crew into thinking time would run out promising them a violent fight to a painful death. The skull and crossbones design on Colin's flag belonged specifically to Richard Worley, a pirate from New York who met his death by hanging at the Royaltown harbor in the year 1719."

"Ah, the Navy has spoken. So it is a real pirate's flag," said Jean Louis, "Did you know that, Colin?"

During this discussion, I noticed Colin glance back and forth to Wilson, Brantley and Bobby. Wilson shrugged, wiping his hands on his faded shirt and Bobby drew his hand across his neck signaling cut the discussion.

"Why, Bobby, that is the same flag we have," said Fern, "You brought some home from the last United Daughters of the Confederacy meeting we attended. I went to the meetings. You hung out with your buddies. One of them gave you the flags."

Bobby shot her a look meant to annihilate. She shrugged.

"Hey, I'll take one if you have an extra," said Jean Louis.

"Sorry, I don't have any more. They are just reproductions of a symbol used by Confederate supporters during the Civil War," Colin said.

"Oh, that's it, the Knights of the Golden Circle," chirped Meg, "now I remember."

"That's some name," said Jean Louis, "does that group still exist?"

"Oh no, it disbanded in 1863 long before the war was over. It's just the stuff of legend and heritage," said Colin with a tick in his voice. He cleared his throat with a guzzle of wine. "I thought it would be fun to fly it."

"Who could have imagined this much fuss over a pirate flag?" Meg glanced at Colin. Her voice cracked.

Except this was no pirate flag. This particular arrangement of skull and crossbones matched the Grand Seal of the Knights of the Golden Circle, later reorganized as the Order of the Sons of

Liberty. And I knew from my research no date of disbandment of the Sons of Liberty has ever been documented. Marco asked me why I was so quiet. "Just thinking," I said.

"Thought so."

Dana began to clink a glass with her spoon. "I have an announcement. About Mardi Gras. Next month. We have decided that Supper Club should be a masked ball. Everyone in costume. We'll have reams of Mardi Gras beads for us all. If you don't have a mask, I'll get one for you. Mario will make exotic Brazilian delights as he is designing the menu. A night of carnivale. So get ready."

"I can wear my southern belle outfit," said Meg to no one in particular.

"Meg, we wouldn't expect you to wear anything else." Marie Justine caught my eye, nodded and I understood that she couldn't bear Meg's clap trap about southern belles.

The rest of the evening settled into the rhythmic hum of conversation punctuated by an occasional laugh. Our table laughed about things I don't remember now. I studied shirt collars or jacket lapels for copper pins with snakes but none were in sight. Guillermo told Marco that he would take Walter, Jean Louis, and him out on his boat fishing anytime. Adelaide cornered Patricia about new products for her hair while Eliza and Fern whispered to each other.

We left that night full of good luck cheer for the New Year. The star porch lights held back the blackness of night and lit the path to our cars. Darius and Chantal waved from the doorway, now fully initiated into the magic of Supper Club.

The black BMW parked in front of us belonged to Wilson Garrett. On the right lower corner of the back window, a small sticker stuck to the glass glowed in the swath of light from the porch. Stickers on cars are clues to the driver's politics, sense of humor, and even club memberships or college loyalties. The Auburn University label told me about Wilson the alumnus. The white sticker, blank but for the skull and crossbones used by the Knights of the Golden Circle, suggested something else altogether. I scanned the departing cars but Brantley and Adelaide sped away, too far from view. Marco urged me to get in. I told him to drive by Bobby and Fern's car on the way out. I waved to Fern. I studied their back window. A white sticker tucked into the lower right corner matched the one on Wilson's car.

Marco said nothing on the way home. He was used to my brooding, interior occasions. Halfway home, he rested a hand on my knee.

I knew they wanted me to give them the coin. Ask for help. Next comes the ruse about going to the coin collector in Atlanta. Then it happened. The punch in the gut that sudden insight throws you. A deep blow. Drains you of color. Makes you sweat a little bit. All this time I had focused on the symbols. The handshakes. The snakes. The copper pins. The turtle. But it's not about the turtle. Not even the coin itself. It's about the numbers on the back of the coin. They are the key. A code to something hidden that they covet. A code to lead them to more gold perhaps? Too bad they blew their chance last September when I found it. They should never have treated me with such dismissive indifference.

Guillermo's admission that he knew of Ian Wilkes confounded me. Ian had a picture of the numbers of my coin I so naively gave him early on. Had he shared it yet, with his gang?

A red flag fluttered steadily in front of my closed eyes, like the ones flown on water safety flagpoles at the beach. Red meant unsafe conditions, riptides, and undertows that you cannot see but nevertheless suck you under into blue oblivion. You survive by swimming with them, not against them. That's what I would do. But only after I reassessed Ian Wilkes. The handsome scholar would take a walk with me this time. Next week couldn't come soon enough.

"What are you thinking about?" Marco broke the silence.

"I am thinking that something is going to happen soon."

"I think so too." He reached for my hand and drew it to his lips. He kissed it like a bird, softly, tentatively, again and again.

Menu

Tortilla Soup with Roasted Corn
Avocado, Red Onion and Grapefruit Salad
Salsa and Blue Corn Chips

* * *

Cerviche (fish, onions, lime juice)
Mini Chicken Empanadas
Enchiladas con Queso with Shredded Pork
Wheat Flour Tortillas

* * *

Tres Leche Cupcakes
King Cake with Cream Cheese Icing
Sopaipillas with Strawberries and Honey

* * *

Carménère, Pinot Grigio

February

"What is going on? What's this fly out into the night with no explanation?" Marco met me at our front door, with a voice like ice and fiery coal eyes.

I grabbed his hand and pulled him to sit down next to me on the couch. "You won't believe what just happened. Eliza decided to break the seal on the letter of instruction. Chantal and I had argued for it. How silly to believe in a curse. Were we not rational thinkers, skilled scientists? She caved, disobeying the instructions passed down intact through generations. We all shared in the act of defiance."

"Okay. You are in it together. That's not new. What happened?" Marco refused to sit down and paced back and forth instead.

"I'm getting to that. Eliza was home alone while Wilson attended a meeting of local Realtors at Goatfeathers Restaurant in Blue Mountain."

"Okay. And?"

"She was busy scoring a slit in the grout around a terra cotta floor tile in the corner of the kitchen pantry."

"Harley, cut with the blow by blow reporting. What the hell happened?"

"Just listen. She lifted up the tile to get to a hole in a shallow subfloor. That's where she had hidden a small metal box with raised intials, EP and a cross. She placed it there just after they moved in."

"What's the big deal about hiding a box?"

"It's not just the box. Someone attacked her. Slipped a dark felt hood down from above encasing her head. Then he yanked it tight around her neck. At the same time another pair of hands took the metal box which had fallen from her hands. She tried to remove the hood but one of them smacked her across her covered face. Then came a second hit from the opposite direction. Luckily she fell across the hole in the floor but then one thief tied her wrists behind her back."

"Luckily? She isn't still tied up?" Marco stopped in front of me and grabbed my arm.

"No, sweetie. Listen. She wriggled herself free by pulling her tied hands under her butt. Then she put her legs though and could stand up. She sawed the rope away with the scalpel she used to score the grout. Too easy, she told me. All the threads sprung away."

"So she is free?"

"Yes. She's fine. So then back to the hole in the floor."

"Hole in the floor? That's more important than Eliza?"

"Just listen for once. The hole is the reason for this mess. What was in the hole. Anyway, she pulled out an envelope that was taped to the underside of the intact adjacent floor tile. Then she called me in tears and I flew down to help her."

"You didn't think I should come with you? So much for sharing life's adventures. Is anything broken, should I check her out?" Marco's voice chilled the air between us.

"Nothing broken. But she hurts like hell. Whoever hit her was clever. The whack muffled through the dense fabric left no trace of a bruise or scrape. Even her wrists looked only slightly swollen. The attackers knew how not to leave a mark."

"I know the type. It's a guy who abuses but doesn't need to show his handiwork to feel powerful," said Marco. "You have called the police. Or is this a secret from them, too?"

"Yes. It's a secret. No. She doesn't want to call them. She doesn't want Wilson to know anything about this. She already replaced the tiles. Nothing looks out of place."

"Why not?"

"Her private stash is a secret from Wilson. It has to do with her great great-grandmother. And the coin," I said.

"The coin? You knew about this, but wouldn't tell me?"

"I would have told you eventually. You know I always do. It's more urgent to figure out who knew about the coin. How could they have known that tonight she would have dug out the tile?"

"That's what I want to know. How did they get in, unless it was an inside job and they waited. They must have heard something to know she would dig for the box tonight."

"We just don't know." I tried to concentrate on all our discussions. We purposely did not discuss anything at Supper Club.

"What is she doing now?"

"Soaking in the tub, lighting candles, and reading a magazine, so when Wilson comes in, he'll find her far from the kitchen and flush from a hot bath. She will see what he does, what he says."

"You're convinced he's involved?" said Marco.

"We'll see. But I think so."

Silence hung in the room like a wall between us. I had to break it. "Who could have imagined something like this might happen? What does this mean for our quest? Everyone in Supper Club knows we have a gold coin that matches the one in the portrait."

Marco's face hardened. His eyes narrowed. He ran his hand through his hair. "Our quest?"

"Yes, Eliza, Chantal and me. We are in it together."

"I see. And Eliza won't call the police? You don't think this is a police matter? Theft and assault?"

"No, she thinks and I agree this is an inside job, a family matter. So it's a matter of pride with her."

"You are pretty sure it's Wilson?"

"Well, he has been obsessed with the portrait of her great-

great-grandmother ever since I mentioned the coin matched mine. Somehow he calculated if he waited long enough, she'd admit to having the coin."

"He knew already. He knew she had it even if she never said so. He knew from another source." Marco sat on the edge of the ball chair across from me.

"How do you know that?"

"Think about it. The coin had to be made at the foundry on the plantation. Surely the great great-grandmother didn't actually pour the molten gold. Some slave did and under the supervision of another man in charge. Do we know if she designed it? Who put the numbers on it regardless of what they mean?"

Marco's observation stunned me. It had not occurred to me that Eliza Powell's hallowed secret might also be coveted by a parallel cadre of men. Over generations had they believed it would lead them to a prize? Whose curious eyes watched a sweaty, shirtless thick-armed man drizzle lustrous liquefied yellow gold into three tiny, deliberately-designed coin molds in the white-hot fires of a plantation foundry? Spies? Knights of the Golden Circle? Eliza's great great-grandfather?

"Marco, should we move our gold coin from our house?"

"I already did."

"When? Without telling me?"

"Last Friday, after Supper Club. I took it to work the next day, and I forgot to tell you."

"Why didn't you tell me? I'm not the only one keeping secrets?"

"It's not a secret. I forgot to tell you. You left for work before me. I noticed an SUV driving slowly in front of our house. On a gut feeling, I grabbed the coin and took it with me. It's locked in my desk at the hospital. No one knows it is there," he said. "I should have told you sooner."

"Anything else I need to know?"

"I think the police should be called. I know you and Eliza

won't, but I am going to speak to Walter McElwain. He'd probably have an opinion on how to handle this. Before you object, I'll only tell him what he needs to know. No details of your quest, since apparently I don't know them all either."

It took us all evening to regain our usual easy rhythm. All the fuss over Eliza, and then to find out my own coin had been moved without my knowledge. It was my coin. My quest. I am in charge of it. Not Marco.

*

Dana, the hyper-organized distributor of organic nutrition supplements, e-mailed us about Supper Club early in February. She and Mario are friends of ours apart from the group. On occasion we'd join them at sunrise at their house in Watersound for a six o'clock run with their pair of golden retrievers along the swish and slap of dawn waves. Whether under the chilly glaze of winter or the warm wrap of summer, the dogs would plunge into breaking waves aiming for the Frisbee Mario had tossed in only seconds before.

They work hard and play hard. Mario's veterinarian clinic is in Blue Mountain and Dana treks all over to the health food stores, pharmacies, and organic emporiums that dot the Panhandle. That's her day job. In late afternoon she sheds her office clothes for taut leotards and sheer floating skirts cinched around her firm waist. With an iPod plugged into speakers and a finger sized remote, she repeats riffs of music as she calls out commands en français to aspiring beginning and intermediate young dancers, putting them through their paces at a dance/fitness center on 30-A.

Sometimes I'd see her rub her left Achilles tendon and watch as a momentary flash of extreme sadness would flit across her face. Unless she told you, there would be no way to tell from her light step and perfect posture, that a dancer's career-ending tendon tear still twinged after all these years. Dana excelled at performance.

She had commanded us all to a February Bal Masqué. We were the dinner and the show. A backstage drama starring some members began to unfold a week before the Mardi Gras Supper

Club. For a change, I chose to make a dessert. The cupcakes. Fern claimed the king cake. Brenda said in an e-mail she had the perfect pan for baking and a cake plate for the occasion. She also had the tiny naked baby charm that must be baked into the king cake. Fern, having no shortage of platters, graciously agreed to use Brenda's equipment.

In the afternoon of the day Fern fetched the baking pan, platter, and plastic baby from Brenda, she called me while I was at my office. The ringing mobile phone broke my attention from the paperback in my lap, leaving Starr Elliott on the ledge and me exasperated.

"Harley," said Fern in a tense voice that verged on tears, "I went to Brenda's house. She keeps her cake plate in a storage cupboard in her basement. I waited in the dining room while she dug it out. I killed time looking at her arts and craft, mahogany breakfront. She has all sorts of old-fashioned crystal and painted plates stashed in it. Behind one glass door, there was a gold coin and a metal box labeled with initials EP sitting next to a faded Confederate bond and a copper pin with a snake on it. Next to that was a small book decorated with skull and crossbones propped up behind the stash."

"You saw all that?" I felt my blood pressure climb.

"Yeah. The coin looked like the one you found. But I don't care about that. It's the book. The book! It's the book I gave Bobby just this past Christmas. These books are rare. I recognized the distinctive marks from wear and tear on the cover."

"There must be some explanation." Distracted, I visualized Eliza's coin and box on the shelf.

"Yes, there is. Neither Brenda nor Glen give a rat's ass about the Civil War. Bobby is stashing his things with Brenda right there under Glen's nose, and I don't mean only the Civil War crap. He's having an affair with her. God, am I stupid." Her voice strengthened as anger replaced hurt.

"You are not stupid. We trust our husbands until they give us a reason not to. This is rather damning evidence," I said.

For the next few minutes Fern ranted and raved about killing Bobby or divorcing him, forgiving him or kicking his sorry self out of the house, and his memorabilia too. Soon Fern sounded more like herself. We agreed to watch the two of them a little longer, to prove our hunch correct or not. Not a word to a soul, we promised. That bought the time I needed to confer with Eliza who to date had yet to extract anything from Wilson. She believed he hit her that fateful night. Something about the pad of the palm that hit her felt familiar. Maybe it was the awareness of topography only a wife would know.

There was no going back to reading the novel. This was like being in one. I dropped it deep into my briefcase and checked my e-mail once again before closing the computer. Two new messages, but only one was important. Ian Wilkes e-mailed that he'd see me at Supper Club thanks to a special invitation arranged by Meg Coffee and okayed by the hostess Dana.

On my way down the steps of the building to my car, I rang Eliza on her cell phone. She picked up. In a few quick words we chose the new Hofbrauhaus in Pier Point to rendezvous. This upscale open-air mall of shops and restaurants along Highway 98 in Panama City Beach had only recently opened but being twenty minutes from 30-A, it was unlikely any Supper Club member would find us. Secrecy was becoming more important.

A smiling young woman dressed in a white Bavarian blouse with shirred scoop neckline and puffy sleeves took our order. Beers all around. We sat tucked away in a corner table against a wall where we could see everything and everyone. I felt like a mobster.

Just after the waitress brought us two heffenviesen beers in tall slender glasses, Eliza poked me. Her upper lip sported a foam mustache and her wide-open eyes shifted toward the door. I followed them to see Glen Royal walk in with his thumb tucked into the back of the low-slung yellow capri pants glued onto the body of a deeply tanned woman balancing on glittery kitten heels. The ends of long blonde hair teased up in the back fell onto bare shoulders and her halter top struggled to keep her voluptuousness in place. She was a stranger to us, but not to the back of Glen's neck which she stroked with one hand, then worked her fingers into his shoulder. They had obviously been there before. He pulled a chair out for her with his hook, and they snuggled in together off to the side far from us. I told Eliza they had more reason than us not to be noticed.

"Have you opened the envelope yet?"

"No. When I look at it I see the spectre of my great great-grandmother issuing the dictum about the coins and letters being opened only in the presence of the other coins. I am scared. It's completely irrational, I know."

"It does seem a bit out of character for you, the scientist, the physician, to be spooked by this. I wouldn't have taken you for being the mystic sort that scares easily. You are almost sentimental."

"It could disappoint us, you know. What if it is some silly statement about the family tree and the coin means nil. Perhaps we have concocted a story with historical implications simply because it is fun, you know, like playing Dungeons and Dragons. Maybe we are creating the game as we go along and roles for ourselves to play in it," Eliza said.

"And, maybe we enjoy the mystery more than knowing the facts. Once you open it, then we are in post-climactic mode. But, someone wants that coin badly enough to rough you up to steal it. It is not an overgrown charm for a bracelet. It is your call, however."

"I'd like to open it with Chantal present anyway. There might be something in it that refers to her family. What would great great-grandmother think if she knew the great great-granddaughter of her slaves was a new friend of mine, and we were in a supper club together?"

"My hunch is that she will answer that very question in the instructions about the coin. Clearly one coin was given to Kate Carter, former slave, now free woman. We are wasting time, though, we need to get your coin back. Either you or I or both need to pay a call to Miss Brenda tonight or tomorrow, to get that coin and before

Supper Club."

"Before Supper Club?" asked Eliza.

"Absolutely. We need to reclaim the control of this game. We know where it is. We need to go get it."

"Well, let's just go borrow another plate from her."

"Yes, I'm sure she would have the perfect platter for my cupcakes. Let's call her now. Glen is still sitting over there with his playmate of the month, and Brenda might be home alone."

"Good plan." Eliza dialed Brenda's number.

Luck broke our way. We sped over to Brenda's house in Dune Allen, the most westerly part of County Road 30-A, just past Miss Lucille's Gossip Parlor. Brenda met us at her front door with a wine glass in her hand, a wide grin, and a touch of throaty laughter in her voice. I followed her down to the storage cupboard to fetch a tray while Eliza scoped out the loot in the glass breakfront. Brenda jabbered about dishes and the menu for that month. She asked me what costumes Marco and I planned to wear. In truth at that moment, I hadn't a clue. She had considered going as Peter Pan and Glen as Captain Hook but he wanted to go as the one-armed man from *The Fugitive*. But, he didn't have a wife, I mentioned, and she giggled, "Yeah, guess he's trying to tell me something." I prattled on a few minutes more to give Eliza time to work. When I could no longer stall in the basement we ascended to the kitchen. Eliza sat on a chair staring out the window.

"Look's like we got what we wanted." She winked at me while pointing to the platter in my hand.

"Yes, this silver tray will be perfect for the cupcakes. Brenda, you are so sweet to let me borrow it," I said.

"Can't wait to try them, I love desserts," said Brenda.

I slid into the red Mini with Eliza who locked the car door like a scared child keeping the bogeyman at bay. She flashed the gold coin once again resting inside the metal box and said, "Onward to Marco's office." With a swerve onto Highway 98, we soon delivered Eliza's recovered heirloom to the secret confines of the locked desk in a locked office belonging to one Marco Polo, MD.

"You call Walter McElwain if Wilson or anyone else gives you any trouble. He knows how to be discreet but effective." With a kiss to my cheek he added, "I'll be home about 8. I promised to cover a couple extra hours in the ER so one of the younger doctors could attend some family function."

"Did we just commit a crime?" said Eliza as we climbed back in the car to leave for home.

"We didn't break and enter anything. The coin is yours; we recovered stolen property taken during a violent physical assault," I said. "There's no record of the theft, so there's no record of its recovery. What would Brenda or Bobby do? A report to the police means exposing their affair. Glad we have Walter." The tall pine trees swayed in the gusty wind. The sky was gloomy with dusk and the shadows amassing from roly-poly clouds.

"We might have ruined a friendship. If Brenda participated, then there's no love lost. She could be oblivious to the whole thing if she just told Bobby to put his pile of treasures there because she's smitten with him," said Eliza.

"What else was in the treasure trove besides the book and the coin?" I drove past the intersection of Highway 331.

"Hmm, a few more coins, a heavy metal object in the shape of a bell, sort of a paperweight, a jewel-encrusted broach with matching earrings, and a tiny ladies pistol with a mother of pearl handle. Yes, that's it," said Eliza. "No wait, there were two miniature clay dolls painted with tribal markings on the face. Why?"

"You remembered all those things in that much detail?"

"Okay, so I have a nearly photographic memory, what of it. Comes in handy."

"I'll say. Those items might have value if sold in the right antique store. The book especially could be a collector's item. You know we may be on the wrong track."

"I don't understand. Are we on any track at all?"

"Sort of. I keep reviewing the events of the past few months from the start of our recognition that my coin and your great great-grandmother's coin bore the same markings. No consistent pattern emerges from the Civil War boys, at least not one we recognize. It could be that we are looking for a conspiracy that doesn't exist. What would be the point of one? Are we blind to what is in plain view? No doubt there are two sides, us and them."

"Hmm. The smack on my head was real enough. The theft was real. The black hood was real. The coins are real. No, there is nothing imaginary here, but you are right, we may not really know what we have gotten into." Eliza touched her face, still sore.

We reached her car, parked in the city center of Rosemary Beach near the post office.

"See you at Supper Club. Let the show begin," I said.

"Not a word to anyone." She put her forefinger to her lips.

*

Marco loves to dance. Tall, graceful, he leads with the deft hands of a nimble fisherman responsive to the rhythm of waves while handling the rod and reel. Casting out and reeling in. The same maneuvers twirl me about the dance floor, whether the swing or a tango, or our favorite dance "walk the floor." "Just call me Fred," he announced, the morning of Supper Club. "Just call me Ginger," I answered.

His tails were ready, still wrapped in plastic from the cleaners. Ginger's gowns always floated as she danced because the skirts were either cut on the bias or tiny rows were pleated into the waist. My coppery gold halter dress had that same type flair plus the added benefit of a sequined-trimmed bolero jacket. We could imagine arriving just off the set of Flying Down to Rio. Marco dug out his top hat, a relic from another party, and dusted it off. Although women like Ms. Rogers did not wear hats in the evening to formal events, I decided a small comb covered with fake flowers tucked into my curls could convey a Latin air.

With the cupcakes arranged in a spiral on the borrowed platter, we waltzed into the living room of Dana and Mario's Watersound home to ribbons, masks and beads, a virtual Mardi Gras. Gold, green and purple crepe paper encircled balusters of the staircase like stripes on a barber pole. Comedy-tragedy masks perched in corners, watched out over us, and a few even had eyes added by Dana. Pink Oriental lilies were squeezed into any available space and sweetened the room like a candy store. Huddled in the corner were five men in grey dress uniforms including capes trimmed in red. The swords hanging from their hips gleamed in the warm light from the candles scattered around the room. Bobby tucked a Confederate cap under his arm while Brantley sported a wide brim affair with a plume rising from a gold band.

"Whoa, who do we have here?" Mario took the platter from me. "Is this some sort of Fred and Ginger thing?"

"How did you know?" Marco smiled.

"Something about a top hat, I'd say."

"You look rather spiffy yourself, is it Marc Antony?" I said. "That must be Dana or rather, J. Lo over there -- did she tape or glue herself into those scarves?"

"I told her it was risky, the heat from cooking might melt this spray-on stuff," said Mario, "but she likes to gamble. Here have some beads." He reached into a box and pulled out purple, green and gold throw beads, and gave them to us. "Hey you musketeers over there, how about some beads?" Mario tossed a handful toward the coterie of soldiers who had turned in unison to face him.

They did indeed strike an impressive pose, decked out with medals, ribbons and brass buttons... And those swords. A copper pin with a snake on it adorned the left lapel of each uniform. Skull and crossbones had been embroidered into the right shoulder of each cape, a Knights Templar cross on the left shoulder. Ian Wilkes, the John C. Calhoun Professor of History, stood with them in uniform, the fifth member of what I had thought was the Supper Club four. This display of regalia confirmed that Wilson Garrett, Bobby Carlyle, Vernon Brantley and Colin Coffee belonged to a group greater than merely the four of them.

The sight of Ian Wilkes without his Hawaiian shirt scared me. This must be serious for him to forgo his personal trademark and don a Confederate soldier's getup. I supposed they used these costumes for battle re-enactments. Replaying ancient history like that never made sense to me.

Marco took my hand and whispered "Say nothing. Let them reveal by intent or by accident."

I felt his secure grip on my arm and admired my clever Wisconsin boy, wise in the ways of gangsters, practiced in the skill of observation. Before one word could be fired off, Meg Coffee sashayed in between us, "Hello, hello, don't y'all look spiffy."

She had to be Scarlett O'Hara, preening in her hoop skirt and puffy capped sleeved gown. Her abundant bosom shoved up in a corset was oddly attractive since her waist appeared smaller than it normally did. There was something to be said for good foundations as my grandmother used to say. She went to her grave in a zip-up girdle.

Meg said Colin was Rhett Butler. It took all my willpower not to point out that Mr. Butler never donned a uniform, blue or grey, making his actions even more heroic. That was a significant point in the novel. But, I digress.

The musketeers sheepishly hung the Mardi Gras beads around their necks, desecrating their holy uniforms. Colin swore just loud enough for us all to hear. Ian stepped toward me.

"You must be out of your clothing comfort zone." I said.

"You have no idea. So this is Marco Polo? I can see why I've had no success in seducing your wife." He winked at me, then shook hands with Marco. "A tall, dark-haired Italian is stiff competition. But I'll keep trying."

"Trying is all you can do. I know what she likes." Marco slid his hand up my neck and into my hair, fondling it, holding me close.

"All's fair in love and war." Ian bowed.

"Enough. You sound like schoolyard rivals." My cheeks blushed from this debate.

I kissed Marco while keeping an eye on Ian and left them both for the kitchen. With tray in tow, I found three other Southern belles. Eliza, Fern, and Adelaide huddled together like three giant cream puffs, their hoop skirts in pale pastels, ruffles in white eyelet, their bodices squeezed to the point of bursting, forcing their cleavage into full display. Adelaide and Eliza listened while Fern whispered to them. Adelaide stood at attention when she saw me as if to stop the conversation. "It's okay," said Fern, "Harley knows everything."

"Yes, that Harley does." Dana added walking in with masks. "She's a super sleuth by trade. Sociologists, always on the lookout. Isn't that right, Harley?"

"Something like that." I pointed to her hands.

"Oh, here. Masks. It's a Bal Masqué, and no one is masked. We are going to dance and exchange partners, sort of like musical chairs. We'll keep switching until the music stops. Then whomever you are dancing with, becomes your partner for charades."

Adelaide groaned at the mention of games. She tried to beg off, but Dana ruled. Fern told her to drink a little more, that always helps. Eliza examined Dana's taped-on scarf dress, "Just how did you do this?"

"Mario was only too willing to help. And lots of spray glue."

"Dana, where do you want the karaoke?" called Spencer from the front hall. He set the square and cables on the floor. He readjusted his brown wig with straight bangs across his forehead, the feathered back reaching just above his shoulders. His blond ponytail hung out below like the slim tail of a stingray. His brown and beige striped bell bottoms and shirt with balloon sleeves were cinched together by a wide tooled leather belt and turquoise buckle.

"Near the TV is fine," Dana said. Patricia followed him carrying CDs of classic and recent rock although 33 $1/3$ albums would have better matched her long red batik skirt, ivory peasant blouse, and a wig of waist-length hair. Multicolored bangles jingled on her wrists.

"Looks like we'll be singing *I Got You Babe* later on," said Mario handing them some shiny beads.

"Ahoy mates," boomed a voice from the doorway. "Make way for Billy Bowlegs and his gypsy queen." The Panhandle pirate bowed deeply, sweeping his cocoá colored three corner hat in front of a red sashed waist and grey knickers. Black boots that folded over with a cuff clicked on the tile floor of the hallway as Guillermo strutted toward the living room. Consuela stepped silently, her ballet flats soft on the tile even as the petticoat of her crimson circle skirt rustled back and forth. She tied an unbuttoned camp shirt at her waist over a tank top reminding me of Ava Gardner in her heyday. With a paisley head scarf snugly knotted at the side, tendrils of escaping hair framed her large dark eyes, and hovered near splendid gold hoop earrings. The Southern belles still fussing in the kitchen gave up a collective "wow" when she delivered the tray of lettuce wedges to the side table.

The costumes continued as Chantal and Darius arrived shaking everyone's hand as if they were running for office. Her iconic purple sheath dress with v neck and wide black patent leather belt, topped with a choker of pearls gave it away. Darius wore a white buttoned-down collar shirt with long sleeve cuffs rolled back three quarter, carrying a sport coat flipped over his right shoulder. Chantal admitted to us that since she liked Michele Obama's look she decided to copy it for tonight's party. "Of course, I am not tall and slim like Michele so I may just look like a purple jellybean," she said. "Where's my mask? With that on, you'll never know."

"That's right, no one is wearing a mask," said Dana, "It won't be fun if we don't wear them for a little while. All y'all put them on."

Eliza grabbed my arm. We walked back to the living room. We stood with an eye on the caped soldiers now expanded to include Fred Astaire and Billy Bowlegs. "Ian attended the raising of the Confederate Flag by the Sons of Confederate Veterans along Interstate 65 in Alabama a few years ago," she said. "Some people say he's crazy because he'd always show up in Hawaiian shirts. This is the first time I've seen him parade around in a uniform."

"So?" I studied them, how close they stood to each other. How loud they laughed or talked. Whether any two broke off in a side talk of their own.

"Something is going on for Ian to wear a uniform. He's just not a dress in a costume kind of guy." Eliza shook her head.

Before I could reply, Marco handed me a glass of wine. "Turn around, you don't want to miss this."

Red dots on her cheeks, an enormous rhinestone tiara pinned into a red mop top wig, Dairy Queen, aka Reese McElwain, waddled into the living room. Hanging from straps across her shoulders, a wire circled around her, encasing her torso in a white sheet, pulled taut at the hem, about mid calf. Her arms were covered by tight white sleeves decorated with red diamonds, the sort seen on a paper cup of a milk shake. She wound long swaths of white chiffon around her shoulders and neck to suggest whipped cream. The red wig was the cherry on top, the tiara because "I am the queen," explained Reese. "Figuring out how to do Burger King over there was simpler. I used an old frame from the day I made one of the kids into a blueberry. Same principle, hang from shoulders, two parallel circles-actually they are hula hoops. Use beige for the bun, Walter wears a brown shirt for the burger, and I wrap a red tie around his neck for a little ketchup seeping out. The crown was left over from some Shakespeare costume. You don't want to see my basement."

Dana took the pot of soup from Dairy Queen and disappeared into the kitchen. The Southern belles galloped out en masse to see the royal competition. Dana taunted us with the promise of a best costume prize. Fred and Ginger were too safe for a prize, but I felt elegant anyway. And I was thankful that I didn't have a hoop skirt to drag around all night.

"Bon soir, laissez les bon temps rouler," boomed Jean Louis as he entered the crowded living room, sporting a 99 numbered blue jersey. He raised his arms in the style of a hockey player who just shot a goal and turned around. "For those of you who do not know this number, it belongs to the Great One, a hockey player, a fine Canadian."

"And for those of you who don't watch hockey too much, this is the official refs uniform," said Marie Justine. "So if Wayne Gretsky here, gets out of line, I just blow this whistle, and he must do what I say."

"Is that anything you say? I hope?" Jean Louis grinned and raised an eyebrow. "I like a woman in tight pants, black and white striped shirt, and a whistle. This hockey thing is a good gig. Now, where can I get a drink?'

"Oh, Jean Louis, that's enough. You'll scare all these nice folks. Dana, where would you like me to put this cerviche?"

Supper Club progresses like a Broadway musical. There are the days of rehearsal when we discuss menus, choose items, or share platters before that particular Thursday. Then the opening act. Our arrival and the setup of potential conflicts. That night, the costumes diverted some attention away from the private suspicions held by some of us about each other in the group. The frivolous celebration, the infectious uptempo mood that Dana surrounds us with should have been strong enough to thwart any squall. But, act two opened in an uproar, when characters could no longer hide behind costumes that took on a life of their own. The unmasking came early.

The first ominous note sounded when the front door slammed shut. Glen and Brenda strode in to the merry crowd with stone faces. Dressed in jeans and a yellow shirt, he wore a trench coat unbuttoned but belted around his waist, with his left arm in the sleeve, the right sleeve empty, swinging around.

"Hey Glen," called Wilson flipping the corner of his cape to one side, "what's the deal?"

"He's the one-armed man from *the Fugitive*," said Brenda, her lip curled. "And, I'm the wife he doesn't have."

Silence. A few clumsy seconds passed until Adelaide chirped, "Is that why you are wearing white powder on your face?"

"Hey, baby powder always soothes everything," said Mario. "I use it on my feet when they are sore." Silence again. "Okay then, let's get this party started. Where's Sonny and Cher? Crank up that karaoke." He ushered Glen toward the wine while Brenda took the avocado, red onion, and grapefruit salad to the dining room sideboard.

Marie Justine intercepted her. We could hear Brenda laugh as she rustled her short pleated skirt with her hands and clicked her stilettos on the floor. Fern whispered to me, "She may be dead to Glen, but she's alive and well with Bobby, that two-faced hussy rat."

"Hyper down. This is not the place to confront her," I said. "Time is your friend. Timing is everything."

While Spencer and Patricia set up the microphones, linking the karaoke player to the TV, Chantal called me to join her. I left Marco, Jean Louis and Walter debating the benefits of double rod downriggers and 10 pound ball weights, line test and the requisite surf rod length. Measured in guy inches of course. The testosterone meter had sprung off the dial.

"Harley, Reese and I disagree about news anchors. Who is your favorite news anchor?" said Chantal. "Mine is Jon Stewart of *the Daily Show*. His wit. His mind. Doesn't hurt that he's cute too."

"Well yeah, he's ten out of ten I'd say. Love his guests. Is he really a news anchor?" I said.

"He talks about the news. Keeps everyone honest." Chantal gave up a heavy sigh. "And looks so good doing it."

"Yeah, but for me, it's Stephen Colbert. Hundred out of hundred. A thousand out of thousand. No contest. Hottest guy in the industry. He is so quick, misses nothing. Charming. Sophisticated. Every woman wants him."

"You two can't be serious. They're rascals." Reese put her hands on her Dairy Queen hips. "How can they compare to Shepard Smith? Boy next door smile. His suits are impeccable."

"Oh please," said Chantal, "He's so uptight he probably wears a man girdle. Now Jon Stewart? He's the master. He has perfect timing. You know what that means. He's a thinking girl's man."

"But Colbert, is a lion. Stealthy, savvy, ripping sex appeal. And his hands. Have you ever seen such handsome, sculpted, expressive tools? Just think of those firm long fingers, and where they might go? You know, he admits in his book that he loves missionary position. But is he on the top or bottom?"

"Hmm. Guess as long as you are face to face it qualifies as missionary," said Chantal. "Let the converting begin."

"You both are disgusting." Reese could not suppress a smile. "I can't believe I am participating in this."

"Ah, come on Dairy Queen, admit you would kill to spend an evening with Shepard Smith?" said Marie Justine eavesdropping nearby. "I always loved Peter Jennings. So elegant, intelligent and, as you know, he was a Canadian. Sad that he's gone. Oh well."

"Okay. Okay. It would be a dream come true to have dinner with Shepard Smith." Reese grinned and added, "at a restaurant where the light is low and there is a single short red rose in a tiny crystal vase on the table.

"Oh la la," said Marie Justine. "Consuela. Did you hear this secret desire of our dear Reese?"

"Oh please, who has time to fantasize about the men in media. Do you have any clue what it's like to have a Latin lover every night." She gave us a slinky shake of her head. "Lucky me."

*

Sounds of helicopters cut our words off, and for a moment we looked to the window. Then the opening riff of Steppenwolf's Magic Carpet Ride at full blast crashed around us. Spencer turned the volume lower as he danced with one clenched fist, rocking out to the music. "This is just a test, don't worry. The latest hits, ballads and singable songs are standing by. Who's up first?"

"Hope he has some Madonna," said Reese, "Walter won't allow her songs in our house. But I love them."

"You mean the same Walter who flirts all the time with us won't let you play a little Madonna?" I said. "What gives?"

"Oh, he's a lot of fun for sure, but he's quite the tyrant on some things. We all learn to live with things, don't we?"

"Now's your chance to do what you want. We'll back you up. Dana can start then hand the mike to you. You'll have to sing," said Marie Justine. "You aren't singing anyway. It's Dairy Queen cutting loose."

The plan set, we shuffled into the living room. As Reese passed near me she tossed me a "here goes nothing" look of despair. Dana had lowered the lights and the flickering candles cast shadowy pirouettes into the corners. The masks, which everyone dutifully donned, created the last bit of distortion needed for us to be set free. I remember the evening as other worldly, where scenarios played that otherwise might have remained unaccomplished. The Dairy Queen began to sing Madonna's Respect.

Walter the Burger King stood still, his ears red, eyes wide, even in his mask. After the song, the Burger King and Dairy Queen started bumping bellies to get past their complicated costumes to kiss. Later, when we assembled the meal in the kitchen, Reese said, "A little Madonna now and then doesn't hurt anybody."

Unfortunately, the libertine atmosphere of costume play doesn't always provide happy endings. While Spencer and Patricia alternated as karaoke DJ's, other scenes began to expose unraveling lives. Eliza, Chantal, and I were on alert to any words exchanged that could explicate or implicate any or all in the theft of the coin and the roles Bobby and Brenda played in it. We spread out that night to watch and to listen.

Fern and I adjusted the chairs at the additional tables set up for that night. Mardi Gras beads surrounded and draped from little statues of saints and voodoo dolls lined up next to a candle as the centerpiece on each table. A tiny mojo bag rested on each napkin, a little party favor for each of us. Fern pointed toward the hallway and I looked.

"Did you bring it?" Bobby held Brenda with a sharp grip to her elbow.

"No. It's gone. I thought you took it with you the other night."

"Shut up, bitch. You are so stupid" Bobby spit on the floor.

"I am fed up with all this sneaking around. If you don't have the guts to leave your sugar mama, then I'll tell her. Everything." Brenda's neck veins popped out like pencils. "What's the big deal about a coin anyway?"

Bobby let go of her. "You idiot. I could have gotten millions for that coin. Without that money I am stuck. If Fern finds out about you and me, I'll be cut out without a dime."

"You loser. It's never been about me, just that stupid coin and your dream of easy money." Brenda smoothed the front of her skirt. "I need another drink." Bobby followed her toward the table on the screen porch where Mario had set up that night's bar, clicks from her heeled stilts fading away.

Adelaide strode in from the kitchen. She asked if we saw the spectacle in the hallway.

"We saw it, but couldn't hear what was said." Fern lied.

"Fern, I've suspected for a while that Brenda and Bobby were an item," she said, "but Harley didn't want me to tell you."

"That's okay. I have known for a long time too, but I didn't know what I wanted to do about it. I still don't." Fern plopped down on a bar stool. "I want to be smart about what I do. He is the kids' father after all. Keep this between us for a little while longer, please."

"You are a better woman than me," Adelaide said, "I'd cut him off where it hurts the most, and I don't mean money."

Meg called from the kitchen that she was about to distribute the tortilla soup in oversized martini glasses. While it struck me as complicated to serve soup while we were still singing, talking and walking around, sometimes it is best to follow orders. Marco, Jean Louis and Guillermo had escaped to the screen porch to avoid singing and the better to discuss fishing. The group of grey soldiers had split up by now, dutifully mixing with wives and others.

Ian Wilkes and Walter McElwain were deep in conversation,

leaning in toward each to whisper something. Walter laughed and slapped Ian on the shoulder. A hamburger and Confederate solider. The Dairy Queen waved to Walter who broke away to join her.

Ian Wilkes sauntered up to me, soup in glass, spoon in hand and said, "Let's take a walk."

"You are avoiding me this evening."

"It's complicated," he said.

"You have met Walter before?"

"Yeah. At a Salvation Army fundraiser. Long time ago."

"That's respectable enough. However, I did not put you with those silly Civil War clubs that glorify days gone by. A tricked out Confederate uniform that fits! You are a respected historian for heaven's sake."

"Jim Reed called me. He thinks you should take the coin to Han Li in Atlanta too."

"Ah, ha. You don't want to admit it. Okay. Now why would I call Jim Reed? I gave you pictures of the coin front and back. You could have identified this coin long ago. It's not the coin, but something else. There is something bigger, a game, but I can't decide if we are on the same team or not." I slurped some soup from my glass without the spoon and put it on a nearby table.

"You are difficult in business." He adjusted his cape, exposing the skull and crossbones of the Knights of the Golden Circle grand seal.

"You have no idea how difficult, Sir Knight." I adjusted his collar.

Ian pulled me to him, putting one hand at the small of my back, holding me firmly against him. "Dance with me, Harley." He took my right hand and pulled it up and began to lead me slowly, like a minuet. But it was no dance I'd ever danced before. I placed my left hand lightly on his shoulder and felt the heat of his cheek against mine. I could feel the contour of his body change, through my silky gown. Deftly, he guided me with small turns, his hands secure and in charge of our direction.

"Are you going to tell me some secret, now, about the coin?" I slid my right leg between his legs to pivot as he pulled me around in a turn.

"Nothing to tell. But, things are not always what they seem." He spoke, still holding me against him. Then he dipped me very low. His strong arms supported the arch of my back. He pulled me up to him.

"There's lots of that going around tonight. Perhaps at the stroke of midnight we will slough off our disguises and all will come clear." I stepped away from his arms. I shivered.

"That, Harley, will not happen this midnight. I shall take my leave." Ian Wilkes bowed and strode back to the cabal of grey.

Eliza and Chantal watched us from the dining room. "Who knew that Ian could dance," said Eliza, "and that you could be so daring. That almost looked like a tango."

"Hey, aren't we supposed to be spies here? I danced with him to try to get him to talk but he didn't give me a thing. Nothing to report. We're on our own as far as the coins go."

"Coins, right. Got that. But, line of duty? Who are you trying to fool? Harley, you like him and you can't hide it from us," said Eliza like a diagnostician. "Anyway, all we have is the letter. We should read it. Soon. I'll arrange with you."

"Wow. You are ready?" Chantal put her arm around Eliza.

"Ready. Time to move this investigation along. Seeing these fool men together is making me angry." Eliza paused then said, " By the way, Harley, where did you learn to dance like that?"

*

Meg, the Southern belle approached to retrieve the empty martini glasses. She feigned a thicker accent than usual, enthusiastic for her part of the act. The karaoke quieted down, Glen crooned a ballad I never liked even in its heyday. Mario sang Evil Ways like Carlos Santana. So smooth. Suppertime approached so I aimed to the powder room off the main hallway. It was there I gave thanks for the architectural detail for which Mario had spent a fortune.

Their two-story Dutch colonial house adorned with cedar shingles and white trim over grey clapboard stood on a street in Watersound West Beach. Their neighborhood of tree lined streets and manicured lawns mimicked a compilation of New England cedar shingles with rooflines lifted right out of Holland. Mario and Dana chose this house because it backed up to the dunes of the Deer Lake State Park, a permanent refuge for the birds, plants and animals of the sand. According to Dana, Mario insisted on placing transom windows above all exterior doors and even a few exterior windows to capture the sound and breeze skimming off the Gulf. The better for light and fresh air, said Mario. So that is how a transom window, pulled open above the privacy window made of glass block in the powder room of their home, changed everything.

Their powder room shared a wall with the screened porch. Unbeknownst to anyone, I scooted in for a quick stop. As I washed my hands and dabbed my nose with a tissue, voices drifted in from the porch. Stern ones. Frustrated ones. But definitely not discussing the wine. I stepped onto the rim of the toilet and peered out through the crack at the bottom of the open transom window.

"What gives?" Wilson scowled at Ian. Colin flicked his shoulder as if Ian was a mere private instead of a high ranking officer. "Where's the picture. How hard is it to get Harley to cough up a picture of her damn coin?"

"It's not that easy. She's real curious. And sharp. She's already figured out that the coin has a Confederate connection. If I push too hard she'll clam up. We won't get anything. I need more time." Ian stood nose to nose to Colin. He looked at Wilson as if to dare him to move.

"And if that's not enough, Bobby here has screwed everything up." Brantley raised a fist and held it in front of Bobby. "Losing it at your girlfriend's house. That's real smart. And those bitches were smart enough to get it back."

"Well, y'all used me just fine. Made me hit my own wife." Wilson looked at the floor. "How much would these coins get at auction, Colin?"

"Millions. With proper documentation. Millions. I can create the necessary provenance and even create other works of art with a provenance to go with them. A dentist doesn't learn the art of ceramics for nothing. Create porcelain caps for some bimbo trying to stay young or create priceless antiques, take your pick."

"Eliza's great great-grandfather's instructions are worth nothing without the coins," Brantley said. "Mr. Powell held the Political Degree of the Knights. That's the highest, the third degree. He conceived of this plan, the three coins, the latitude and longitude of buried gold and silver engraved on the back, the seed money for the next wave. He knew that by reorganizing the Knights of the Golden Circle into the Order of the Sons of Liberty, the trail would grow cold. Those Yankee sons of bitches would run square into a brick wall. He depended on us to fulfill his vision."

"Shit, Brantley. What are you talking about?" said Bobby. "Do you think this is about the South rising or some bullshit like that? What do you think we are doing this for? Hell, I just want the coins and the gold they'll bring us. If we manage this right. Did you miss something here?"

"I don't know, Bobby, did we? It's pretty convenient your girlfriend can't produce the coin. Maybe you want it for yourself?" said Colin.

"Idiot. That interfering Harley and her posse have it. It wouldn't mean anything to anyone else. And hell, Wilson, you must have missed something. Eliza hasn't said a word about what happened. Those chicks know something we don't, god damn it," Bobby replied.

"Hell if I know. Eliza could be holding out on something. Those Blackmon women are a pretty closed set," said Wilson. "What should we do now, professor?"

"Yeah, you are the big brain here," said Bobby. "Or are you in with Brantley here to secede from the Union?"

"I can revisit Harley anytime seeing as I've already softened her up. She's a sociologist after all. They think they are super dectecitives, always getting to the back-story. You can entice them with crumbs, little clues of aberrant behavior from which they might discover some long lost sub-group or tradition. They adore deviance. I'll serve her up some and get back to you. Don't lose hope," Ian said, "and Colin, keep those antiques in production. The authentication too."

"We better go in, I'm sure Dana is dancing around trying to corral us into eating," said Wilson.

The shuffled steps of the grey soldiers wafted through the open transom. They were in retreat, at least for the moment. One last sound floated in, a slap on the back and Ian saying, "Brantley, buddy, keep the faith." Then silence.

I waited for a moment, gauging the time needed to walk from the porch to the dining room. I couldn't emerge from the powder room too soon and have them think I was eavesdropping on the tiny platoon. A knock on the door startled me. I opened it to find Marco standing with a concerned look on his face. I reached up and kissed him hard, my hands cupping his face. I kissed and kissed until he pushed me away with a "What's with you? Later, darling, not here." I gripped his hand wrapping his arm around my waist. I leaned toward his ear whispering, "It's all coming clear. I'll tell you about it on the way home."

We picked up plates from a table that included Bobby and Fern, Brenda and Glen, Consuela and Guillermo, and Ian Wilkes. Ian pulled out a chair next to mine instead of near his grey brethren. No doubt to soften me up some more. He sat down. His thigh rubbed against mine. Guillermo sat on his other side and thankfully engaged him in conversation. They must have known each other because they seemed too chummy for a first time meeting. Marco and Bobby discussed wine and Consuela told me about her latest painting. Fern sat in sullen silence while Brenda glared at Bobby. All the while we managed to consume the chicken empanadas and cerviche. I loved the crunchy blue corn chips con queso and hot salsa.

Guillermo entertained us with stories of the high seas and pirates he fought in his naval career. "Filmy. Dirty. Sweaty. Foul-mouthed and brutally aggressive toward each other. No pirates' code, Jolly Roger flags, or redeeming swashbuckling uniforms. Just thugs."

"Did you see any pirates with hooks?" Glen clicked his a couple times.

"No, but Captain Hook at Madame Tussaud's Wax Museum cuts a dashing figure," Guillermo said.

This harmless discussion about pirates fell away into awkward silence when dessert was served. Fern and I excused ourselves to serve the desserts we had prepared. It was a relief to get away from Ian, who had assumed a proper decorum at the table but occasionally managed to touch me. Marco did too. I felt like a sandwich that night. Squeezed from both sides by men each unaware of the other. At least I hoped so.

I focused on my job as dessert server. Each plate had a fat cupcake and a slice of king cake.

I moved around the tables balancing plates.

"Harley, you and Fern are presenting a masterpiece. I am so glad to see my platters, as I don't use them." Brenda took a cupcake from me.

Bobby choked on his wine. Brenda pounded him on the back. "Can you talk? Can you talk?"

"Yes." Bobby's squeaky voice broke through coughs.

Fern patted Bobby's hair. "Honey, be careful." He nodded. Then she found her mark. "Meant to tell you, Brenda, I just love your dining room furniture. Especially the breakfront. The one filled with your antique glass and other collectables."

"That's nice," said Brenda, "I am so glad you noticed."

Before any more words could be uttered, a laugh rose up at the dining room table. Spencer stood up, his fingers holding the naked baby charm. "The baby is mine. Course, this means I bring the King Cake next year."

Fern and I slithered off to the kitchen to fuss with the remaining dessert plates. "I enjoyed that," she said.

"I know you did. Remember, timing is everything. You need to think about what you want. Preparation will be your friend."

In the mean time others had gathered platters, costume accessories, to say goodbye. I caught Eliza and Chantal. "Breaking news. Will call you tomorrow."

The rapidly closing last act of February's Supper Club resolved the evening but not the troubles simmering just below the surface of friendships and marriages. The Bal Masqué hid nothing. Some left happy. Some left angry. Some left exposed. I left confused. About Ian Wilkes.

Marco guided me toward the car, his hand around my waist. "You have something to tell me?"

"When we get home." And I did. Everything. Well, almost everything.

Menu

Poached Eggs Salad

Toasted Sourdough with Walnut Oil for Dipping

Quiche Lorraine

Shrimp Boulette Salad with Citrus Vinaigrette

* * *

Steamed Broccoli in a Gruyere Cream Sauce

Onion Sage Mashed Potatoes

Lima Beans with Heirloom Tomatoes and Basil

* * *

Trois Viande Tourtiere

Cheese Toasted Baguettes

* * *

Normandy Apple Tart with Cognac Whipped Cream

Blueberry Pie with Vanilla Bean Whipped Cream

* * *

Burgundy and Bordeaux

March

The days rushed by and suddenly it was March. The dormant shrubs and trees began to grow again in soft new green under the toasty sun. Budding oleanders and Lady Banks roses trailed close behind. Frosty winds blowing from the north and west could still shatter the arc of spring. The look of spring, but the chill of winter. Our flipflops at the ready, but shoes still rule the day.

One such day, an unrecognized number flashed on the caller ID of my cell phone as I pulled into the college. I ignored it.

Ian Wilkes' car sat a few spaces from mine in the car park. We had not spoken since Supper Club last week. He had the picture of the numbers on the coin. Why the lie to his compatriots? Whose side was he on? If there were sides at all? Why couldn't he take me into his confidence, especially if he was conducting some sort of social historical research? Historians rarely use participant observation techniques like sociologists, although depending on his research question and study design he might elect to do so. I wasn't sure how he regarded me. The tension. The dancing. They were real. But what was the point? He had begun to be slightly predictable: flirty whenever he wanted information from me. I didn't like that he was playing me or that I might enjoy it. I reached my office door. A chirp alerted me to a new voice mail on my phone.

I proceeded like a robot: open the computer, toss my brief-case into a chair, and fill a cup with coffee. Only then, did I ring up the voice mail. A soft, even voice asked me to call Eva at the head-quarters of the Muscogee Nation of Florida and left the number.

The same articulate voice answered the phone. "Muscogee Nation. May I help you?"

"Yes, I am returning your call, this is Dr. McBride."

"Hello, this is Eva. I called you on behalf of the chairwom-an of the Muscogee Nation, Hannah Hunter. She wants to talk to you about a private matter and not by phone. She desired to include another woman but did not have her name or phone number. She indicated you would know who this is and to have her accompany you."

"Yes. That is my friend, Chantal Carter." I held the phone tighter as my curiosity grew.

"The Chairwoman requests that you come to the original schoolhouse. It has a plaque on the side saying it was built in the late 1800s. This is our headquarters. It's in Bruce, Florida."

"We would love to meet with your Chairwoman. Let me get a hold of Chantal and check her schedule. I'll call you right away to set a date." I dug a pen out of my briefcase and grabbed a note pad.

"That will be great. Thanks so much. Look forward to hear-ing from you. Good-bye." Eva hung up.

I called Chantal immediately. She insisted we must take Eliza along with us. We had to wait for Eliza to finish minor surgery clinic before we could share this unexpected call. By the end of the day, I had called Eva back. We arranged to meet two days later at noon at the Muscogee Nation headquarters. In the meantime I realized how little I knew about them other than the Musical Echoes festival they host each year in Fort Walton Beach.

The meeting with the tribal leader reminded me of the syn-chronicity Guillermo had described. But it could be more than that. Marco called it karma, the break we needed in our search for the intended purpose of the coins. He holds a belief that special tribal elders have an intuition, a consciousness, a capacity for presentiment that science cannot explain. He grew up with the native tribal elders watching over him and his brother, over all the children playing at Indian Beach on Big Crawling Stone Lake. His belief was forged in experience. It was real.

Meanwhile, I anticipated the upcoming meeting with fear. The throbbing in my right hand had grown steadier. The episodes had become more frequent and stronger over the past months. It grew bolder, hotter, whenever there was a breakthrough on the search. I deceived myself into thinking it was a pinched nerve in my neck that made my hand twinge. That wasn't it. I knew. But how could I begin to explain it to Marco or anyone else and not be labeled crazy, or overdramatic at the least. So for now, this specter's pain remained my secret.

Eliza, Chantal and I sped off to meet the chief of the Muscogee Nation on a day when the crackly dry atmosphere made the sparkling water of the Choctahatchee Bay dazzle with a dusting of tiny rainbow crystals sprinkled on the horizon. As my red Mini climbed to the top of the bridge on Highway 331, the bay spread out on either side of us, disappearing on the west to the Gulf and to the east to a bayou bordering Eden State Park that led to the Choctahatchee River. The shrimp boat Cheri Dawn had anchored at the shore of the east bank next to the highway, their "Fresh Shrimp" sign swaying in the breeze. Magically it is always there, bidding us hello or farewell. I look for it whenever traveling this road.

Our destination, Bruce, is east and north of 30-A, an hour's journey. At Freeport, we turned onto State Road 20 to State Road 81 a few miles east. We turned at Church Road and found the old school house, now the tribal office and a records room containing historic documentation. A gift shop with embroidery, paintings, belts and baskets took up an additional wing of the building. Eva ushered us into a room where three chairs had been placed in a semi-circle facing a long table. One wall was lined with bookshelves tightly packed with books and folders. Another wall was covered in framed embroidery, the once white cloth aged to ivory, its bright blue stitches faded to soft violet. A middle-aged woman with short, wavy, salt and pepper hair stood in a corner gazing out the window. She wore a soft grey shirt and traditional skirt trimmed in double multicolored braid rings.

"Hello, I am Hannah Hunter. Thank you for coming." She wore a cordial smile and pointed to the chairs. Her beaded necklace caught the sunlight as she stepped toward us shaking each of our hands.

"I'd like to begin with some background about the Muscogee Nation of Florida," she said, "because it is relevant to our meeting."

I was hooked like a bluegill. Eliza and Chantal shot knowing looks my way.

"We, Muscogee, are a tribe of Creek Indian people whose ancestors were one of the tribes that made up the Historic Creek Confederacy." Chairwoman Hunter folded her hands on the table and leaned toward us like a professor in a graduate seminar. "This Confederacy signed eleven treaties, count them, eleven. Eleven treaties with the United States government between 1790 and 1833, which ultimately led to their forced removal from traditional homelands. Our ancestral tribal leaders of the Muscogee Nation, however, rejected the Creek Confederacy's ill conceived treaties. They refused to be dispersed and erased. So they fled. They moved the whole community from Daleville, Alabama, tracking south, following the Choctawhatchee River to Bruce Creek. Here they re-established their community, traditions, and homes. For over 175 years we have fished, hunted, farmed, or ranched faithful to our heritage and customs. We sustain the organic link of continuity over time to our ancestors through the practice of traditional ceremonies."

I studied the fine face of dark oval eyes and tanned complexion in front of me. Could Ms. Hunter be the mother of the young girl at the gift shop? They favored each other. It took all my energy to concentrate on her words, because my hand throbbed hard and fast. Heat shot up through my forearm. My thoughts raced ahead to a story taking shape in the fringes of my brain that could be plausible. And possible.

"You see, Dr. McBride, my daughter overheard you and Ms. Carter speaking about the loss of her great great-grandmother's metal box that grieved her to her death. The description made by Ms. Carter rang a bell. She called me right away. I realize it has been over three months since you both visited the museum gift shop, but it has taken me that much time to consider what to do. You had given your card to Iris. She gave it to me. I contacted you when I was ready to speak. Now if you will indulge me a few minutes more, some specific history is in order."

"Take all the time you need," I said. Chantal crossed her legs and held her knee tight like a parishioner trying to hang onto the sermon. Eliza squirmed in her chair.

Chairwoman Hunter dug into the deep pocket of her skirt, retrieving an item lost over a century ago. She placed a small metal box on the table in front of us. "My people, the Muscogee, settled in Bruce in 1852. By then it was not only illegal to trade with Indians, it was under penalty of death that we could declare ourselves to be Indian at all. Either you were white or colored but not Indian. We did not have a reservation. As I said, we lived off the grid. Such as it was then. Such as it is now, until recently.

"We didn't suffer the indignity of a reservation, the government's method to imprison people they don't want. We suffered the tyranny of invisibility. We were there, but no one could see us. Jim Crow laws forced us to hide even deeper. Our tribal government, traditional ceremonies and culture could not be subject to public scrutiny. We could not afford to have our existence be discovered. We had to cloak our identity from the outside world all these years. It is the ultimate irony, that now, in the twenty-first century, we are ordered to present historical evidence, and official documents, to verify our existence if we are to be awarded the privileges and rights of a fully recognized nation of native people under the law of the land.

Mind you this is the same United States government that forced us to hide in the first place. This struggle for recognition of our existence as the Muscogee Nation of Florida is a struggle for survival that is not yet won."

"And this?" I pointed to the box with my left hand. My right hand was jammed into my coat pocket, throbbing away. Sweat formed on my forehead.

"So what does this tale of woe have to do with the metal box sitting in front of you? It has everything to do with it. You see, after the Civil War, there was tremendous migration of newly freed slaves traveling west and south in search of opportunities. It helped to put distance between them and the plantations they had once worked. Our people, although based in the Bruce area, hunted and traded in the region. One trading party ventured to what was then called Camp Walton where soldiers, traders, whores and missionaries mixed it up. Its location near the water drew in transients both honorable and dishonorable. The people were of no matter to us. But its existence as a key destination for trade, to acquire the things we needed and to sell our goods, did matter to us.

Skirmishes broke out from time to time between different traveling parties. The hatred between whites and freed slaves became a flash point for the rage of broken dreams, new dreams and widespread poverty. Our people could get caught in these conflicts even though we did not believe they were our fights. Our fight was grander. The fight for recognition as a sovereign nation. We are still fighting this grander fight, as I have described. This is the context for the story of how this metal box came to be in our possession."

I inched forward in my seat. Please hurry up. My hand is aching. No rubbing or shaking makes it go away. Get to the point. I knew what was in the box.

"At the end of the war," Ms. Hunter said, "some of our traders came upon some newly freed slaves who had been attacked and robbed near Camp Walton. They had come from the East, as most did, from the Apalachicola River, even further north from the

Chattahoochee River. As our traders journeyed closer to Camp Walton, they confronted a mangy gang of thugs lugging goods stolen from these freed slaves. Details are not important. Who can say what exactly happened. One thief had a metal box which he persuaded a young Indian to trade for meat, or so the story goes. The young man knew it belonged to the freed slaves who by then were long gone. He took the box to his father, the Chief, because it was marked with a cross. The box was welded shut and for some reason the thief had not yet pried it open. This box has been handed down, unopened since then, through the descendants of the chiefs. It remained unopened by custom, but I suspect they were superstitious about the cross and initials on the front. I can think of no other explanation, but once the tradition was set, it was respected."

The Chairwoman leaned back in her chair and a wry smile lit her face. "When my daughter heard your stories and told me, I thought, after much consideration, that perhaps the descendant of the rightful owner had been guided to us. It is not ours to keep if it is yours by right. That's why I called you. Ms. Carter, I believe this is the box that belonged to your great great-grandmother."

She pushed the roughly three by five inch shallow box toward Chantal. She picked it up gently in her hands and ran her finger over the initial KC embossed on the side, just below the simple cross. The rusted weld might give way with scraping from a small penknife. I gave her one from my key ring. Chantal scraped the spot with the flat screwdriver head. It gave way. She pulled up the lid to see a gold coin sitting wedged between pads covered with red satin, a turtle on one side, and numbers on the backside. The third coin.

"It's a match." Chantal's face wrinkled with joy.

"Are there papers?" said Eliza. "I suppose that would be too good to be true."

"Perhaps under the coin?" said Chairwoman Hunter.

Chantal lifted the sides of the red satin revealing a yellowed envelope folded to fit the box. "I'll wait to read it with yours, Eliza," she said and tucked the note back under the satin.

My hopes for immediate explanation were dashed. I couldn't insist Chantal read the note if she wanted to wait. But they didn't have the restless sleep and strange pulsating feeling in their hand that had been mine all this time. I couldn't bring myself to tell them then either. At least not at that moment. Eliza looked visibly stunned at the sight of the coin. She couldn't absorb any more.

"My great great-grandmother said that someday the three coins would come together." Eliza ran her shaking hands through her hair.

"So you, too, believe a force has brought this to pass?" said Chairwoman Hunter.

"Yes. According to my great great-grandmother, someday the coins would assemble. For what purpose I don't know. It makes little sense to me, but it is a closely guarded secret of her female descendents. This whole thing began when Harley found a coin washed up from the sea. We believe it belonged to my great great-grandmother's sister who was lost at sea in a shipwreck. Chantal's great great-grandmother was the housekeeper at the family plantation," said Eliza. "Only with the three coins together am I to open the letter from her. I resisted until now, because I believed that I must honor the instructions handed down by her." She looked at me and Chantal, "We'll read tonight."

Chairwoman Hunter said, "Yes. Don't delay. These matters begun in another time are calling out to be resolved in your time, however odd it may seem. I am satisfied that our stewardship of the box is finished, and that it has found its rightful owner. It makes me happy to return it to you. I am glad my nosey daughter eavesdropped on that day." She stood up. "Your great great-grandmother intended these toward some good purpose."

Eva and the Chairwoman escorted us to the door. "Please give Iris our thanks," said Chantal.

My red Mini flew up the bridge over the Choctawhatchee Bay, almost even with the pelicans diving for fish in the silver grey water on either side of us. I considered how networks collide with each other even when separated by generational time and space. Is this merely synchronicity? What word could explain this saga that enmeshed the three of us?

"Even when we read these papers tonight," said Eliza, "I don't think they will have all the answers for us."

"Maybe, but we'll know more than we do now," said Chantal. In the rearview mirror, I saw her lift the box to her nose and inhale, as if to absorb the history contained within.

"We'll know more than our Civil War buffs know, and that is a beautiful thing." I drove into the hospital parking lot.

We took the metal box with the coin inside to Marco who met us at his office. Chantal removed the envelope and slipped it into a plastic folder Marco had given her. He locked the box into the false bottom of the top drawer of his desk.

"Hey, you good looking gals," he said, "Do me a favor."

"Anything," Eliza replied.

"Walk out the rear of the building and over to the shopping mall next door. Stop in a store or two as if you are shopping. Maybe have a margarita at the new Mexican place. Leave your car parked where it is for a while."

"Okay, why should we do this?" said Chantal.

"Because on the chance, be it ever so slight, that you have been followed, it will seem less likely that you have dropped something off for safe keeping here if you don't just leave right away. If you go spend some time together, it suggests you visited me, but then that was just part of an afternoon girl's outing, which doesn't suggest anything."

"Even if we were trailed to the Muscogee Nation and back?" said Eliza.

"Right. A little distraction and deception never hurt anyone. Do it for me. I'll be here working in the office for the rest of the day until late. If I think the coins are not safe, I'll move them. Trust me."

"We do, darling," I said. "Let's go."

When we reached the mall Chantal put her hand on my arm

189

and asked, "How does Marco know to be so careful? I can't decide if he's paranoid or practical."

"It's a long story. He grew up in the shadow of the mob, gangsters, that sort of thing. Let's have a coffee and I'll tell you if Eliza doesn't mind hearing it." She didn't. So we had espressos at the bar in the new TexMex joint and I told Marco's story. Again.

An hour later we headed for 30-A. We agreed to meet at my house that night around seven. Our stated purpose, that is, what we would tell our husbands, was to practice making baguettes as a surprise for Marie Justine, that month's Supper Club hostess. I had the ingredients for dough handy to stage the event although none of us had the slightest intent to bake bread. This was to be the night for answers.

Just before seven that evening, Marco drove away heading toward Cocoons to meet Spencer Dell who had invited him to watch a basketball playoff game on TV. Even Marco didn't know about the papers that went with the coins. I had never confided anything about papers to him. This was a women's secret after all and somehow I relished the power of that secret until we had to share it.

Eliza and Chantal arrived as I uncorked a bottle of wine. We gathered at the dining table, each of us placing a photo of our respective coins in front of us. Oh the power of digital photography and a smart phone. It had been simple to document Chantal's coin before we left it with Marco. It felt good to know the coins were locked safely at the office. The photos were his idea too, another safety precaution. Eliza raised her glass and we toasted the women whose coins they were.

"Don't know about you but I think this is rather eerie," said Chantal.

"Yeah. Like some apparition will form at the end of the table and will talk," said Eliza. "I believe in science."

"Ok, you two. Enough. Let's just do this. I'll watch while you read. If any ghosts appear, I'll vacuum them up with my Dust Buster. Eliza, you go first."

Eliza eased a slim sterling letter opener, another family heir-loom she'd brought with her, along the envelope flap. It gave way instantly, the glue having long disintegrated. She pulled out 2 sheets of ivory paper, yellowed over time and peered at them. Slowly she began to read.

Dearest Daughter,

If you are reading this, you are in the company of coin and kin. Your father, God rest his soul, died in battle. I acted immediately knowing the Order of the Sons of Liberty would arrive as soon as they heard of his death. It's all written down. What was done. What was undone. Kate Carter's Bible holds the information you seek. Our fortune was at stake, as were our souls.

Elizabeth Rainer Powell

Union Springs, Alabama 1864

"That's it?" said Chantal.

"That's it. I knew this wouldn't tell us anything. Why can't this be easier?" Eliza passed the letter to Chantal while she examined the second sheet. "Look. It says 'War no more. Gold compounds.' There is a triangle drawn below it and an X in the middle. What does it mean? Quick, Chantal, open yours."

Using the same letter opener, Chantal worked the edges of the folded flap on her envelope until it gave way. A single ivory paper contained the same words and picture of a triangle with an X in the center. "Now what? They match," Chantal said.

"Where's Kate Carter's Bible? Do you have it?" I said.

"Yes. At my house. It's framed in a shadow box." Chantal put her paper back into its envelope.

"Let's go." I grabbed my car keys. "Now!"

We sped down 30-A with my Mini in the lead. I flew by the cut off to Crooked Creek. Suddenly blue lights began to swirl and the roar of a cop car covered me. I had to be going fifty at least in a thirty five mile zone, when I slowed and pulled over. The others crept by and each signaled they'd be waiting at the house. The car door slammed and an officer approached, shining a flashlight at me.

"Harley, where's the fire?"

"Walter? You are retired!"

"Ah, now and then I pick up a few shifts to help out the boys. What are you and your posse doing out speeding down 30-A? You pretty gals are not exactly teenagers."

"We are tracking down some info about my coin. Sorry if we got carried away."

"Twenty miles over the speed limit carried away, little darling. I'll just give you a verbal warning, about the speed, this time. But, Harley, this coin thing of yours. I worry about you. If you need me, just call me. Here's my card. Call this number, not the house."

"Sure, Walter. Will do. And thanks." I pulled out, anxious to join the others. I watched him back around and park on the cut off, ready for the next speeder. His card was plain, a name and number. That's all. I'd think about him, later.

I raced up the stairs two at a time. Chantal and Eliza had the shadow box on the kitchen table, one screw left to loosen.

"This Bible has not been out of this box for years. My grandmother used it for years, until my mother framed it. She worried it was too fragile for daily use."

Eliza lifted it out of the box and examined it. The pages were thin like onion paper. She took her slim knife and teased at the paper lining the inside cover. The front cover did not budge. The back cover felt padded. Again, she patted the edges until she found a slight bubble, where the glue had dried. With the tip of the knife,she incised between the leather cover and the paper lining. It gave way.

"Look. There it is. Be careful," said Chantal.

"I will. Don't worry. I am surgeon."

"Yeah, well don't cut it." I said.

"Shut up. Let me slide this out. It's been folded a long time and is very dry." Eliza pulled a tiny forceps out of her pocket. "I threw these in just in case."

She pulled the folded paper from its home in the cover and placed it next to the book. With the knife and forceps she unfolded it, layer by layer. There were two pages

"One is from Eliza Powell's diary," said Chantal. "I'll read."
June 21,1864.

Rain has made everything muddy including my spirit. Mr. Powell has little time for me having seceded both financial and domestic spheres to me and does not want to be bothered. His time is spent in affairs of the war. Soon he will return to the battlefield, where he is happiest, surrounded by like minded men. The clinic is growing and I told him that I needed more space. The barn or the stable, he agreed to. I shall assess their conditions tomorrow.

Mr. George, my butler, came to see me in a fearful state. He described Mr. Powell receiving three visitors but did not bring them to the house. Mr. George followed them to the smithy because one of them kept looking everywhere as if on the lookout but truly so as not to be seen. Mr. George, admitting he watched and eavesdropped from the rear side, said Mr. Powell cursed with a smile so evil the men waved their hands in unnatural ways. He stoked the fire in the forge, and the men poured liquid gold into molds. They chanted like a prayer speaking of more land and more slaves. Mr. George does not scare easily and he risks discovery to protect me. Something is not right. I told him to stay close by the house and near our beloved Kate.

I lied to Mr. Powell saying I saw visitors from the window and chastised him for not bringing them round. He apologized but it felt insincere. His next words troubled me greatly. He has decided on his own, to which I objected to no avail, to mint three gold coins to serve as clues in his plan, with the Order of the Sons of Liberty, to hide and later use our combined Rainer and Powell family gold for long term aims of the Confederacy. Today he completed one side of the coins. On his return from the war, he intends to engrave location markers on the blank sides and distribute them to designated sentinels. Meantime, I am to keep safe, the coins and his portfolio of documents related to these plans, while he is away. Pray, God, this will not come to pass. I will speak to Maggie tomorrow.

Eliza Rainer Powell

"No answers. Only more questions. What does the other paper say?" My hand throbbed and the heat was unbearable, but I could not tell them. Somewhere along the way, I had surrendered to the belief that these physical signs could only belong to Maggie, a spirit unreconciled, seeking a way of being in our here and now. It was too absurd to disclose to anyone. It was our secret.

"Let me see, here." Eliza scanned the second sheet.

"*Dearest Daughter,*

The answers you seek are secure by my heart. Find my heart, find the answers.

Love,

Eliza Rainer Powell

"Another clue. Another riddle. What is the point?" Eliza leaned back from the table and crossed her arms. "This is nuts. What was she trying to prove by making this so difficult?"

"She was afraid," said Chantal, "All of this scattering of clues is to hide her actions. We can detect from this entry alone that she and her husband did not agree about the war. She called Kate 'beloved,' and worried about George because of the risks he took to protect her family as well as his own. She did something contrary to Mr. Powells's plan and wants us to understand what and why."

"So where is Eliza Powell's heart? In her grave? Eliza sighed and put her head on the table. "That's in Union Springs, Alabama."

My right hand lay motionless in my lap. Steady beat, calm. I thought of the first time it beat. In front of Eliza's Powell's portrait. The vivid colors pulsating through her face. I knew the location of her heart.

"It's the portrait. Not the grave. In your house, Eliza." I stood up to leave. "If Wilson is not at home, we should go now."

"I'll keep these papers in this Bible where they have been all these years, and put it in the piano, just like Rick did with the letters of transit in *Casablanca*. No one ever looks there." Chantal took the book to the living room. We could hear her move the hammers up to make the space where she could slide the Bible out of view.

"We must hurry. Wilson could be home in an hour. That's not much time." Eliza grabbed her jacket.

"Time enough. Let's go." I led the caravan to her home.

Eliza and Chantal parked behind me, three houses away. We gathered at my car. Eliza's house lights were on. Wilson was home.

"Why is he home so early? What are Bobby, Brantley and Colin doing there? Wilson never said anything about having the guys over," said Eliza. "We can't go in now."

"That's obvious," I said. "You'll just have to get it yourself when he isn't there." My hand cooled down and the pulsation slackened.

"Should be easy enough. Then call us. We can meet back at my house again, just in case we need to see all the clues together," said Chantal. "I do have a question. Although Mr. Powell entrusted his papers to Eliza Powell, what makes us think there weren't copies? His buddies might have had copies too."

"Good point. We don't know. Until we get the paper from the portrait. We are still in the dark." I stepped toward my car door. "We'll be waiting to hear from you."

"Hey, don't lose sight of how historic our day has been. The coins somehow have drawn together. Your great great-grandmother's wish has been fulfilled. What are the odds, given a shipwreck, robbers, Native Americans and time itself? Surely we can decipher the meaning of the coins once we get the remaining paper."

Chantal and I left Eliza at her house. I walked into my own and saw the bread baking tools we didn't use. I stroked Daisy and Tulip and decided to read awhile before Marco turned up. I pulled the Starr Elliott novel out from under the cushion in my ball chair and relaxed into its curve.

At six o'clock the next morning, the phone rang. Marco picked it up and swung it over to me as he rolled over twisted up in sheets. I answered with the husky voice of sudden wakefulness.

"Mom, is that you?" A voice dear to me crackled.

"Maria, where are you?" I said.

"Here, at work, in Tunis. Mom, what is going on there? What have you gotten yourself into now?"

"Nothing, what are you talking about?"

"Mom, your name showed up tagged on an INTERPOL list. For surveillance about illegal trading in cultural artifacts. Even

Gamal has called me about it. What mess are you in?" Maria said with a voice of exasperation well known to me.

"You must believe me, there is nothing going on. I cannot imagine for a moment how my name is on any list. Does it say what artifact?"

"Gold coins from 19th century, Confederate States of America," she said.

"This is unbelievable. Is there anything about contact numbers for who might want to buy if I had anything to sell?" I fished for a pen in my night table drawer. "Give me any numbers you have."

"The name is Omo which doesn't help. It's just a front name for the real buyer. There is no number. You can't call this person, Mom, it doesn't work that way," Maria said. "I just want you to be careful. You haven't told me anything yet, by the way. Is there something to this?"

"I don't know. There is something going on here. Can I e-mail you, encrypted?"

"You'd better, right away. You have the instructions how to send it. Tell me everything," she said.

"Everything else all right? I mean, with you?"

"Yes, I'm fine, other than the shock of seeing your name on INTERPOL. Gamal is going ballistic about it. Now get out of bed and send that e-mail. Bye for now. And, tell Dad I love him."

"Bye, dear."

Within minutes I fired off an explanation. Marco had made a pot of coffee and brought me a steamy mug. "What's next?" he asked. I didn't know.

*

The next few days disappeared in the drudgery work of wrapping up the spring semester's courses. Eliza called me daily, exasperated because Wilson was hanging around more than usual. He was there when she left for work and there when she got home, always in his office. He didn't have any evening appointments nor anything else at the moment.

"I can't complain because he thinks he's being a good guy by being around more," said Eliza, "But I think he's up to something. I caught him on the upper balcony with binoculars watching the sea. He's no bird watcher. I think he'll be gone most of Saturday. Why don't you come over and help me."

"Okay." I agreed.

On the morning of a Supper Club Thursday, I dismissed my class early and went outside to sit under the sun on one of the park benches. The sharp air made stringy clouds out of the steam from my coffee mug that reached to the sky.

"May I join you?" said Ian.

"Shouldn't you be saying 'let's take a walk' or something vaguely sinister like that? Or are we still dancing?" I took in the golden locks of Ian Wilkes. "Back to your usual uniform I see. What, no cape?"

"You noticed?" Ian laughed.

"Where have you been by the way? You don't answer e-mail, or voice mails. You showed up at Supper Club in full Civil War regalia, then go missing from work when all the rest of us faculty are here slaving away. You dance with me as if we were lovers and then go missing. I'd say you are having an affair with someone else. You've dumped me. I thought we wanted the same thing. Information." I smiled and sipped my coffee. It tasted great.

"We do want the same thing. I am sure of that. Harley, I cannot say more, but you must trust me. I am not your enemy or competition," he said.

"That may be true. But I am confused. Why didn't you give the numbers on the back of my coin to the other members of the Order of the Sons of Liberty, the re-organized and active Knights of the Golden Circle? I know there is power in those numbers."

"Ah, Supper Club. So indiscrete. I have warned Brantley about it. Let us just say, I don't share all the ambitions of the group. These multiple ambitions actually make it dangerous. You say you know there is power in the meaning of the numbers. Then you must also know that others could use that power toward different ends." His blue eyes stared off into the distance. He looked troubled.

"To which end will you use the power, Professor Wilkes?"

"To the honorable end if I had the power. I haven't been able to decipher the meaning of the numbers," he said. "Have you?"

"I know a lot of things, Ian. One of them is to play one's cards close. But I would like to know what you think of Han Li the coin expert? Is he an honorable man?"

"Han Li? What does he have to do with anything?" Ian asked with startled eyes.

"You tell me. You told me to see him, but I never did. Jim Reed mentioned I should see him too."

"You never did? You have not been to see Han Li? You are sure?"

"Ian, I have not been to Atlanta in a year. I don't intend to go either. So you tell me what is going on, and why you have that shocked look on your face," I began to worry.

"I can't say anything more, Harley. Trust me. Think like the sociologist you are, and you will understand everything is not always as it seems. I must go." The Hawaiian shirt peeked out below a jean jacket fled on a new pair of thick-soled athletic shoes toward his car. His tires squealed as he sped away from the college that day. Flexible hours are a perk for faculty members. Neither of us could live without them. I left early too, but with Supper Club in mind among other things.

*

Marie Justine and Jean Louis live down the street from us in Seagrove Beach, the old coastal town almost a century ago known as Russ's Hammock. Like Grayton Beach, its sister community populated by travelers from Point Washington about five miles north, development came late to Seagrove Beach. In 1949 Seagrove Market opened, owned and operated by town founders Molly and C. H. McGee and their son, known as "Cube". The dirt road of 30-A did not connect Seagrove to Grayton Beach until the road was paved and a bridge was built over Western Lake. Most of the oak trees edging the bluffs along the sea, which gave the town its name are gone, replaced with houses and condos. Just enough haphazard cinder block homes, A-frames, and brick ranchers remain among the shiny new clapboards and stucco houses to hold onto its quaint feel a little longer. We can walk to their house.

Marco carried the tray with hors d'oeuvres-sized quiche Lorraine I baked from my own French Canadian grandmother's recipe. I even made the crusts with lard, in defiance of all health warnings against it. The mix of Gruyère and ham in the egg and cream filling melted in your mouth. Marco had tasted one for good measure, so my confidence was high. The trois viande tourtière would be an adventure for the uninitiated, but Marie Justine's mother's recipe crushed any competition. The Supper Club members were in for a breathtaking meal, and they didn't even know it.

Under the archway above the courtyard we met Brenda wearing a slip dress that hovered just below her thong. Tonight she could have used the leggings she wore so religiously. She was armed with a basket of baguettes, and Glen carried a bottle of wine in the crook of his arm like a football. The baguettes made me smile since not one was baked the other night. Glen picked off a tiny quiche with his hook and popped it into his mouth.

"Jerk." Brenda's lips curled back like a snake about to bite.

Glen grinned but otherwise ignored her. We said nothing and trailed them in. Thankfully Jean Louis waved us in at the door.

"Come in. Hey guys, how are you?" he said, full of gusto. "Get yourselves a drink and head toward the pool. Marie Justine has ordered us there for hors d'oeuvres."

Marco placed our tray on the bar height table, the four chairs pulled away, lined up in a row to the side. Consuela and Patricia both sporting the latest sweeping swirl skirts and tight cami tops perched in two of the chairs deep in conversation. Adelaide, decked out in orange capris and cinnamon jacket, and Brantley, who must have found an old bottle of Vitalis somewhere to get that smooth hair look, stood near Fern and Bobby, too far away for me to hear anything. An enormous Sago palm anchored the corner of the fenced pool patio and next to it Wilson spoke to Colin nodding his head. Oh, to be a tiny grey salamander with a neon blue tail, hiding beneath the palm soaking in the tawdry plans of men. I confess a tendency toward melodrama. Anyway, the two maintained the posture of a senior officer instructing a junior officer in a plan the junior must implement. Perhaps it was third degree knight to second degree knight. Marco tapped me on the waist and told me not to stare.

Spencer and Guillermo dispensed a lush Burgundy wine ordered special by Jean Louis from Bobby's shop as we stopped in front of the temporary bar set up in the corner of the living room. I left our Zinfandel on the table to open later. Jean Louis's favorite rocker Kid Rock, blared from the surround sound speakers overhead. Last month he was on a Metallica campaign. Before that it was all Kinks, all the time. Marie Justine almost tore out the speakers. Just then she stomped out of the kitchen toward the wall of electronics in the living room. With her jaw set and her blouse collar up over the straps of her striped apron tied in front like a barkeeper, she punched a button or two and strode back to the kitchen. Gone in mid-note. A few seconds pause. A tuneful guitar twanged. Martha's Trouble, a Canadian folk/rock group, filled the air. "Don't you dare change it." Marie Justine called orders from the kitchen. Jean Louis shrugged his shoulders and grinned, the forever petulant bad boy that we all loved.

Reese grabbed my arm. "To the kitchen." Brenda and Adelaide stood next to each other, bread scattered across the table.

"Wasn't I to bring the bread? What's this?" said Brenda.

"You have the baguettes. I had the sourdough for dipping in walnut oil," said Adelaide.

"And your point is?" said Brenda.

"It's not one bread fits all. There are two different requirements in this menu so the breads are different. You can't use a Sister Shubert's roll for everything, you know." Adelaide sneered a lip.

"Oh, you are dissing Sister Shubert's and me now. Or is it just me?" Brenda's voice grew louder.

"There is nothing wrong with Sister Shubert rolls," said Adelaide, "but you can't tell one bread from another. The world's just one big Parker house roll to you."

"What are you trying to say? Or, don't you have the guts to tell me what you really want to say?" Brenda held an uncut baguette in her hand like a machete.

"Oh, I have the guts to say it. I don't know if you have the guts to hear it. Hear it in front of our friends in the kitchen." Adelaide chugged a gulp of Burgundy.

Fern leaned toward me and whispered, "What's going on?"

"Nothing." I led her away. Marie Justine took control of her kitchen shooing everyone but Adelaide and Brenda out.

"If you two have something to say, then say it. If not, button your lip. Take it outside. Not at Supper Club. This is supposed to be fun. A night with friends. I intend to have it that way," said Marie Justine. Adelaide put her basket of sourdough toast next to the walnut oil on the island where the buffet would be served. She walked past me and swore, "Brenda's a slut." I pulled her back towards me and shoved her toward the front door.

"Why does Brenda set you off? What's her behavior to you anyway?" I said. "She's not doing anything to you or Brantley."

"Look. Her fooling around with Bobby could be bad for more than just her marriage. If Fern knows and takes action...well, I can't say more, but it could affect lots of people," she said.

"Adelaide, I still don't understand how. What effect?"

"God, are you thick. Money. What else? There is money involved that she could totally mess up because she wants Bobby. She has no idea. She's just a stupid gym rat. Okay? Get it? I need to get more wine." She stomped off.

Reese and I watched her make her way to the bar. We tried to reconcile this side of Adelaide, with her usual flaky self. Reese broke the moment with a simple statement. "Adelaide doesn't care about the affair because it hurts Fern or Glen but because it could hurt her in the wallet, although I don't see how."

"You are right. This is not about friendship. Sort of makes it even less of our business. We should not interfere in this, we'll only catch blame. Reese, I think we just keep out of this. Fern does know about the affair. She's dealing with it on her own time table. She will need her friends later, so I know your support will be called on eventually."

"Harley, I still think you are a heathen, but I'll always want you on my side," said Reese with a shake of her head.

"Well, I still think you are a holy roller deluxe, but we all need at least one in our lives." We walked together toward the crowd standing by the pool.

Dana approached then and pointed toward Adelaide who had rejoined Brantley, Fern and Bobby. Brenda stood in front of them laughing but no one else laughed. Glen walked over to them, but Brenda stepped back from him. Everyone's eyes focused on their taut faces rigid with tension like a furnace about to blow. Eliza and Marie Justine stepped away from the kitchen and stood in the doorway. Chantal and Darius had just arrived with blueberry pie and vanilla bean whipped cream.

"Brenda, let's go home, I don't think you feel well." Glen reached his hand toward Brenda as he took another step closer.

"Since when do you stay home, you freak?"

"Let's go Brenda, this is not the time or place," he said again.

"No, it's never the time or place, is it?" She turned away from him and raised her voice higher. "How do y'all like the show?"

Glen moved again, grabbing her arm. She bucked, taking a step backward. She shook her arm loose, propelling Glen forward into the pool. He plopped in with a wide splash, the burgundy wine from his glass seeping into the water like blood. Frantic like a little kid, he used his hand to pull himself up, his hook heavy in the water dragging him down. Marco and Mario jumped in to pull him toward the shallow end and the steps where he could climb out. Brenda stared. Catatonic. Then she began to laugh hysterically. Consuela and Patricia eased her toward the living room. Meg and Dana followed right behind. Marie Justine fetched beach towels from the poolside cupboard. Eliza took them to the men. Reese filled Chantal in on the fireworks although none of us knew what spark lit this explosion.

Brenda and Glen left together a few minutes later. Supper Club continued slightly bruised. Marco and Mario made a quick visit to our house for some dry clothes while the rest of us drank more wine and assembled the supper. Marie Justine's unflappable savoir faire carried the evening. Soon we were chatting about the favorite Junot topics, hockey, Genever, and the houseboats in the canals of Amsterdam. And of course, rock and roll.

The tables had been set with pure white dishes and Euro slim straight flatware. In the center of each table stood a holder with four flags. The Stars and Stripes and Maple Leaf were clearly known to us, but the other two stumped us. Darius figured it out, one blue and white flag with a fleur de lis in each quadrant was the flag of the French Canadians of Québec. The other, the flag of French Canadians of Ontario consisted of a green half with white fleur-de-lis and a white half with a green trefoil. Fresh rosemary sprigs from the garden were clustered at the base of the holder. Only one tall white candle lit each table, giving a lean and clean look, like the tables my grandmother set in Montréal.

The statements Adelaide made about money kept interfering with my attention to the discussions of goat cheese versus brie or what makes an heirloom tomato an heirloom. Eliza and Chantal sat at different tables and neither with me. I couldn't consult them. Marco detected my silence and whispered to me to quit thinking so much that it showed.

The trois viande tourtière tasted like my grandmother's, and it pulled me away from 30-A for a few minutes. The Normandy apple cream tart had been a family standard as well. How quickly we travel away from home. How infrequent our visits, even through the family cuisine, now thought to be too rich in butter, too much cheese, too much cream, too much work to prepare. It is still a splendid repast, at least every once in a while. I am grateful Marie Justine insists on it every time they host Supper Club. Jean Louis pours us more wine, and I see my grand-père and grand-mère at their table. I listen to Jean Louis lecture in that charming French way.

"Do you know where this carafe came from?" Jean Louis asked us all. "It is supposed to be a one-of-a-kind carafe hand blown in Cairo, Egypt. I have papers that say it dates to two centuries ago under the Ottoman Empire. It is authentic, just like the ten other ones sitting on the shelf at the souk, you know, the market. I bargained for it and got it for five Egyptian pounds instead of the five hundred the poor chap demanded."

"How did you do that?" asked Adelaide.

"I told him I was with the cultural attache of Canada and was investigating fraud in antiques. He caved in, explaining that the fake paperwork impresses tourists and they give a better price. He assured me they would understand it is not a genuine antique. He promised to tell me if he ever encountered true fraud, and he would of course call the police," Jean Louis rolled his eyes. "Of course I believed him, eh?"

"Is there much of that around?" asked Reese, "I mean illegal trading in antiquities? I read recently the Carnegie Museum in San Francisco is accused of conspiring with crooks."

"Oh, it's a big industry. It's on INTERPOL's top five list of international crimes. All you need is a front, though the real wheeler dealers use middlemen who create the provenance for goods that are not true antiques but passed off as real. Some create paperwork that says it is a fake but substitute the real thing to cheat the system and collect the payments personally. There are several variations, all layers upon layers, no direct path to anyone or anything if they can help it. But, they do slip up, usually when they get greedy. Too much exposure trips the alarm of the police."

"How do you know so much about this?" Bobby swirled the wine in his glass.

"I did work years ago for the Canadian government when I was young, in the border patrol out west. We'd catch smugglers usually trafficking in Asian antiquities. After a few frigid winters, I decided to find a job in warmer climates. I went back to school to be a civil engineer and the rest is history."

Colin whispered something to Meg. She nodded. Before I could study any other reactions, noteworthy or not, Chantal served the blueberry pie, Marco's favorite. Soon enough, Supper Club came to a close.

"A bientôt," called Jean Louis to us as we left. See you later. Marie Justine cornered me and commanded I call her tomorrow to ventilate, as she says, about the incident. I promised. Marco and I strolled back to our house a few doors down.

"INTERPOL" he said. I didn't answer.

We met Tulip and Daisy, each secure in their favorite chairs. The light on the answering machine flashed red against the cinder block walls, reminding me of a nineteen fifties spy movie. Marco pushed the button.

"Hello, Dr. McBride, this is Eva at the Muscogee Nation. Chairwoman Hunter wanted me to let you know that we had a break in at the headquarters early this evening. Nothing is missing but her office was ransacked. She wanted you to know and to be careful. Thank you very much. Goodbye."

On Saturday morning, I picked up Chantal to swing by Eliza's house. There wasn't much time. Wilson was out for a run. I told them about Eva's call at the same time we peeled back the dried out brown paper seal on the back of the portrait. Sure enough, a small folded paper was tucked in between the canvas and wooden spacer. Eliza used her forceps to pull it out. Rather than risk confronting Wilson, we left straightaway for Chantal's house. Eliza opened it.

September 21, 1864

It has been a month since I received news of Mr. Powell's death at the battle front. His body has not yet been returned and I am beginning to doubt we will ever receive him.

I fear the Order of the Sons of Liberty will appear any day. I refuse to release the gold coins to this group whose aims I believed to be ill founded and immoral. As the widow and by right, I choose to act differently. Therefore, all Mr. Powell's papers related to this foul mission in my possession were burned in a fire by my hand. Furthermore, I have granted freedom to Mr. George and Miss Kate and their children.

The coins were engraved according to my instruction. My actions were encrypted within a phrase and a diagram. Together the coins and papers indicate the good purpose to which I committed our fortune.

The cards have shown me a future of uncertainty, chaos and death. I shall meet my fate with honor.

Eliza Rainer Powell

"But what does it mean?" Eliza took a deep breath. "She even invoked the tarot cards. We now know the numbers on the back of the coins are hers and meant to convey her message, not great great-grandfather's message."

"The coins plus the information on the papers. They have to be interpreted together," said Chantal.

"We should keep this with the paper in the Bible. You feel your house is secure enough?" Eliza slid the paper toward Chantal.

"Yes. Trust the piano. And our German shepherd, Jasper, and our alarm system," said Chantal.

"We must sort this out but need more time. Sorry, I can't stay to do that today. Meantime, all of us should think in historic terms, the context of her day. She is writing in that frame of reference." I rubbed my hand against my leg, but nothing relieved the tingling which had begun the moment I saw the portrait.

"Let's all be in touch to find a time to do this," said Eliza.

One phrase played and replayed on my way home. "in my possession" meant Eliza Powell's personal bonfire did not necessarily include all copies of his papers related to the coins. There could be authentic papers about these coins held in trust by the other men. My head began to ache and this time, my hand did not settle down.

Once home, I pet the cats and then flopped into my ball

chair. The newest *Starr Elliott* stuck out from behind the cushion, but even that could bring me no comfort.

Menu

Three Bean Salad

Lemony Sage Potato Salad

* * *

Steamed Asparagas with Hollandaise

Roasted Summer Squash with Herbed Butter

Mustard and Roasted Red Peppers

* * *

Buttermilk Oven Fried Chicken Fingers

Angel Biscuits with Butterfly Pork Chop

Aged White Cheddar Grits

* * *

Grandmother's Banana Pudding

Butter Pecan Ice Cream

Lemon Bars

* * *

Pinot Noir or Merlot

April

"Fern shot Brenda."

"When?" Darius put on his calm lawyer's voice.

"Less than an hour ago," I said.

"How do you know this?"

"Fern called me from the emergency department. She's wounded. Brenda is critical. She needs a lawyer and asked for you."

"Sure she wouldn't want Chantal?"

"She asked for you. That's all I know. I'm on my way over to see her now."

"Has anyone contacted Bobby or Glen?"

"I assume the emergency department has, but beyond that I doubt anyone else even knows about this."

"I'll be there fast as I can," said Darius.

If getting the most shocking phone call I ever heard wasn't enough, Tulip escaped out the front porch. I finally pulled her out from under a palmetto patch. I text messaged my students to cancel the afternoon class.

I barreled down 30-A, heading west where it would eventually link up with Highway 98. At the four-way stop where Miss Lucille's Gossip Parlor stood, I remembered Reese's sighting of Bobby and Brenda only a few weeks ago. I glanced at the cars in the parking lot. Empty but for a couple of minivans.

The window gave him away. There sat Bobby with a coffee, lit up by the morning sun for all to see through the big, squeaky clean picture window. I floored it through the intersection and slammed on my brakes, parking on the shoulder of the road. I flew in the door and slid onto the chair in front of Bobby. He was posed like a peacock in a fresh new mint green golf shirt that still had the press marks in the sleeves. He had pushed the front of his brown hair straight up back with a dab of mousse affecting a Euro stud look. An Atlanta Journal Constitution real estate section, folded open with a few ads circled by magic marker, lay next to his cup of coffee.

"Waiting for someone?" I leaned forward, my hands folded like an detective.

"Ah, yes, as a matter of fact." He slid the newspaper to the side out of direct eyesight.

"I see. Well, just thought you should know something. Fern shot Brenda. They are both at the emergency department." I formed fists and leaned closer.

"Oh my God!" All color drained from his face.

"Fern's okay. Brenda's critical in case you're interested. I'm on my way there now. The emergency staff has been trying to reach you for over an hour." I hissed to prevent screaming at him.

"My cell phone is call forwarded to my private wine cellar phone, so it hasn't rung. I am not taking calls at the moment." He looked at his watch, then up in the air, the way you do when you calculate time in a different time zone.

"A separate private phone number for a wine cellar? What are you doing Bobby, running a secret business?" I stood up. "I'm on my way to see them. Consider yourself informed."

He said nothing as I left, still sitting motionless at the table by the window when I revved up the Mini. In five minutes I reached the driveway for the Sacred Heart Hospital and parked near the Emergency Department entrance. The receptionist waved me in, recognizing Dr. Marco Polo's wife. Marco held a phone to one ear and signaled to me with his free hand. His blue scrubs were blood-stained. A hemostat still hung from his pants pocket. His face grim. I went to him as he hung up the phone.

"It's bad. Brenda died here in the trauma room. The bullet clipped her aorta and tore into her heart. She bled out, never had a chance. I could see she was DOA as the paramedics ran the gurney into the room. I had to try. I had hoped it looked worse than it was. Fern is in that corner room, a bad lac on her forearm, getting stitched up right now. She doesn't know yet. I have to tell her. " He placed his hands on his hips and took a deep breath.

"I'll come with you? Fern called me. That's how I know."

"Yeah, I think she'll need someone with her. Where is that jerk, Bobby? The secretary has been calling him nonstop. His cell number forwards to some automated answering thing, not his usual voice mail. There's no answer at the wine shop either."

"That's because he was sitting at Miss Lucille's Gossip Parlor presumably waiting for Brenda. I saw him there on my way here. I stopped and told him. His phone is forwarded to another private line at his wine cellar. That's why you can't reach him. Then you're not going to believe this. He didn't rush to follow me here. What about Glen?"

"That explains Bobby. Glen's cell goes straight to voice mail. Where the hell is he?" Marco spoke with an indignant exasperation he rarely showed.

"You know, Glen is a realtor, perhaps he's out of range or with a client. I don't know if or when Bobby will show up."

"Unbelievable. Come on then, let's get this over with. You know, she shot Brenda with one of Bobby's black powder revolvers, at point-blank range. She told me that he keeps his Civil War guns loaded at all times. That lead ball could have gone anywhere, and she'd have been okay, but straight, close and into the heart. I hate to say this, but she meant to kill," said Marco.

"How can you be sure?"

"Those old revolvers require you to pull the hammer back first before you shoot. You can't just pick one up and fire away like they do in the movies. She had time to think about it. She probably knows how to shoot a black powder revolver from all those re-enactments she's attended over the years."

We walked past two cops, one writing on a clipboard. Marco rapped the back of his hand on the exam room door and pushed it open. Fern lay on the narrow bed, her pale head on a small pillow. Her left arm draped in sterile cloths rested on an arm board perpendicular to her. A resident physician tied a knot on the last stitch then patted her sewn laceration lightly with a sterile two-by-two gauze pad. She applied an antibiotic cream to it and then wrapped it with a final outer dressing.

"Harley, I am so glad you are here. Marco, how is Brenda? I called 911 right away, there was so much blood." She covered her eyes with her right hand and began to cry.

"Fern, listen." Marco sat down on a stool next to her. She turned her frightened eyes to him. "Brenda is dead. She never regained consciousness. I tried everything, but you are right. She lost too much blood, and the bullet struck her in the heart."

"Oh my God! I never meant to kill her! You must believe me. It was self defense. I was home alone in the kitchen when I heard something. You know I never lock the doors except at night. Then, there she was standing behind me, bulging out of her sports bra. No shirt, wearing black biking shorts and flip flops, sweat dripping down her face. Even her hair was sweaty and limp. She held that butcher's knife in her hand. Not mine, her own. She kept chanting that she'd had enough and was tired of waiting for him. She sneered that I couldn't give him what he needs, that Bobby only stays with me because I have money. Over, and over again. But one thing didn't make sense to me. She began to scream on and on about me stealing Eliza's coin and that ruined everything for her. I have no idea what she was talking about. What coin of Eliza's? She screamed this at me several times in a row and then she started to lunge at me. She was in the hallway. I grabbed the gun from Bobby's desk. He kept it loaded. I knew that. But, I swear to you that I did not intend to kill her, only scare her. She kept shouting and jabbing the knife in the air. She got closer. When she cut me, I fired. God, I sound like a TV show." Fern turned to me, and I took her hand, helping her to sit up.

"I called 911 right away. The police came with the paramedics. Have you called Bobby? He'll hate me for sure. Am I going to jail?" Tears poured down her face, dripping onto the fresh bandage.

"The cops are outside the room, Fern, anytime there is a gunshot case. They will want to talk to you. As for Bobby, he's been informed you both are here but not the details. He's not shown up to my knowledge." Marco stood up. "Harley will stay with you, I'll be back."

I squeezed his hand and he left the room. Fern's blood spattered pink T-shirt clung to her, turning brown as the blood dried. She sat hunched over on the bed, bare feet dangling above her sandals. "Oh, Harley, I've killed her. I didn't mean to. I wanted to scare her, sure, to make her go way. I hate Bobby." Her eyes searched me for support. "It's been nothing but lies, our whole marriage."

"Fern, there is something I should tell you. It may help to explain one thing Brenda said to you. It's about Eliza's coin."

"You mean there is a coin? I told her she was insane, crazy to make this crap up."

"Remember the gold coin I found. The one that matched the coin in Eliza's great great-grandmother's portrait? That coin was hidden in Eliza's house, but someone beat her up and stole it. When you borrowed the platters from Brenda, you saw it next to the Civil War book you gave Bobby. You told me the book was next to old coins including a gold one. So Eliza and I knew that Bobby was involved in that theft. We got it back when we went to Brenda and borrowed more dishes. Bobby was angry she lost it. We all saw that at the last Supper Club."

"So you stole the coin?"

"Well, Eliza repossessed what had been stolen from her." I paced back and forth in front of her.

"For God's sake, why is it so important?"

"We are certain that Bobby and probably Wilson Garrett, Brantley Vernon and Colin Coffee are involved in some secretive business, but we don't know exactly what yet. Something with the Civil War but we can't figure it out."

"Oh my God. The Order of the Sons of Liberty. They are scary; they can hurt you. You must stay away from them. They will hunt you down if they think you know anything about lost Confederate gold. They'll kill you to protect it."

"Are you sure? Bobby and those others don't seem like the crazy type. Maybe they like to play dress up in soldiers uniforms, but killers?"

"This can't be true." Fern sighed, slumping like a defeated athlete. "Your coin and Eliza's coin must be recognized as long lost clues to the treasure stashes. These can be sold on the black market for hundreds of thousands of dollars. Collectors will pay huge amounts for the thrill of owning a clue that is genuine and that may lead them to more gold. People will steal and kill for them."

"You know this to be true?"

"They are dangerous. Believe me. Don't get mixed up with them."

"Okay, enough. This is not the priority now, you are. We can deal with the coins later." I lied to her out of sympathy. The coins were the priority to me. First Eliza was hit, then the Muscogee Nation. Someone is tracking us and getting closer.

"I'm so afraid." She wailed like a little child. Like a spoiled rich child.

"Me, too. A little." I refocused to the moment, the tragedy of it all. "Fern, I called Darius as you asked. He's on his way. And say nothing to anyone. Those are his words. You don't have to talk to the police yet. Tell them you are waiting for your attorney. There is someone I am going to call."

"Who?" Fern shivered and closed her eyes.

"Walter McElwain. He's a cop. Sort of retired. I'd feel better if he knew. He looks after us, unofficially, of course."

Before she could answer, Darius walked in dressed in a dark suit, white shirt with blue and silver silk tie. He conferred with her as I stood outside her door, scanning the hallway for her absent husband. Marco saw me and nodded toward the trauma room. Bobby staggered out of the room with tears dripping down his face, staining his new shirt. He reached for a nearby chair and swung into it, expressionless. A nurse whispered something to Marco. He approached me. "Glen is on his way in."

"I don't think Glen ever confronted Bobby, but he knew. Glen has his own girlfriend. I've seen her. Is Bobby going to see Fern?"

"Doesn't look like it. He should, but maybe he can't face her. Who knows what demons are torturing them. I wish we didn't know as much as we do. That phone business with Bobby is odd. Reminds me of this friend of my father's who ran a bookie operation out of his attic. Special phones. Different lines. The cops knew too and made their sports betting there. Wouldn't surprise me if he had some secret deal going on. Hell, a wine cellar would be a perfect place to hide people or things."

"Look, Darius is walking over toward Bobby."

We watched the two men converse. Bobby's head shook in agreement. Darius placed a hand on his shoulder. Bobby wiped his eyes with his hands and followed Darius to the room where Fern sat in a blood soaked shirt with a beating heart, broken from shattered promises. Fern told me later that Bobby said only "I'll do anything to keep you out of jail." He confessed nothing about Brenda or the affair.

The police talked to Fern, Bobby and Darius, but they did not take her with them. They could arrest her later if they or Glen pressed charges. Bobby left without a word to any of us. It fell to me to drive Fern home. I later found out he went straight to see Wilson Garrett in Alys Beach. Marco changed into fresh scrubs and went to see other patients. Just before we left, Glen walked into the trauma room to see his dead wife.

He reappeared within minutes, ashen but coherent enough to ask where he could get a beer. The hospital personnel detained him long enough to sign some papers after which the police spoke with him. He left without noticing us. Fern and I watched a transport person wheel the sheet-covered body of our friend Brenda down the hall to an elevator. Her red stiletto heels rode along in the clothes basket beneath the gurney. He pushed the B button for basement, where the morgue took in the day's dead.

*

Once home, Fern insisted I leave.

"I feel fine. At peace, actually." She climbed onto a bar stool in the kitchen. "I'll let you know if I need anything."

"We should mop up the floor. The police are through here. Where is a bucket." I opened a closet and found a mop in an empty bucket. Fern sat still. She put her head down on the countertop and sobbed.

There wasn't much blood on the floor. That's the way with internal bleeding. Hence, the term. Cleaner. But, fatal.

"You'll call me." I spoke like a professor to a student.

"Yeah. Don't worry about me. Bobby won't be violent. He's too calculating for that. He'll want to control the spin, once this incident became public knowledge. Can't let it affect business." Fern gave me a weak wave.

While rumbling down 30-A as fast as possible to Seagrove Beach and my safe haven love shack, I hit the speed dial to Eliza to give her the news. I figured the occasion of a dead member of Supper Club justified breaking my no-phoning-while-driving rule.

"So that explains Bobby's sudden visit. My God this is shocking. But it explains why he is so agitated. I can't talk now. I need to listen. Wilson and Bobby are in the dining room totally outraged about something. I'll call you back later," said Eliza.

I swung into the driveway. Daisy and Tulip were sitting on the front steps waiting for me. How did they get out? I never let them run wild outside. They rushed to my feet and rubbed my legs with vigor. Then, much sooner than I expected, Marco pulled in and slammed his car door shut.

"Hey, my replacement wanted to pick up some extra hours, so he came in early. I was glad to get out of there. Why are the cats outside?"

"I found them out here. Waiting on the steps." I nudged the door. It opened. "Marco. I locked the house when I left today."

Marco pushed it back. He stepped into the house. I followed with the cats, one in each arm.

The door to our bedroom was closed. We never close it during the day so the cats can get in to sleep on their favorite pillows.

Marco opened the door.

Chaos.

"That son of a bitch Bobby did this. " I stepped around the drawers pulled out from the dresser. Underwear and socks thrown around the room. T-shirts and shoes tossed everywhere. Our closets stripped bare. The once neatly hung clothes rumpled into heaps on the floor. My jewelry box dumped. Every bauble tangled.

"Why do you say that? Shouldn't we call the police?" Marco stood motionless. "How did he get in here anyway?"

"He and Fern have a key from when they'd stop in and feed the cats while we were away last year. There's no forced entry. He let himself in." I grabbed the pocket-sized camera from my briefcase and snapped pictures of the mess. "We should call Walter."

"Why not the police. Walter is retired. What can he do?" Marco picked up a pile of golf shirts.

"Walter is the police. I don't think he is very retired. Plus he's our friend." I pulled his card from my wallet.

Walter McElwain pulled into our driveway in an unmarked cruiser within 10 minutes. His Bermuda shorts and black socks made me smile. Could it be a uniform? He's actually undercover?

"Tell me why you think it's Bobby?" Walter stood at the door and surveyed the mess. He picked up Daisy and stroked her.

"Bobby watched me leave for the hospital. He sat there with

a coffee cup and didn't move. This must explain why he didn't show until later. He came here first to look for the coin. Should I be saying coins? Someone ransacked the office at the Muscogee Nation. He's at the top of my suspect list."

"You think someone knows you went out to Bruce?"

"Not from anything Eliza, Chantal or I have said. Some body knew we were there. I only told Marco after the fact."

"That's true. She never tells me anything ahead of time." Marco slid a drawer back into the chest.

"I confess, Harley, I don't know what you and the gals are up to. If you want me to help, you'll have to come clean with the whole kit and caboodle. If you don't think anything is missing, no need for a police report."

I walked Walter to his police cruiser. "For someone retired, you sure get around."

"And you are keeping a secret. A deep one. That's no good. People can get hurt. Brenda's dead. That coin is partly responsible."

His words stung. And he was right.

Marco and I began the tedious task of restoring order to our room, working around Tulip and Daisy who insisted on nesting in the piles of cloth. They made us laugh. We spoke to each other of many things that afternoon. Eventually night came and we slid into bed, exhausted. Only later, when Marco turned out the light, and I snuggled against his side, drifting to sleep did I realize Eliza never called me back.

*

I woke early. A dull hue colored the day. I left Marco to sleep in. The ugly stories of Fern and Brenda, Bobby and Glen, bothered me because Walter had made me aware of my own role in them. Who could have predicted Brenda's knife wielding attack. Could Fern have been better prepared if she had known about the coin? Should we have told her about it? Would it have made any dif-ference? I rang up Eliza ,sure she was on her way to her clinic.

"I was just dialing you," said Eliza. "Call Chantal. I won't have time once I get to my office. It's minor surgery all morning. We must meet somewhere today. I have something to show you. It's about my great great-grandfather."

"And, the coins?"

"Yes, and more. How about the coffee shop inside the new Target at Pier Point, say 4 o'clock?"

"Fine. Before you go, someone broke into our house and ransacked our bedroom. Nothing missing, but it was a big mess. We think it was Bobby."

"I saw him last night, extremely agitated. He couldn't contain himself last night, but he never spoke about Brenda. He's a cold one. Heartless. How did Fern put up with him all these years? What could Brenda see in him?"

"I don't know. We'll talk about it later. See you tonight."

*

The kitchen light through the plantation shutters outlined the silhouette of a woman sitting at a counter. I knocked on the door and entered. Fern looked up, eyes red from tears. She offered me a cup of coffee. The kids, she said, were coming home later that day from their spring high school field trip to Atlanta. They were good kids, they'd understand. They had always been closer to her than their father. She counted on their loyalty to her.

"Bobby never came home last night."

"Did he call?"

"No. He probably crashed at the wine store. I don't know what I'd say to him. Sorry I killed your girlfriend?"

"There are probably some things he should say to you."

"Yes. I am sure we'll be saying a lot of things. Darius wants to handle the criminal case now. When it is clear what will happen, that is, if I don't get arrested, then I'll file for divorce. Guess I'd switch to Chantal. She's the divorce lawyer."

"Fern, Glen has a girl friend. I've seen them out together. She's not a client although that's how he explains her."

"Hmm. I didn't know that. Does it make any difference? I

killed Brenda. It's dragging me down like a stone pulls a body under water. Suffocating. I can't pull myself up away from it."

"You should not be alone."

"I'm not."

"Hi, Harley," said Marie Justine walking in from the hallway. "Glad to see you. I stopped by last night to return a platter and found Fern in rather deep distress. She told me everything. Jean Louis is out of town for a few days, so I stayed last night to help."

"I thought Bobby was going to be here. I didn't know Ivy and Deuce were gone." I felt guilty that I had left Fern aling in her house yesterday.

"Well, I can stay all day if needed." Marie Justine putting her arm around Fern. "That's what friends are for."

Fern nodded and closed her puffy eyes. With Fern's agreement, Marie Justine and I divided up the Supper Club member list to inform them of yesterday's tragedy. I realized Walter must have said something to someone to keep it out of the news. At least for now.

I left for work, studying the clouds while stopped at a traffic light. The water under the bridge rippled with white caps and the wind from the Southeast signaled storms. The tips of the palm trees fluttered while the slender, dense, ornamental grasses that lined roads and decorated car parks swayed back and forth in the gusts of moist air.

Ian Wilkes' car was parked in its usual space. Today the red Mini pulled up next to it. I stopped at his office before going to mine.

"Ian, I have something to tell you." I stood in front of his desk. He looked up, reading glasses balanced on the tip of his nose.

"Fern shot Brenda yesterday after Brenda attacked her with a knife. Among other things, she ranted on about a gold coin. Brenda died in the ED. Marco couldn't save her. A Civil War black powder revolver loaded with live ammo. A lead ball chewed up her aorta and heart."

His tan face turned grey. "Where is Bobby?"

"I don't know. He didn't come home last night. Maybe he stayed at his wine shop? That was Fern's guess."

"This is not good at all," he said shaking his head.

"Well, that's insightful. Fern is afraid of the Order of the Sons of Liberty. She thinks they will blame her for Brenda's loss of the gold coin, that you and I both know was stolen from Eliza. But, Fern didn't take it from Brenda's house. I know who did."

"Who?"

"Does it matter? What matters is that your get rich scheme by selling it has been wrecked."

"Harley, it is critical that I know where the coins are. I know you think I am in league with those guys, but trust me. The Order of the Sons of Liberty is a sham. It means nothing. It's a game. No knight is going to appear to take revenge. It's not that at all."

"You're involved in something, Ian. You know it. I know it. You don't want to say what. Okay. But listen to this. Some Knights of the Golden Circle or Sons of Liberty, you call it what you want, ransacked not only my home last night but the office of the Muscogee Nation a couple of weeks ago. You or someone of your gang has been tailing me."

"So it has turned desperate. Harley, I must ask you to leave. I am sorry about Fern and Brenda, but there is nothing I can do about it." He stood up and walked toward the door, waiting for me to exit. So I did, without a word.

*

I ran a bit late getting to the coffee shop at the Target. Chantal and Eliza sat at a table in the rear, with cappuccinos steaming in front of them. The waitress brought me a third when I plopped into a chair.

Chantal volunteered that charges against Fern were unlikely given Brenda's aggressive threatening behavior and Glen has no desire to destroy Fern's family by sending her to jail. She stirred the steamed milk in her mug with a spoon then licked it clean. "Go on now, Eliza, tell us why we are here."

"The night of the day Fern shot Brenda, Bobby showed up at our door, sweaty, alcohol on his breath and fidgety. Rage against Fern over Brenda's death gushed out of him, you know, 'heartless bitch,' 'her family never accepted me,' that sort of thing. However he never talked about Brenda directly in a personal way. Wilson and I managed to calm him down. Then Wilson told me to leave them in private. Of course they are good friends. But I don't trust them either so I listened from outside the room. Couldn't hear what they said very well, but I saw Wilson take a yellowed paper from a book on the shelf and examine it with Bobby. He put it back in the same place. Wilson called to me that he was going over to Bobby's house. I went to bed, and Wilson came in later."

"But Bobby didn't go home. Marie Justine stayed with Fern," I said.

"Where did he go?" said Chantal.

"I don't know. But, I do know when Wilson left early today, I went to that book, an old book about hunting in the Deep South. I opened it pages down and made them flutter. Sure enough, a yellow, very old paper tucked into the pages floated out. I read it."

"And?" I pulled a fresh bag of M&M almonds from my purse and ripped it open. They rolled around in the torn bag as I dug for a few and then offered the bag to the others.

"It is the instructions for the coins. The original plans as my great great-grandfather wrote them. We already know from Eliza Powell's diary that he commissioned the coins in the first place."

"For God's sake, tell us what it says." Chantal pounded the table with her fingertips.

"It's dated May 5, 1864, the year the Knights of the Golden Circle reassembled as the Order of the Sons of Liberty." She began reading with a quiet voice.

The long term viability of the Confederate States, even against a loss to the United States, must be supported. My wife's and my family fortunes are hereby pledged to the Confederate States of the Golden Circle. Our gold will be held in three separate secure locations.

Thusly, I have personally minted three coins to denote three locations. The turtle, being our official symbol for money, validates them as officially belonging to the Order of the Sons of Liberty. The numbers engraved on the back will indicate where the treasure is buried, by latitude and longitude.

The coins will be held secure by a third degree member of the Order of the Sons of Liberty because a third degree member will safeguard them in alliance with other sentries, who will hold the exact maps of the site. Together they will provide a web of protection. The maps if stolen will give away nothing. The coins if stolen will not give precise whereabouts. Only together, in alliance, can they reveal the location of the hidden gold.

On my return from the battlefront, in coordination with third degree members, the locations will be chosen, the maps drawn.

Should I fail to return from the war, the coins may be retrieved from my wife, who has my papers and coins in safekeeping for me. The pledge of our fortunes stand. I trust the Order of the Sons of Liberty to carry on the plan.

This paper bears my official stamp as does the exact copy held by my wife. There can be no doubt to their authenticity or intent.

Stephen William Powell.

"That gave me chills. " Chantal sat straight up in her chair rubbing her arms.

"No wonder Eliza Powell would not go along with this," I said, "It's madness."

"If she burned all Mr. Powell's papers, then what is this?" Eliza pointed to the stamp. "Sure looks authentic to me."

"Must be the copy he entrusted to a member of the Order." I said, "Where did Wilson get it?

"Don't know. Secret files," Eliza said. "He's a member of several Civil War groups. Any one of them could be the Order of the Sons of Liberty."

"This doesn't really change anything. We know what your great great-grandmother wanted for the coins. They assembled as she directed. She's running this show." My right hand began to throb even though I had held it tightly in my other hand.

"That's true, but it's frustrating we haven't figured out what

Eliza Powell's numbers mean yet even though Mr. Powell meant the numbers to be longitude and latitude, " said Chantal. "Remember when we plotted the numbers as longitude and latitude all we got was an empty spot in the Mediterranean Sea. So they can't be that. Has to be something else."

Eliza folded the paper with care. "Let's keep this safe with the other papers in the Bible." She gave it to Chantal and said, "What we do know is that the men are operating under these instructions, unaware they no longer apply to the coins. They don't have Eliza Powell's papers. They don't know what we know.

"So what now?" asked Chantal.

"We know Mr. Powell gave this letter and maybe other documents to a brother in the Order. Somebody thinks this letter is not only real but still valid. You've been beaten and robbed, my house ransacked, and the Muscogee Nation office turned upside down. This doesn't strike me as over. Bobby's concern for the coin outweighs his concern for Fern or his kids. Brenda, poor her, only wanted attention."

"I didn't see anything about Brenda in the paper yet, an obituary or funeral plans," said Eliza.

"Could be too soon. Glen is unpredictable, I said, "You should know that Ian Wilkes is involved with this group. He may think this a serious historical document."

"Ah, him," said Chantal, "the history professor. They are all about primary references, original documents. His contacts probably run deep in these parts. Yeah. This is not over."

We left that meeting with more knowledge but less certainty. Historic documents alone cannot reveal all aspects of intent. Trickery and deceit are tools for the ages. Great great-grandmother Eliza's diary entry date meant she knew with certainty her husband met his ignoble end on the battlefield. She couldn't have believed herself free to change his instructions if she thought he would return. This new discovery, this yellowed paper read by Eliza this morning troubled me. Its very existence proved there was and is a clandestine organization afoot. Perhaps it is a forgery. A forgery written recently that could pass for the real thing. Like a provenance Brantly Vernon so willingly offered to construct. I said nothing to the others already driving off in their cars. I sat in the red Mini, replaying it all, but couldn't find it, that one slightly remarkable word, action, or sound that could make all this fall into place. I drove home chanting "Ian, Ian, Ian," hoping the mantra would open my mind.

*

Seaside. Seaside is worshiped as the vanguard of the modern age. It is the mother ship for all the "New Urbanism" communities along 30-A. Seaside was the first to sell the notion of building a town from zero, all at once. The shops, the post office, a school, the houses, and presto, a beach side city would emerge that residents would never want to leave. Committed loyalists are everywhere.

Adelaide works at Pizitz, the home furnishings shop of casual elegance where the élan of French countryside meets 21st century modern, in the original arcade of shops on the street level. Million dollar condos are found in the floors above. She can see the town's grassy square from the store window, a half circle amphitheater sloping downward to a band shell stage where outdoor concerts and plays are held. On occasion, when blankets are spread across the ground secured on the corners by picnic baskets and coolers, adults stretched out on top, glasses of wine in hand, day or night, you might think you are on the lawns of Wolftrap or Ravinia. Across the perimeter lane of this crescent lawn, residents and tourists bustle in and out of Modica Market, an emporium of wine, exotic olives, cheeses, plus all the other mundane things you need on vacation. Their hot cinnamon rolls, fresh each morning are the best. Just across the street is Sundog Bookstore, where I first met Eliza years ago.

I poked my head into Pizitz that day to ask Adelaide if she could come with me to Modica's. She declined because of an approaching appointment with a decorator. "Have you heard from our poor friend, Glen?"

"He took Brenda's body back to Luverne, her hometown and had a small family funeral. Their two sons were there. One of them works on an oil platform for a company in Texas. The other is a crew member for some NASCAR driver, so he's on the road with that circuit," I said picking up a glass to check the price. "He probably didn't reply to the usual Supper Club e-mail, I'd guess."

"I don't expect he'll want to come, although it might be good for him to be with friends. Fern and Bobby are not coming. That much I know," she said.

"They are trying to regroup because of the kids, but I doubt it works out. Anyway, I'm off to get some asparagus at Modica's." I pulled the shop door open to leave.

"You, asparagus? Thought you hated it too much to cook it. But don't worry your pretty head about it. Say, I'll let you in on a secret." Adelaide moved the pile of receipts to the side of the register. She looked around to see if the coast was clear. "I know my reputation for cooking is low, but Supper Club will be wowed by the chicken and pork chops this time. Want to know how?"

"Of course."

"I'm having Modica's prepare it for me!" She stuck her chest out and beamed.

"That's a great idea. Everything they make is delicious. You'll enjoy the party more. Good for you."

"So you don't think it's awful that I'm not cooking them at home?"

"Not at all. Supper Club is about friendship. No doubt we'll be rehashing the Brenda, Fern, Bobby triangle, not to mention Glen. Gotta run." I walked toward Modica's weaving through the stainless steel tables and chairs out in front, crowded with families and couples, noisy with life.

*

The phone rang once. Then nothing. Then again, long and steady. I answered, "Maria?"

"Mom."

"What time is it there?"

"Midnight. Look, Mom, I think you should talk to someone. Your name is still on the list. Gamal is worried about you. I know you want to play super sleuth, but this is real. And it's nasty. You and Dad could be in real trouble," she said. "First it's ransacking. It only escalates. Mugging. Even kidnapping. You need to talk to the police."

"Keep Gamal out of this. My life is none of his business. Get it? Do you?"

"Okay. Okay. I get it."

"So you think there's something to all this? As for safety, you sound like your father."

"I know there's something big going on. Dad knows what he's talking about. Listen to him."

"He'll love it that you take his side, as usual, I might add."

"Mom, just do it. Promise?"

"Promise. I'll talk to someone tonight."

"Hey, you are not talking about this at your Supper Club, are you? That's not the place to talk about this if I understood your e-mail correctly." Maria's voice grew strident.

"There is someone coming who is a retired Navy intelligence officer. He's legit and a friend."

"I don't know. If you are sure you can trust him. Otherwise, I'll get a name for you. "

"It will be okay. Go to sleep honey. I've got to steam some asparagus for tonight."

"You? Asparagus? Transformation complete! You are turning into a Southerner." Her voice softened.

"Never. I'm only a Southern appreciator. That's all I can aspire to be. Now, don't worry. I'll call you in a few days. Love you."

"Love you, too."

I love my daughter but she annoyed me today. She's in complete alliance with her father. As usual. I did not sense the risk that Maria or Marco registered. The thrill of the mystery. Yes. But, frank danger? No way. Not me. I just knew I wasn't alone in my quest. The pulsation in my hand had convinced me of this. I went back to steam the asparagus. The vegetable I detest the most.

Marco came back from surf fishing early and stood by waiting to carry our contribution to the car. I put a bottle of wine into my sloppy purse and slid it onto my shoulder. We took off toward Seaside, the sun hanging below a ridge of clouds as if resisting the closure of a picture perfect spring day.

Seaside roofs, tall and short but all made of tin, glowed pink in the last bits of day. The pastel-colored clapboard cottage homes trimmed in white were each grander than the last. Steep, sloping rooflines, second floor screened porches, circular staircases, and watchtowers shaped the town horizon like a fairy tale city. The narrow interior streets converged at various roundabouts which moved the traffic along toward other lanes and alleyways. One such lane led us to Adelaide and Brantley's home built in the oldest part of town.

Brantley greeted us on the front porch, a wide open air veranda that wrapped around most of the house. You could imagine Southern belles sipping mint juleps ensconced in the pairs of plantation rocking chairs grouped around low tables scattered about. He held open the mahogany door to their living room bathed in turquoise and white, with accents in dark brown. The '50s-era sofas designed low to the ground were curved around a central round ottoman made of woven sweet grass. I placed the tray of crunchy asparagus on a tray in the center as instructed by Adelaide the day before. Marco followed Brantley to another room off the kitchen where he had set up bottles of Pinot Noir and Merlot courtesy of Bobby's store. A few bottles of chilled white Bordeaux stood by for the white wine drinkers. I aimed for the kitchen.

Adelaide and Patricia told me to move the chicken from the caterer's foil pan to an ivory ceramic platter with scalloped edges. The pork, already repositioned on a similar platter, was garnished with sprigs of curly parsley. A bowl of lemony sage potato salad sat nearby. Patricia admitted it came from Cocoons but Spencer had made it.

Eliza and Wilson arrived, followed by Consuela and Guillermo. We all spoke briefly in the dining room, lit from above by a chandelier of a hundred individual lights whose wires were then braided together into one big industrial-looking cable. Two round glass top tables seated six with chairs also made of woven blond seagrass. On the adjacent screened porch, she had set up cafe tables and chairs, the metal type you see in Paris. Easter egg trees, little metal sculptures dangling hand-colored eggs from white string stood in the center of each. Foil-covered chocolate eggs tossed carelessly across the tabletop dotted the white table cloths with bursts of spring color.

In came glamorous Eliza, turned out in a mauve silk wrap around blouse over billowy retro palazzo black pants. "I can't take him any more. The complaining. The whining. You'd think he had a hard life or something. I'm fed up with the whole thing."

"What whole thing?" I gave her a glass of wine.

"The mystery of the coins. What do they mean? Does it really matter at this point?" Eliza shrugged and took a few steps toward the living room. "What more is there? We know that Eliza Powell changed their original purpose to suit her own. Why not let the boys know our women's history trumped their little game of knights of whatever it is. We won."

Until then, Marco and I had told no one about INTERPOL. I pulled Eliza to the still empty screened porch. "There is more. Much more." I glanced around to be sure now one else would hear. "My name is on an INTERPOL list as the seller of a Confederate gold coin. Even Maria is worried. This is much bigger than even Eliza Powell could have imagined."

"So that's it? They are involved in criminal activity? Selling the coins? They are not theirs to sell. What should we do? I don't think I can stand this much longer. Living with a man who hits you to steal your family's heirloom? I am going to be sick." Eliza broke out in a sweat along her hairline, then wiped it off with the back of her hand. She dabbed sprinkles of her white wine on her face and fanned it with the palm of her hand. "There. I'll be all right."

"Look. I am going to get some help tonight. If we hold on a little longer, we can catch them in the act, as the old saying goes. If we expose what we know, they could accuse us of being girls with too much imagination and time on our hands." I squeezed her shoulder. "Give me one more month. After that, if nothing has changed, we'll convene our own Civil War group."

"Okay. And, Chantal? She needs to know too," said Eliza.

"There she is, just coming in. You let her know. I'm off to get help. " I stepped away.

"From whom?"

"Guillermo. That's all I can say. We'll talk later."

I whispered to Marco about Eliza. He did not object to her knowing about INTERPOL. We agreed with Maria the time had come to get some perspective from someone here. We decided to call Guillermo to help us. Snappily dressed in a pale yellow golf shirt and pressed khakis, Guillermo gathered us on each arm and led us away from the growing din of the chatty crowd.

"Now you two, I am glad you called me after Maria's message that your name, Harley, was still on the list. She and I have been in touch so we now can act together on the team. This is much bigger than you could imagine," Guillermo said. "But we are very close to discovering how your name ended up on INTERPOL. "

"You have known about this all along?" I said.

"You didn't start anything, Harley, but stumbled into an ongoing operation. Usually that is disastrous, but in this case, you have actually helped."

"What should we do?" asked Marco.

"Nothing. Do nothing. The investigation will not last much longer. It is critical that you both act or react normally to events such as they may happen, so I won't provide you with details. I can promise you, we are only a few weeks away from an arrest."

"Is anyone in physical danger?" I asked.

"There are contingencies for everything, but no, I don't think you need to worry about that. If you need to reach me, call Jim Reed and tell him you need a book about Billy Bowlegs. I'll call you back from a secure line."

"Jim Reed? He's a spy?" I gasped.

"Naw, he's just a decent guy, a rare book seller."

"Yeah, right, you expect me to think that, Mr. Billy Bowlegs?" I regretted being sarcastic.

"If Guillermo says he's just a rare book seller, then that's what he is. We leave it at that, dear," said Marco wearing his official doctor eyes. "That's how this works."

Before anything else could be said, Dana and Mario walked in. "Where's the party?" Mario opened a door and peered in. "Whoa, there's some serious history in here. Where's Brantley."

"I'll go get him,"said Dana. "Let's ask him if we can see his stuff?" Her hair was whipped up into a ball with chopsticks stuck into it. She wore a black leotard top with bell bottom jeans. She skipped off with ballerina steps and returned pulling Brantley along by the hand with a few others tagging behind.

"I'm flattered you'd want to see my memorabilia. The Southern heritage is to be honored not flayed at with ignorant jokes or insulting stereotypes," he said.

The Coffees, newly arrived, joined the rest of us in the library. Meg was poured into a red camisole with built-in bra that clashed fiercely with her red hair. Colin sported a lime green plaid madras shirt. How odd. They were not their typical color coordinated selves that night. I could hear Colin greet everyone with a voice always a little bit too loud.

The musty room smelled of shelves packed with old mildewed ledgers and books with cracked spines. Confederate bonds, certificates, gold and silver notes framed on acid free board, protected with museum glass hung on the walls like banners. Battle-worn shreds of flags secured in shadow boxes hung on the opposite wall. A curio case contained coins, lead balls, small books, and brass buttons from uniforms. One shelf held a couple of Confederate uniform caps and a ceremonial officer's sash and gloves. A mannequin wore the complete grey uniform, a saber hanging from the waist, a rifle held upright, balanced in its hand.

"That's creepy," I whispered to Marco.

"What do we have, a time warp?" Jean Louis, wine glass in hand, flashed a grand smile. "Let's see, there's a lot of money in here that won't buy anything."

"It did once," Brantley said. "And, it might yet again."

"Amen, brother Brantley," said Meg, "don't count the South out yet."

"The South or the Confederacy?" countered Jean Louis. "Looks like the South is doing just fine. The Confederacy? That's probably better left where it is. Dead."

"You wouldn't understand," Meg said, breathless with angst. "You don't know what it is like to be the despised minority in your own country."

"Me, a French Canadian? Listen, Meg, the very fact you could utter such nonsense shows you don't have clue about me, Canada, or probably much else," Jean Louis said. "I think I'll go back to the living room where it is the 21st century."

Marco and I drifted back too, along with Dana and Mario. Patricia and Spencer reminded us that not all Southerners worship the past. "Stick with us." He showed off his most recent flaming jabberwocky tattoo on the biceps of his arm already covered with skulls, stars and moons. Patricia sported longer locks than her usual and urged me to let my hair grow out for a while. "Look here." She pulled the waist of her cropped jeans lower. "How do you like my new tat? It's a yellow fin tuna just like what's in the smoked tuna dip."

Reese and Walter approached us. Reese kept looking behind her as if she'd seen a ghost. "Glen is here."

"That's great," said Patricia.

"He's not alone." Reese whispered with a frog in her throat. "He's brought a blonde with.... I can't even say it. Look for yourself."

"The biggest tah tahs I've seen in real life." Walter tapped his round belly. "She ordered them two sizes too big."

"In real life? Walter, have you seen them somewhere else? " said Reese. "Is that what you are telling me?"

"Honey, now, it's just an expression. Look here they come, be nice," he said.

Glen and the same blonde we saw that day at the German restaurant approached us.

"Hey y'all, I'd like you to meet a client of mine, and a friend, Candy. She's looking to move down here permanently, so I thought it'd be nice to meet some folks who live here full time."

"Hey, nice to meet y'all." Candy shifted back and forth from one foot to the other as if her shoes were too tight.

Glen went to bring her a glass of wine. We did our best to chat with someone who clearly wished she were somewhere else. Her eyes darted about, never once speaking eye to eye to any of us. She hung on Glen literally, her thumb firmly tucked into his jeans back pocket. The Merlot in her glass disappeared rapidly at regular intervals, but I noticed she maintained her balance on her black wedge sandals.

We gave, at best, a half hearted effort to bring the full charm of Supper Club to support Glen as he picked up his life, less than a month after the death of his wife. I couldn't help but notice that she sported a tattoo similar to the late Brenda's, an orange smiley sun with blue feathery things surrounding it. Only the top half was visible above her low-rise white jeans. At least it didn't clash with her ribbed tangerine shirt that set off her colossal bosom. Consuela, simply demur in a strait indigo linen skirt with a white Nehru collar blouse embroidered with black, appeared with Adelaide who wore a yellow flowered sundress and black cardigan with three quarter sleeves. They called us to choose our plates and attend to the buffet.

Eliza and Wilson, followed by Chantal and Darius picked up plates at a table for six. I hurried to grab the other two. Guillermo and Consuela sat at the table nearby. She whispered she made the angel biscuits in honor of Brenda, who ordinarily brought all things bread. The absence of Supper Club stalwarts Fern and Bobby bothered me. Supper Club inserts a familiar routine into our lives. The loss of Brenda was permanent. The absence of the Carlyles was probably temporary. The Modica fried chicken, pork chops and grits were meant to be comfort food. But I am from the North so they brought me no comfort. I just wasn't hungry. Even the desserts, a most civilized way to combat anxiety, stress and a whole host of ailments didn't entice me. You couldn't be more down home Southern than banana pudding, made with full cream and extra banana extract. The butter pecan ice cream, homemade by Reese in her Salvation Army ice cream maker made the ice cream addicts swoon. I picked at a lemon bar, the tartness cut by the squishy layer spread on top of a buttery shortbread crust. My hand began to throb and I hid it in a pocket.

Before we left, I passed along Guillermo's advice to Eliza and Chantal. We agreed to give it a few more weeks, using the next Supper Club as our deadline. On the way into our house, my cell phone vibrated in my pants pocket. I missed the call, because my arms were loaded down with the asparagus platter, but the voice mail chirped. The message from Fern asked me to call her in the morning at home, adding she was all right. She had something to show me. I closed the phone, but then reopened it. The number of the last received call was unknown to me. Fern's call came not from home or her cell. Where was Fern?

"Marco?"

"What sweetie?" He opened our front door.

"I think this is the beginning of the end."

Menu

Walnut Olive Tampenade on Pepper Corn Crackers
Prosciutto and Apple Wraps

* * *

Vintage Carrot and Raisin Salad
Grilled Cobia Cakes
Broccoli and Cheese Tartlets

* * *

Royal Red Shrimp & Cayenne Gruyere Grits
Caramelized Onions
Heirloom Tomato and Basil Brochette

* * *

Pineapple Upside Down Cake
Chocolate Amaretto Mousse

* * *

Savignon Blanc

May

May belongs to the locals. Spring breakers have come and gone. Memorial Day at the end of the month kicks off the official start of summer tourist season. So the next four weeks of deserted beach bliss remind us why we love 30-A. The traffic is still light. There is plenty of space on the sugary sand to pitch your own umbrella over a chair and towel. The water, tinged turquoise to ultramarine blue rolls in on frisky waves. The Royal Reds, scarlet shrimp from the local deep water habitats, taste like tiny lobsters and suddenly appear in the markets these delicious scant weeks. You can lie on the beach, watching the fishing boats move east to west scouting for cobia, a tender white fish that runs only in the spring and only from east to west. I'm not much for lying on the beach but walking gives me a lift every time. The sunny May afternoon I walked on the beach with Fern, however, turned out to be anything but a lift.

Fern had called me from a strange number. To play it safe, I called her back on her home phone early the next day.

"Harley. I need to see you today. It's not an emergency. But, if you can." Fern spoke so low it was almost a whisper.

"Are you okay? I can meet you today. Where?"

"Let's meet at the San Juan Avenue beach access and walk east to Eastern Lake." A couple of hours later, we did. Under a bright sun and a gentle sea breeze from the South. Flabby waves rolled onto the shore that day. Fern's search for clarity kept reeling me in, but not for the drama of her complicated, unfolding personal life with Bobby. It's what I kept learning about Bobby that hooked me.

We took the short boardwalk to the steps that cut through dune scrub, oak shrubs, wavy ground vines and lithe grasses. Tiny grey salamanders with blue tails slithered along, abruptly darting under boards if we stepped too close to them. Footprints of dune mice and mockingbirds were etched into the sand and crisscrossed between bushes and dune grasses. Despite its peaceful appearance, activity never ends on a sand dune. Reaching the top of the steps, we gazed out at the vast blue of the Gulf of Mexico. Fern took a deep breath and headed toward the shoreline. I followed her, descending toward the beach where we tossed off our flip flops and sank our feet into the soft sand.

"The night I called you, Bobby had stayed in Birmingham. It was a long work day at Fusion Gallery. Lots of new swanky glass objects came in and I had to price them. But, you know me. I can't give up my daily beach walk even after a hard day. So I got back to my house late. The lights were left on but the door was locked. Ivy and Deuce, long since off to worlds of their own, forgot to leave a key under the mat for me."

"What did you do?"

"I wasn't alarmed. There's a house key in the wine shop. I just had to find the spare front door key for the store." She put her arm on me to stop. "I walked to the wine shop and found the key behind the outside lantern. I let myself in and went right to the drawer near the computer keyboard, next to the antique cash register we keep for show. The house key was inside. It was with another brass key strung onto a piece of leather string which I did not recognize."

"Surely it's to a safe or a special wine case with exotic labels. Something like that." I considered Bobby devious by half. Who knows what the key fit.

"Too big for that. It fit at least a door. I tried it on a locked closet door that I've always been curious about, and it worked." Her voice lowered. Fern choked slightly, "It wasn't a closet. All these years I thought it was a supply closet, but I was never sure. I had never tried to open it. I stayed clear of Bobby's doings, respecting his empire especially since he always felt superior to my family. That was stupid, you know. Hell, the Carlyles are only a couple generations out of the slag pit."

"Fern, don't disparage his family, neither of you come from the indentured servant crowd. It doesn't matter now, anyway. If it wasn't a closet, what did this door hide?"

"Stairs. Stairs down to rooms I never knew existed." She began to walk again, still bending close to me. "I had been to the wine cellar below many times, but these stairs did not lead to these rooms."

"What sort of rooms?"

"Dark, musty rooms with linoleum tile floors and low ceilings. One room had a desk and chair. One had a twin bed made up with sheets, pillow and a blanket. A toilet and sink were semi-hidden in the corner by a folding screen. There were three different telephones on the desk and one computer hooked to a high speed modem. The walls of the other room had been lined with stainless steel shelves. These shelves contained all sorts of knick-knacks, ceramic figures with Asian faces, carved wooden masks, some cloth stuffed dolls with button eyes and yarn hair. They all looked old, at least a hundred years old, but there is no way they are authentic."

"What are you suggesting?" My heart raced. I'd have to tread with baby steps.

"Don't you think it is obvious? They can't be real antiques. There are too many of them. He's selling fakes. And, I haven't told you about the cases full of old coins, which probably are real but need provenance. I know from my own work at Fusion that if we sell some expensive art or antique, there needs to be something that certifies its authenticity."

"This is a pretty serious crime. Fraud. That's the name of it. There are international police that watch this sort of thing if you sell across national borders."

"I don't know the details," Fern said, "but those phone lines worry me more. Who is he calling? Hell, it's like a mafia room from a movie, but it is real. You know he probably creates fake documents with that computer. Use any old-looking paper, especially that yellowish onion stuff. Singe the edges. You can create a very atmospheric look."

"Where would he get the figures, the objects themselves?" I sloshed through the water. Inside I was thinking about the conversation I had overheard back in February in the Obstbaums' bathroom.

"Pay anyone enough, they'll make anything for you. For a sociologist you are pretty clueless. Maybe it's just you talk about business but never really have to do the business." Fern stared at me, swinging her arms back and forth.

"Ouch, Fern, that hurts. You think I live in an ivory tower?"

"Well, what would you know about running a business?" She began to walk ahead.

"Only that I grew up on the South Side of Chicago, daughter of a saloon keeper, Fern. A man who ran a bar and sold lunches and dinners to the neighborhood mill workers, and teachers, and plumbers, and let's see, what else. I know a thing about running a 'small independent business' as it is so sweetly called today."

"Don't get touchy. I didn't know. It's just that after all these years, Bobby probably doesn't make his money selling wine, but from some shady God-knows-what." She bent over as if she had a cramp. "What am I to do?"

"I don't know."

"And I haven't told you the worst."

"What's that?"

"Glen is suing us for wrongful death of Brenda. Darius says it won't work. Still, it's a headache because we have to be deposed about the affair."

"That cannot be easy for either of you." That's all I could muster. I still smarted from the sting of her slam about sociology.

"That's for sure. The horror of taking a life hangs over me. I can't sleep. I swear I see Brenda's ghost in the windows. Every errant sound in the house makes me think she'll appear. Her screeching voice still rings in my head. What she said about Bobby and that coin."

"That stolen coin, Fern. Bobby and his Civil War buff friends beat up Eliza and stole it. Fern, you must know something about them."

"Look, my father was a Mason. He and my uncles held all sorts of offices in the various Sons of the Confederacy organizations. I grew up on the outside edge of secret societies. I learned from a very young age that you don't ask about them. If Bobby wanted to join a group that had a few secret handshakes or costumes, well, it didn't strike me as odd. If you dig where you are not welcome, they can make life very uncomfortable. You don't want to mess with them. I don't want to mess with them." Fern stopped to stare out at the sea, the wind jostling her short hair.

I noticed her roots needed attention from Patricia. I brushed that uncharitable thought aside and tried to think of a way to help her out of these various messes.

By the time we walked about a mile, Fern's need to talk had focused on her general malaise and decision to divorce Bobby. She obsessed about how soon Darius could make the wrongful death suit go away.

"I want Chantal to handle the divorce proceedings. But I can't implicate Bobby in the stolen coin affair. I'd be too afraid of retribution by him and the other thugs invoking their historical rights and all that."

Whether the threat was real or not, she feared them. Fear, shame, honor, such things mattered in the private, provincial old South world to which she belonged. We turned to head back, leaning into a brisk wind.

"Fern, take me to this room, I want to see it for myself."

"Now? Right now?" Her face morphed into a mask of fear.

"Yes. If Bobby's not there, let's have a look. I need to see it."

"Okay. But we have to hurry. Bobby traveled to Pensacola for the day. I don't expect him back until after dark."

The scarce traffic on 30-A made me speed faster. I swung the car into the parking lot but drove around back to where Fern pointed. Bobby's car was nowhere to be seen. She found the key and opened the door. The lit "closed" neon sign out front hung above a hand written note saying "closed for the day, inventory." That was Bobby's well known sign among friends for when he won't be there to work. We all knew he was too cheap to hire a part-time person.

Fern opened the door at the top of the stairs with the newly-found key and flipped on the light, the shadow lines of the steps marking the way. She leaned over, peering below into the dim room as she stepped hesitantly down, step by step. Finding the light switch, she hit it. The fluorescent tubes buzzed before they shook out their light, one segment at a time. The cold light revealed a room exactly the way she described it. Even the musty, damp odor smelled exactly as I had expected. Who would ever sleep down here? Unless by necessity? Maybe you waited for an overseas call or e-mail to arrive, to conduct business in Asia or other time zones? I walked over to the desk. Fern nervously waited near the bottom steps, the quicker to retreat, abandoning me to my fate.

The glowing green computer light meant it might only be asleep. I tapped the keyboard in front of the dark screen. The groans of a waking hard drive filled the silent room. The screen lit up with a navigation map neatly squared with longitude and latitude lines. The coordinates, listed in a text box in the corner came from Eliza's coin. The point marked a spot in the middle of the Mediterranean Sea which to date had made no sense to any of us. No city. No geological site. I leaned closer to the computer.

The light from the brass trim of an old fountain pen reflected in the screen. I peered more closely at the pen. The metal tip with a split nib was screwed into a shaft that sucks up real ink into its cartridge. A calligrapher might use such a pen to mimic the curves and flourishes of penmanship long out of style. A glass paperweight kept a stack of sepia-colored parchment paper in place next to the pen and a full bottle of black ink.

Next to this set of tools was a masterpiece. I picked up a small square piece of fine leather. Slinky as silk. The type you could roll up or fold and keep for a hundred years. Forever if need be. A spidery grid spun around three points had been drawn by hand with a fountain pen full of black ink. A frilly compass rose of North/ South and East/West took up the top right corner, drawn with the curvy script of the 19th century. The bottom left corner contained a skull against crossed bones, the grand seal of the Knights of the Golden Circle. Incomplete without names at the points, I replaced it carefully in its spot on the desk.

I glanced at the floor around the desk, the mesh waste basket contained an invoice. Unable to stop myself, I picked it up. A special order from one of the local office supply stores, it read, "For all your scrapbook and historic records needs" along the bottom. I stuffed it in my pocket. Fern stared at the bed in the corner.

"I didn't know this room existed," sighed Fern stuffing her hands in her pockets.

"Did you ever see anything about these other phones? In a bill or phone company service, anything like that?" I opened the light in the other room which was filled with bric-a-brac, collectibles, or as Marco would say, "useless crap." Some of the ceramic bowls were fired in a glaze that causes tiny break lines or crackles. The rough edges on hand thrown clay could easily pass for early native pottery but not necessarily from North America. Aztec or Incan motifs had been expertly fashioned onto the figure objects. The very fact of mass production screamed fake, unless you didn't know about the other 20 objects that look just like your original. The scale of the fraud impressed me. It was not a new business. The three phones tempted me to check the last number called, but I didn't dare chance that a computer record could detect my own interference.

"Harley, let's go. I'm scared. If Bobby finds out he'll kill me." Fern climbed the stairs two at a time.

"One second." I pushed the camera button on my cell phone and quickly took pictures of it all, the map, the pen and paper, the computer screen, the shelves. All of it.

Then we froze. A tapping, scraping noise above us. Surely it was too early to be Bobby. Maybe Wilson, or Brantley, or even Colin had keys. Could they have seen my car? I signaled to Fern that we should make a dash of it. Get out now.

She nodded and then took off. I followed close behind snapping the lights off as I raced up the stairs. She quickly locked the door and returned the key to its hiding spot. I scanned the parking lot and yard while Fern locked the outside door. We ran to the car. Once inside, Fern pointed toward the back of the lot and ordered me to drive there. We saw a small flock of crows tussling over a dead squirrel by the window well of the basement. I breathed a sigh of relief. I maneuvered onto a dirt road. There sat Ian Wilkes' empty parked car. Fern didn't recognize it. I didn't say anything.

"This connects back to the main road. I just don't want any-one to know we were there," said Fern. "I just want a divorce. I don't care about this coin thing or that business down there. It's not mine. It's over."

"Okay. No more coin discussion." I pulled up at her house. "I'm a phone call away for anything else." I thought about Ian's car. What did it being there mean? Whose side was he on? Does he now know that I've seen Bobby's basement? And so what?

"Harley, are you okay?" Fern got out of my car. "This was creepy but I'm glad you saw it. No one can say I made it up. Thanks, I'll be in touch." She turned and shuffled toward her empty house.

I drove a few blocks, pulled to the side of the road, and put the car in neutral. I attached the photos to a text message and sent them to Maria and myself.

The clouds gathered above, soft and grey. Just before the

chubby raindrops began to ping on the tin roof of the house, I hopped onto the steps to our screened porch and to the term papers left to grade.

Daisy and Tulip each claimed a chair on the front porch, front legs stretched out ahead, eyes closed, tails curled around haunches. Their faces lifted up slightly when I sat down to join them. The phone rang and the caller ID spelled Meg Coffee. Now what?

It was Meg inviting all the 30-A Supper Club women to a girl's night out the following week at her house first for wine and appetizers. Then we'd all go to the Pub and Prime in Blue Mountain to hear Spencer and his band play. "So far everyone is in," she said. So I agreed.

The text chime rang on my mobile phone. "gr8 luv u, M."

Good. Now my daughter knows what's going on, and maybe I can finish these essays.

*

On the Thursday before Supper Club, the 30-A women gathered at Meg's house in Watercolor. Curiosity consumed us all because the Coffees did not host Supper Club until July. Tonight gave us an early peek inside their fashionable pad in the spiffy neighborhood.

"Colin told me to get whatever I wanted. It only took one day with my favorite catalogs. I went room to room, choosing the look I wanted from whichever one I liked the best. I just bought everything in that picture. You know, the drapes, the furniture, the carpet if there was one, if not, I left the floor bare, just like the picture. I highly recommend it. No decorators for me." She glowed with pride.

"Guess that leaves me out," whispered Adelaide to me. "Not that working in a home furnishings store makes me a decorator, but."

"This is amazing," I whispered back. "I'd heard that people do that, but I've never seen it."

"What are you two whispering about," asked Chantal. She followed us up the staircase. "This is an upside down house, the bedrooms on the first floor, the living space and kitchen upstairs."

"Yeah." Reese huffed and puffed behind us. "Can you imagine carrying groceries upstairs? I mean, you'd be climbing these stairs every time you moved."

"Now Reese, the stairs would keep you young, active, like a stairmaster," said Dana. "The secret to a long life is staying active."

"That's right," said Marie Justine. "My mother will be one hundred and one years old in August. She has two flights of stairs in her house in Canada."

Meg called to us from the kitchen. It sported bright ruby red cabinets trimmed with black hinges and button pulls, exactly like a photo-spread from *Southern Living* a few years ago. A few with glass doors showed off leopard print plates and black wine glasses.

"Who knew she'd be into leopard ware?" Eliza whispered to me. "Who asked them into Supper Club anyway?"

"I'm not sure, Colin is one of the Civil War buffs and Meg tags along. I think maybe your Wilson. Bobby and Brantley must have submitted names. I missed that meeting. It really doesn't matter. We don't want to be all alike. That would be terribly boring." I gave her a half smile.

"That's true. You just never know, do you?" Eliza stepped back to let Consuela step in front. She examined a painting, scrutinizing the signature with severe eyes.

"Meg, where did you get this painting?" Consuela voice wavered, her eyes narrowed to black slits.

"Oh, I think from some Chinese dealer in Atlanta. Colin knows him. Don't you love that? The artist, Frida something or other, is from Mexico I think. I don't know, but it fit the space perfectly and the colors go well with the hallway. It's one of the few things Colin added that he personally wanted," said Meg. Consuela did not reply, but I noticed her looking at the painting more closely.

Meg led us through four catalog bedrooms and bathrooms, each one decorated within an inch of its life but lacking any personal touches. Then back to the kitchen. A tray of cheeses and fruit waited for us on the granite-topped island, Champagne glasses lined up in two rows. We opened some bubbly and kept shuffling around the great room that lay beyond a round frosted glass top dining table with six chairs.

We meandered out to the porch to take in the view. A sliver of the gulf could be detected between other buildings. Another sliding door led to a small studio space containing a barely visible worktable and shelves containing ceramic and porcelain figures and sculptures. Jars of ceramic paint were scattered about the table. Adelaide shielded her eyes from the outside light and peered in. She pulled me over and made me do the same. "I thought sweat shops were illegal in the US. This is some little factory."

"Hey, where is Patricia?" I realized she had yet to join us.

"She went ahead with Spencer to help him set up. She is his roadie, you know," said Meg. "Come on y'all, let's hit the road."

The Pub and Prime has served beer and burgers to 30-A denizens for more years that anyone can remember. Their seafood gumbo and catfish po'boys competed with the pulled pork french fry sandwich for fan favorite. Their smoked prime rib cut like butter. We found Patricia and Spencer at the corner stage conducting a sound check.

"Test, Test," said Spencer into the microphone. Patricia turned some dials on the mixer. "Test, 30-A Supper Club ladies, welcome, test." We waved to him, and to the bearded drummer and bald bass player. Then we filled up two tables in front. Meg ordered a couple pitchers of belly wash, something pale and light. I offered up a silent prayer that all these gals would be fine with beer after wine and then ordered a Guinness for myself. "Test, test."

Patricia slid into a chair between Consuela and Reese. "He's going to cover some Madonna for you." She draped an arm around Reese. "In fact he's going to play a song with each of you in mind."

"That sounds scary," said Marie Justine, "what's he going to play for me? *Oh Canada?*"

"Wait and see. He's rehearsed this set for a few weeks."

"How about the new song? 'Home Depot Kinda Man?'" asked Adelaide. "What is a Home Depot kinda man like?"

"Oh, he's every woman's dream guy. As for singing, I don't know. Spencer wants me to do it, sort of test it," she admitted with a chuckle.

"Do it," said Eliza, "you've got the right outfit."

"Yeah, baby, yeah." Chantal drummed the table top.

Patricia gave in to the slight ruckus, "Okay, for y'all." She stood up and turned toward the corner stage, tight black jeans, black peep toe pumps, and a fitted magenta shirt, the sleeves turned back into cuffs above her elbows, the collar raised in the back, unbuttoned to the split of her bra. Perfect product sculpted her sassy hair; she had everything going on that night.

With a nod to Spencer, the drummer clicked his sticks to start the song. Standing in front of the mike, Patricia rocked on…

I don't want a man who just talks, talks, talks
I need a manly man who paints and caulks.
Somewhere down the aisle by screws and brackets,

Just around the corner from pipes and gaskets,
He'll be there… waitin' for me,
My Home Depot kinda man.

He'll know a jigsaw from a router.
Use heavy power tools, that's no doubter
The whirr of his bandsaw brings a shiver to my spine,
His orbital sander smooths roughness with its whine.

Now he might be wearing a three piece suit
Or blue denim jeans and some cowboy boots
But he'll look up from lighting with a smile electric
From answers to my questions, I'll know he's the expert.

He works magic with his hands
He's as sharp as a tack
He is everything I need, a master at his craft
Just gotta find the aisle that leads to happiness,

He'll be there, waitin for me,
My Home Depot kinda Man,
He'll be there, waitin for me,
Cause I'm a Home Depot kinda Gal.

We stood up clapping and whistling for her. Spencer gave her a salute and bowed slightly. Patricia skipped down the steps to her adoring fans.

"That'll be a hit song one day," said Adelaide with the gravity of someone who has had several beers on top of several glasses of Champagne. "Here's a beer for you." She slid a mug over.

As the evening went on, The Pub and Prime filled up with a display of the two types of locals. Rockers, conspicuous by their tatoos, boots, t-shirts and shorts. The rest known for their khaki shorts, boat shoes, capris or sundresses. Flip flops and pony tails could be seen on any of them, men or women.

A delightful evening to be sure, but my thoughts drifted back again and again to that little craft room in the Coffee house. The one that prompted Adelaide to mention slave labor.

Spencer came to sit with us during the break between sets. Patricia perched on his lap. As devoted groupies, we spoke too loudly, laughed too hard, and flirted for the fun of it. Probably made fools of ourselves. Finally Spencer waved us off and returned to his band mates. The second set did not last as long and finished with some Beatles covers.

*

I sang myself home. But the driveway was dark. The house was dark. Not even a porch light shined. Something was wrong.

I opened the front door and flicked up the light switch. The sudden brightness woke the sleeping Daisy and Tulip, their eyes blinking in protest. "Marco?" I called. No one answered. I rationalized he may have been called to work in the emergency department unexpectedly and failed to call me. He does forget things like that. And emergencies do happen all the time. But, I didn't believe my own made up story. I sat down between the cats to concentrate on what to do. A call to his cell phone went straight to voice mail. Another to his office rang over to voice mail too. The emergency department head nurse said he had not been scheduled for that evening. It had been very quiet anyway. Before I made another call, the green Thrillmobile crawled into the driveway. Marco slowly unfolded out of the car and scuffed toward the door and into the house. His cheek was purple and dried blood covered a scrape on the side of his forehead. I rushed to him but he waved me away toward the couch.

"Harley, sit down. Ian Wilkes robbed me at gunpoint in my office. He showed up dressed like a ninja. I told him to go to hell. He hit me like some whacked-out soldier you see in the movies. He's had some sort of training because one hit and I was down hard. He pulled my desk apart as if he's done it a million times. Almost as if he'd studied desks to know where secret compartments might be. This guy's a pro. The coins are gone." He flopped into the round chair. "What do you know of this guy?"

"Are you hurt? Let me get you some ice for that cheek. Where is the blood coming from? Robbed you? Why? How did he know you had the coins?" I loaded a dish towel with ice and softened another cloth to wipe the blood away. Gingerly Marco placed the icy pack against his cheekbone. I swabbed the scrape to clean it.

"He's nothing but a poser. He talks in riddles like he's Yoda but he's a farce."

"Yeah, but he's clever. He probably followed you to my office. That time you and Eliza and Chantal were there. I think he thinks he's smarter than those other idiots but something doesn't add up."

"What did he say?"

"He kept repeating 'tell Harley to trust me.' He said you'd understand. Do you?"

"He's always said to trust him. He's said things are not always what they appear to be. I thought he was blowing smoke, that's all. I don't think he has ever given me any information but I have probably been a source for him. If he's tried to say something to me it is pretty obtuse. Why would he hurt you for coins unless he's in deep with something criminal? You sure nothing is broken? Do you need an x-ray? Did you hurt him? I hope so."

"Let's say this guy, this Hawaiian shirt thing with the surfer dude hair, is all a cover. Maybe he works for the FBI. And went bad. Or the mob. Or maybe he's just a lone gun." Marco wiped his cheek with the damp towel. He winced trying to flex his fingers to make a fist.

"I think we should call Maria, or the police, or Walter. Did you call the cops from your office?"

Before Marco answered, the phone rang. He grabbed it, "Hi Maria. It's Dad." He listened intently and nodded. "I'll tell her... Exactly as you say... Bye."

"Tell me!"

"INTERPOL has lit up like a Christmas tree. Pictures of the three coins are posted on a secure site, the paperwork in order, a map, the great great-grandfather's letter. Omo, the shady Asian intermediary they have been watching for over a year, is ready with three million dollars. Maria said not to call the local police. The question is, where does Ian Wilkes fit in to this mess and how many others are involved?" Marco sank back into the couch pillows.

"Why no local police? Of course she's probably alerted the Feds here and with INTERPOL involved, it's probably cleaner when it comes to jurisdiction."

"I think you've watched one too many cops and lawyers shows, dear. Let's just wait until we hear from her again before we do anything." Marco offered me his hand. I sat down next to him.

He folded his arms around me. Steady, always steady. And always in league with Maria. It stuck in my craw just a little bit. And the coins, my coin, were gone.

It was too late to call Eliza or Chantal. What could they do? Morning would come soon enough. Tonight, I tended to a wounded Marco.

*

I did not expect to find Ian Wilkes' car parked at the college that next morning. It shocked me that the clandestine Order of the Sons of Liberty still exercises its ideological sway over their members. War enactments. Memorabilia. Hero worship. It did not bring back the coins but working through the people, actions and context since last September is all I could do.

This was the last day of the semester. Grades entered. Free at last. Seniority has its perks too. It allowed me to opt out of teaching any summer courses. Maria wanted to meet us somewhere, anywhere. Only one place we would not go. Cairo. I'd make sure of that. Marco is keen on Lake Como in Italy. That would work. I pealed out of the college car park for the summer and headed toward Seaside.

An empty parking space in front of Pizitz is a rarity but today it was mine. Adelaide looked up from the counter of her workspace and watched me wave.

"Glad I caught you early today. I have something to tell you." Adelaide looked around to see who was in the store. "I have to be careful, so many people who shop here know each other."

"What's up?"

"Remember that strange work room we saw at Meg's yesterday?" She continued to fold a stack of linen napkins. "Well, I heard something yesterday from a client from Mountain Brook, near Birmingham, who is suspicious to say the least."

"What? Meg isn't part of the Mountain Brook scene." I ran my hand across a lovely scalloped plate from Provence.

"You do know that Meg creates provenances, certificates, call it what you like, for stuff and sells them at antiques stores around

Alabama and Florida. You don't? They are like those ceramic cups and saucers, and figures we saw at her house. She goofed up, though, and numbered two different figures with the same number. A client of mine, a doyenne of the antique world, a true antique junkie, spotted this. She's a hawk, and made quite a fuss at an antique store called the White Hen. Accused them of selling fakes or at least faking the paperwork."

"We all know not every piece of junk in an antique shop is actually old or old enough to be a true antique."

Adelaide leaned against a cabinet and crossed her arms. "Yeah, but what really matters is that objects were made by authentic tools of the time with materials consistent with the era they came from. And, old can be quaint or nostalgic, not necessarily a strict antique by years, so it's what appeals to you, the customer. Now, traceable numbered figures, that's a different league altogether. That takes planning to devise the believable history of a manufacturer in a specific time and plausible ownership legacies."

"How did your friend figure this out?"

"She met Meg at the White Hen and saw her white ceramic angel figures in an early 20th century style. She noticed similar ones in a Hoover antique mall, a half hour away. Being a snoopy sort of shopper, she looked closely at the figures themselves and discovered how identical they were. The too perfect paperwork didn't help either." Adelaide began to walk toward a table of linen place mats with matching napkins.

"Were they expensive?" I watched Adelaide glide around the store.

"Well, that's just it. The price point did not scream exclusive or extremely rare and that also bothered my friend. She's got money and will spend it. She's no fool though, and an antique that's a bargain is more likely to be a fake than a seller's mistake," said Adelaide.

"You know a lot about antiques."

"It's just the business. You see a lot, learn a lot in a place like this. I just thought you should know since she's always bugging you about that coin. Reminds me of Brantley. He was always interested in that coin of yours," she said.

"Really?"

"Yes, because he truly believes that someday, Southern dignity will be restored, that states rights will come to fruition in a new Confederacy. That secession will happen in his lifetime if he works at it. He's very hooked into the Texas secessionist movement. Blah, blah, blah. He's crazy. It's his dream to have this Order of the Sons of Liberty become some sort of Secret Service for the new Confederate president. It's nuts." Adelaide shook her perfect hair.

"You don't share his opinion on this?" I couldn't believe Adelaide actually called the group Order of the Sons of Liberty. It was true. It did exist!

"Oh, for heaven's sake, Harley. Do I look like the type who would care about such silliness? It's a rich man's, make that, white rich man's hobby. I live in the present day world. It's a much better one than that world a hundred and fifty years ago. Those guys need to pay attention to the world we live in now, not dwell in the past."

We walked toward the front of the store, near the white slip-covered sofas, and sea grass coffee tables with blue glass vases. She sent her hello's to Eliza and Chantal, waiting for me at Flip Flop Grill in Seagrove. I raced from Seaside over 30-A bursting to tell them this latest piece of gossip. At the same time, I felt slightly ashamed of how much I relished knowing there was a crack in the smooth veneer Meg manufactured so diligently.

*

"I know we said we were meeting over coffee, but I can't resist these homemade cookies." Chantal stood up to give me a hug. "You'll just have to suffer along with us since I got one for you too."

"That's right, Harley, we need this, unless you have some of your M&M's handy." Eliza pulled a chair out from the table. "Isn't this great, we're alone out here."

The late afternoon traffic on 30-A vanished for a while, leaving only the cardinals and mockingbirds to serenade us. I sat down in the warm teak chair and leaned over the table. The blue umbrella fluttered in the breeze. "I have just seen Adelaide and you won't believe what she told me."

"Adelaide? Isn't that sort of risky? Seeing that Brantley is part of the gang of thieves?" said Chantal. "You know I am a skeptic. And I couldn't believe what you told us this morning. The coins are gone. It's an outrage. Maybe Adelaide is involved."

"I doubt it. She convinced me that she couldn't stand any of Brantley's Civil War activities. And, she never liked Meg much. Anyway, this Civil War gang is tight," I said. "She called them the Order of the Sons of Liberty. They are the real deal. Never disbanded. Since a 150 years."

"Are you joking?" Eliza sat straight up.

"No. This is so creepy. They really think they are going to revive the Confederacy! Using our coins!" I bit into the cookie.

"It's madness. Utter madness. But why would Adelaide implicate Meg? Aren't they sisters in the struggle?" asked Chantal.

"I think Adelaide felt sympathy toward Fern because Bobby and Brantley neglected them both by devoting so much time to their secret society. She thought Brenda took advantage of that. She stalked Bobby because Glen never paid enough attention to her. It's all a mess. But that's not the point. Adelaide doesn't care for Meg Coffee because she tries too hard to be high society. She's so into the daughters of this, and friends of that." I cringed inside at how gossipy it all sounded. "But mostly, Adelaide wants to be distanced from Meg in her business world. Adelaide deals in upmarket items and doesn't want her reputation tarnished by association with Meg, who she has learned is a fraudulent antique supplier."

"Well, the alleged fraud. We don't have all the facts. Who made Adelaide the judge?" Chantal's calm voice gave way to anger.

"She's not judging exactly, you have to understand. In her work she hears everything, and passing on information is part of the business. It keeps her valuable to certain customers who send their friends and so on. It's how the elite continue to feel elite. People like to shop where their name or "diddy's" name is known. Anyway, we are off the subject. This is not a class on social connectedness."

"Okay, what was it that Meg was doing then?" said Eliza.

"Just that she's playing fast and loose with her antique hobby and some of the dealers have caught on. She mis-numbered some items and got caught. Adelaide says she's in danger of losing her reputation." I stared out toward the beach. "Tried very hard to like her, but she just bugs me."

"She sure has made it a project to get attached to you. We can all see that," said Chantal. "But I want to know what we do about our stolen coins."

"Maria asked us to wait, give her some more time. INTERPOL is on it. She's our best chance to find them."

"No doubt, she's the only way if we are ever to see them. We're lucky to have her help. If we could only figure out what the value these old coins have in the minds of these guys. Do they really think they will resurrect the Confederacy on the basis of three gold coins?" Eliza sighed.

As the afternoon gave way to the five o'clock hour, we gathered our things to leave. Eliza shocked us all with one last statement.

"Chantal, I have a question."

"Okay, shoot," said Chantal.

"Could you represent me as my lawyer? I intend to sue that lying son of a bitch, Wilson, for divorce. He hit me over my own relic and then stole it from me, the greedy bastard. There's more. I won't go into it now. I can't bear the sight of him. There, I've said it. Sort of feels good. Liberating. " Eliza's face relaxed. No worry lines. No frowns. Pure contentment. A decision made. Even if a hard decision.

"Of course. You sure that's what you want?" said Chantal.

"No doubt about it."

Chantal and I hugged her.

"Keep this between us until I get my ducks in a row."

At the last minute, we remembered to address the Supper

Club menu. Decisions about the menu seemed trivial in the midst of these very serious issues, but we had to carry on. Eliza claimed the Royal Red shrimp and grits. With Brenda gone, the bread was up for grabs. Chantal chose it, citing long hours in court next week as justification. I opted for the vintage carrot and raisin salad. Reese, that month's hostess, no doubt had a sacred recipe for me.

*

The night of Supper Club began with a dusk spring shower. The rapid ping on the roof of our house slowed to a drip as the droplets rolled off the long needles of the pine trees hanging above. Marco, in a bad mood, did not want to go. He was still grumpy from the theft of the coins and sore from the fight. He held Wilson, Colin, Bobby and Brantley responsible even if Ian Wilkes did the dirty deed. Maria had told him that this case was an INTERPOL priority but that held no solace for him if the coins were ultimately lost. I tried to steer him toward the real prize, Eliza Powell's papers and the two drawings, undecipherable but safe in Chantal's piano.

"Talk to Mario and Guillermo, or Walter, or Jean Louis. Spencer will be there too. Just hang with us women, and you'll feel better," I said. "Imagine their surprise when they learn we were on to them. Won't they feel like fools?"

None of my suggestions worked to make Supper Club more palatable to him. I pushed his mother's bowl into his hands anyway, filled with shredded carrots in a light vinaigrette, with raisins and flaked Manchego cheese on top. Being chauffeuse for the evening, I held the car door for him. I leaned in and kissed him hard. That made him laugh but he said his face hurt. We sped off to Rosemary Beach.

Anchoring the east end of 30-A, Rosemary Beach sprawled across both sides of the street and required two stoplights fifty yards from each other to assist pedestrians to their beach or home destinations. I turned right at the light and zoomed past the town hall, a beautiful white stucco building with a scalloped façade, and went up a block filled with shops and restaurants. The grand hotel on the left had balconies at every window. It reminded me of an old European colonial town, where the streets are narrow, but the architecture full of character.

A West Indies motif dominated Rosemary Beach design, with shutters, porches and brown colors lifted right out of a picture book. We wound around the street to the bright lights of a porch with a turquoise stained cement floor crammed with brown all weather wicker sofas stuffed with stone and turquoise printed pillows.

The McElwain's house in Rosemary Beach is located on the south side of 30-A in the oldest section of town. They can see the beach from their patio. A perfect place for a Supper Club night. The entry hall opened into a great room with an open kitchen at the far end opening onto a screened porch. Reese had plenty of stories about how she fought with the architect to put the bedrooms upstairs. She won.

Marie Justine greeted us. "Hi guys." She kissed Marco's cheeks "What happened to you? This bruise?"

"I'll tell you about it later. Not here." I held her back. Marco walked on to the kitchen.

"Harley, you are always into something. That coin of yours will be the death of you. Meantime, have I lost my mind?" She pointed to the walls. "Has Reese redone her colors? I don't remember the turquoise."

"To my knowledge, no," I said, but wondered if she did.

"We'll have to remark about it, if she did redo anything," said Marie Justine, "or her feelings will be hurt."

"How about, it's as lovely as ever, or something timeless like that?"

"That sounds good. We'll say that." Marie Justine stepped away to help Consuela who lugged a large platter. "Where's Guillermo?"

"Parking, he'll be right in." They kissed each other's cheeks in the air like bon vivants.

I spotted Walter, sporting khaki pants and a sport shirt instead of his usual Bermuda Shorts. He was arranging wine bottles like chess pieces.

Marco found Mario, to my relief. Dana called me from the kitchen to see the wooden shelf with containers of herbs just starting to sprout crowding one corner of the porch. "Who'd have thought Reese was a container gardener? She didn't have this the last time we were here, did she?" I confessed I didn't know. Although we see each other once a month, it might well be a year before we see each other's homes. That's true for some of us.

Adelaide stepped out to join us and raved about the tables. All were dressed in yellow and white striped tablecloths with hourglass vases tied with yellow and white gingham check ribbon filled with daisies. A tiny terra cotta pot with a sprouting herb sat at each place setting. According to Reese, proud of her nose for bargains, the alternating yellow and white stoneware plates came from a close out sale from one of the outlet stores.

As if a bus dropped off all its passengers at once, the bulk of the members arrived. They poured in from the hallway to the kitchen to the great room. The usual wine snobs made a beeline for the bar, set up in a room Walter used as a study. Marco hung back, hunkered down with Jean Louis and Mario. Guillermo stood near them checking his watch. Walter walked over and slapped him on the back and shook his hand. This struck me as odd.

Consuela pulled me aside. "Meg's landscape signed by Frida Khalo is a fake. I know Frida's work. She did not paint that, although it is an imitation of her style. I wonder if Meg knows that?"

"I doubt it even matters to her. I don't think she is much concerned with authenticity." I studied Consuela's face, wondering if I should tell her what Adelaide had told me.

"She should have been." Consuela spit her words, sharp like nails. "Come on, let's get some wine. Your Marco is not himself tonight if he has not presented you with a glass of wine yet." I laughed but grew aware that Marco had disappeared.

Walter handed me a glass of wine. "Here you go, little lady."

"Thanks. You are out of uniform." I pointed to his pants. "Where are your shorts?"

"Well now, Miss Harley, I have many uniforms. How nice of you to notice. Can we keep it a secret?"

"Keeping secrets is my specialty." I walked over toward Eliza and Chantal who stood chatting with Fern.

Meanwhile, Darius joined Walter who moments later bellowed, "You can't make a deal with a fool." Their laughter drowned out the other voices. Wilson, Bobby, Colin, and Brantley had assembled together like a prayer group. Nearby, Meg gushed to Patricia about Spencer's band. Spencer and Jean Louis argued about Metallica but did agree about The Band. Reese floated around the house with the calm demeanor of a woman comfortable organizing mass scale meals for school or church functions. Nothing had been left to the last minute. She had the meal under control.

I spotted Marco and Guillermo deep in discussion near the French doors to the porch. Guillermo checked his watch again. He pulled out a thin phone from his pocket and put it to his ear. I couldn't hear his answer, the din of Supper Club in full ascent. Eliza pulled my arm to point at the secret hand gestures flying in Wilson's entourage, followed by an eruption of laughter. Consuela, Adelaide and Dana hovered near the kitchen with Reese. Chantal reminded me Glen had apologized for that night. Something about his girlfriend. A prior engagement. Otherwise, a full count for Supper Club. There were still plenty of appetizers, but Reese, the domestic general, gave us a five minute warning that we'd begin shortly.

The chatter of voices had reached the intensity of woodland birds just before dawn breaks. Then silence. All eyes turned to Ian Wilkes. No Hawaiian shirt. No Confederate greys. Just a plain black linen beach shirt over blue jeans with a hole in the knee. It didn't look right. His blonde hair was slicked back. His face sunburned. He greeted everyone individually, shaking hands, making his way toward his brethren. Their faces froze. Ian closed in on them.

Every last ounce of color drained away from their bodies. The rest of us stared.

"Ian, you are not in Mexico?" Wilson choked. He took a gulp of wine and licked his lips.

"No. It's over." Ian said. "Wilson Garrett, Bobby Carlyle, Brantley Vernon, Colin Coffee and Meg Coffee, you are under arrest for fraud, conspiracy to commit fraud, assault, and armed robbery."

"What do you mean? You traitor," Brantley roared. He lunged at him with clenched fists. "You son of a bitch. All that talk about Confederate honor. You're nothing but a seditious pig." He took a swing, aiming for Ian's head.

Ian caught his arm and whipped him into a half somersault. Brantley crashed onto the floor. Ian drove his knee into his hip, grabbing the other arm and flipping him flat on his stomach. He pulled a Sig 40 seemingly out of nowhere for us to see, especially Brantley.

"Now, it wouldn't be a good idea for anyone to try anything." Ian reholstered his weapon and brought his hand up with a pair of handcuffs. Brantley winced as Ian pulled his hands together behind him, and locked them together with a quick grind. "Okay, Brantley, now who's the son of a bitch? I'm not kidding here. Anyone else try anything and I might not be so gentle." Ian stood erect and alert, leaving Brantley sprawled on the floor.

"You've got nothing on us," said Wilson. "We were in international waters."

"Yes, but the boat belonged to the US Navy so you were actually on U.S. soil. Sorry. You blew it." He spoke into a small transceiver under his left collar wing, "Okay guys. Let's do this."

I watched Colin scan the room searching for an escape. His eyes settled on the second set of French doors to the right of where Marco and Guillermo stood. Then he caught my eye. I glared back. He jumped toward me, yanked my arm, spinning me off balance. He pulled me to him, gripping my arm behind my back. He held me in front of him. "I'm not surrendering to you Ian, you traitor. Little Harley, here, little Miss Yankee busybody, is going to help me." Colin pulled a Khar 9mm, the ultimate cool guy gun, from his pocket and pointed it at my head. "Marco, you annoying do gooder. If you want to save her, don't move. That goes for all of you. Ian, tell your men to stand down!"

Ian barked into his collar. "Hostage, stand down!"

I could see uniforms coming toward the windows pull up with a jolt. My arm burned, stretched to the point that it could explode out of its shoulder socket but I didn't make a sound. I wouldn't give Colin the satisfaction of knowing how much it hurt. Guillermo held Marco back. "Take it easy there, Colin. No need to hurt Harley. Don't make it worse." He patted his side and eyed Ian. "There's always backup."

"Shut up. Just shut up. Now. Nice and easy Harley, we're going to slide on out of this house." Colin began to step toward the French doors. I shuffled with him.

"Harley, now open the door. Wide. Don't try to run because I'll break your arm. I won't let go. Keep away, you pigs." He considered the officers outside, poised but inert.

I stared ferociously at Marco and Guillermo willing their eyes to me, then aimed my gaze down toward my feet. Guillermo raised one eyebrow. I fumbled at the latch on the door. Colin screamed in my ear to hurry. I shook his voice away and took a deep breath. I jammed my three inch spike heel into the top of his bare right foot in between the straps of his leather flip-flops with all my might.

"Son of a bitch!" He gripped me tighter before crumpling over. "You Yankee bitch. You've crippled me. Oh, my God, the pain. My foot's on fire."

I dropped low toward the floor and dove toward Marco. He pulled me away from Colin, who regained his balance and fired two wild shots at us. Marco collapsed, taking me down with him. Everyone in the room ducked for cover. Reese and Patricia screamed as everyone flinched as the gunshot sounds reverberated in the room.

Guillermo fired back at Colin, then Ian tackled Colin from

the side. They fell hard against the concrete floor and wrestled. Ian knocked the gun from Colin while mashing his face against the floor. Police poured into the room. An officer bent over and cuffed Colin. "You are damn lucky Ian pushed you when he did or you'd be a dead man," said Guillermo stowing his backup.

I held Marco in my arms, blood pouring from his left arm. The bullet from Colin's Khar grazed his arm leaving a deep bloody furrow through skin and muscle.

Reese ran to us with a handful of napkins pulled from the tables. I kept pressure on the wound stemming the blood. She wrapped a cloth tightly around his arm.

"It's okay. Just a flesh wound." Marco winced as I continued to apply pressure. "It only grazed me. I've seen what these do if they actually hit you. Just a tiny entrance hole but then it blows the back of you out in shreds."

I held him as tightly as I could. I would never let him go. Wilson and Bobby did not resist the swarm of police that surrounded them. Meg cried as she was cuffed. Reese held a tissue to her so she could blow her nose.

Colin ignored her and continued to whine. "My foot. It's bleeding. It's broken."

Adelaide had run out of her high heeled mules to Brantley still lying on the floor spewing obscenities. "You fool," she said. "How could you? You believed you could single-handedly bring back the past? You actually thought these guys, a dentist, a wine snob, and a trust fund baby cared about restoring the Confederacy? What's going to happen now? Where is your noble cause now?" Walter eased her away. She sank sobbing into a chair. Dana and Patricia surrounded her. Walter returned to Brantley, pulling him to his feet at the same time as he read him his rights.

I stroked Marco's hair. "It's never been about the Civil War, The Knights of the Golden Circle, the Order of the Sons of Liberty, none of it. The secret handshakes, the symbols, the grand seal, even the uniforms. It was all to dupe us into thinking they had genuine devotion to reviving Southern rights and honor. It was all a charade. A decorative front to cover illegal trade in fake antiquities. Fraud. The coins are real but the maps and the story they are selling to go with them are fake. They didn't know Eliza's great great-grandfather's instructions were never carried out, rendered null and void by his own wife. There is no Southern nationalism here. No preservation of antebellum culture. Nothing but rotten greed. Too bad if someone got hurt. And it's all run out of Colin's home workshop and Bobby's creepy underground bunker."

Fern stood silently like a stone, watching the spectacle in a detached way, from afar. She had made her break months ago. This changed nothing for her. She drank almost a full glass of wine in one swallow. Bobby managed only to squeak, "Fern," as the grip of the cuffs snapped into place. She did not reply. One of the officers droned on about his rights.

Meanwhile the paramedics had rushed in and rapidly opened their cases and began to work. One checked Marco's vital signs. The other checked his wound and began to prepare an IV. He protested that an IV was overkill, but the paramedics overruled him. While they attended to him, Marco said to me, "Harley, explain to the others here, quickly what has gone on. They need to know."

"Not now. None of that is important. Just stay still and let the paramedics work." His hair was damp from sweat, his eyes filled with pain.

"No, now. Tell them what's been happening." He frowned when the paramedic applied a pressure dressing to the bloody gash on his arm.

So I told them about the room at Meg's house with all the figures, a studio of sorts. "Adelaide told me about Meg's fake antiques. Only Colin could make these figures and cups. That's obvious. He's a dentist, works with ceramics. Works with molds. Carves and sculpts teeth. It's not a big leap to sculpt a figurine."

"So you both are involved, Meg. Is that why you were so buddy buddy to me, Eliza, and Harley?" said Chantal. "But, Harley, how do they fit in with the coins?"

"Through the Order of the Sons of Liberty. A few days ago, Fern took me to a secret basement under Bobby's wine shop. Two rooms, one with shelves full of the same stuff at Meg and Colin's house plus other art objects. The other room had a desk and three phone lines, a computer, and a bed. Ladies, gentlemen, our Civil War buffs are not trying to resurrect the South, but are running an illegal trade operation in fake antiques. Fraud. International fraud. Meg and Brantley create the phony provenance or certificates of authenticity. Colin makes the items. They must have a source for the other things. Then they sell them to foreign collectors."

Eliza squatted by Marco and patted his shoulder. "So it was never about Southern heritage? Just a front, an elaborate scam?" The paramedics shoved her aside as they continued to work, stabilizing Marco for transport to the hospital.

"But the coins. They are real," said Chantal.

"The coins are real. But don't you see? The story being sold as their authentic reference is a lie," I said.

"What do you mean?" asked Eliza.

"When I tapped the keyboard of the computer in Bobby's secret basement, the sleeping computer woke up. The longitude and latitude from one of the coins was displayed but meant nothing. Then I noticed phony maps drawn on leather made to look like it was an antique. They are concocting a treasure map to go along with the coins based on each coins' numbers with the added tale of Knights of the Golden Circle or Sons of Liberty guarding them to this day. It's all fake. They are using their own authentic history and twisting it into a lie to dupe some naive collector."

"So are you saying the letter from my grandfather, the one I found in the book, is fake too?" said Eliza.

"No. It is real. It fits with Eliza Powell's papers. But other historical documents they concoct for the faux antiquities are fake. There is a receipt from a specialty shop that I grabbed from their waste basket listing the various types of antique paper, ink, and pens," I said, "It's at home. I'll give it to you or maybe the police will want it now."

"I wonder where they make their transactions," said Reese.

Mario, who had stood quietly behind our tiny huddle, chipped in with an answer. "They could be done anywhere. By computer. You know capital is global. It can be wired to anywhere. The pickup of the actual antique? That I don't know."

"I do," said Eliza, "at least I think I know. Look at all that water out there." She pointed toward the view of the Gulf of Mexico from Reese and Walter's home. "If you are going offshore, then it has to be more than 24 miles to escape the territorial waters of the U.S. Don't you get it? Wilson's boat. He takes it out for hours to fish or dive. Wilson and the gang could be out on that boat all day and we'd never know it. The perfect place to buy and sell fakes."

We soaked in the meaning of her words. The scale of the crime and its elaborate nature rendered our talkative group silent for a rare few minutes.

Then there was Meg. The stalwart wife, the co-conspirator, as phony a friend as her ceramic figures. It took some digging for me to dredge up sympathy for her. She called Ian a Judas, a son of a bitch and a host of other names. She hadn't flinched when Ian cuffed Colin and said, "Sorry pal, it should have turned out differently. College is a long time ago." She stood with her back to us.

"What happens now?" said Adelaide. Purple blotches broke out on her neck and shoulders. "When will I see Brantley again?" Dana stayed by her, steadying her wobbly gait.

"Depends on the judge, the lawyers, and the bail. Soon, anyway, I should say," Ian said. "They are going to the federal prison tonight over in Pensacola."

The word prison shook us all. No one spoke a word. The paramedics were ready to transport Marco. Blood had begun to seep through the temporary bandage. His face was grey. My heart began to race as I suspected the wound was deeper than we knew. I could not let go of his hand.

Ian supervised the officers as they took the suspects into custody, loading a large van with metal screen reinforced windows. The paramedics began to roll Marco, on the gurney, to the front door. Ian said, "Stop for one minute." He dug into his pocket and took out three gold coins. He handed them to me. "Sorry about that shiner, Marco."

"You asshole. Harley saved us all today." Marco waved the paramedics on toward the ambulance.

I gave Eliza and Chantal their coins. The three coins together. We still did not understand their message. I ignored Ian and jumped into the ambulance for the ride to the hospital.

Marie Justine told me later after we left, Reese and Walter offered up a prayer for our collective well-being. Chantal and Darius accompanied Eliza, Fern and Adelaide, as they followed Ian and the police with suspects in tow, to help them sort out the immediate legal steps they could begin. The irony of two African-American attorneys helping a bunch of Civil War fanatics escaped no one. Marie Justine and Jean Louis, Guillermo and Consuela, Patricia and Spencer, and Mario and Dana, stayed to help restore some semblance of order to Reese and Walter's home. Our Supper Club had been gutted that night and we were the sadder for it.

Menu

Olives in Cheddar Cheese Blankets

Bacon Basil Tomato Cups

Clam Dip

West Indies Salad

Smoked Oysters on Saltines

Vegetable Crudites

* * *

Mint Chocolate Brownies

* * *

House Red or White

* * *

Good People IPA Beer

Epilogue

On the way to the hospital my phone rang. Maria's official ID shone in the screen.

"Hi Mom. It's over. You're off the INTERPOL list. And your friend Gamal is elated. He was very worried about you."

"Good news, honey, but it's been an awful night here. Ian Wilkes descended on Supper Club to arrest them but they didn't go without a fight."

"What happened?"

"Your Dad was shot in the arm pulling me to safety from Colin Coffee. That jackass was holding a gun to my head."

"Is he alright? How bad is it? How did you get away from him, Mom?"

"Easy, easy. Your Dad is fine. Just a flesh wound. As for getting away? A spike heel into his foot. A girl's secret weapon." I squeezed Marco's hand.

"Unbelievable. Can I talk to Dad? What's that noise?"

I gave Marco the phone. He smiled hearing his darling daughter's voice. He cussed about Ian. "We'll call you later once we are at home."

We pulled into the ambulance bay. Within seconds, we were met by a mob of anxious Emergency Department staff who knew from medical control reports that a gunshot victim was on the way in. And they knew it was their own Marco Polo. The paramedics plowed through the crowd to a room where the physicians and nurses stood ready to receive us.

After X-rays, tests, cleaning, suturing and bandaging, an off duty cop and long time friend of Walter's drove us home. Daisy and Tulip greeted us with their lazy yawns. I poured a couple of glasses of wine and we sat on the sofa exhausted.

"How's your pain, sweetie?"

"It's okay. Just glad to be home. And I'd much rather have this glass of wine than those standard issue pain pills we give out to everyone."

"I guess Ian chose tonight to act because he knew they'd all be together. Made it easy?"

"Easier for him maybe. Can't say it was easy for the rest of us." He took a sip of the Zinfandel and laid his head back on the sofa. "This hits the spot."

"Funny, you'd think all of this would have led us to some answers. We have the coins but still don't know what they mean."

"Let me see those heels you are wearing. Whatever made you think to stab him with them? That was incredibly brilliant, my babe."

"Oh, I don't know. I got mad. Colin was hurting me and so I hurt him back. It was war, baby!" I slipped off my red coral Chanel slides with the three inch heels that my cousin had sent me. Then I noticed the message light flashing by the phone. Reese had called to say that the rest of Supper Club would touch base tomorrow but if we needed anything to call her. What great friends they all were. Well, some of them.

Fatigue caught up with us. When we entered our bedroom I opened the little box and replaced the coin. My hand felt thick. The intruder pulse returned but I ignored it. Marco complained his arm had begun to throb. I helped him to bed, positioning extra pillows under his arm. I gave him a dose of that standard issue pain medicine. He fell asleep quickly and soon I too crawled under the covers.

Daisy and Tulip joined us as usual. Still awake, I stroked Tulip's tail and thought about everything. I thought about my coin. Context, I mused, context. The key to these coins lies in their context. The last thing I remember before drifting to sleep. Context.

*

As expected, the phone rang the next day with calls from Eliza, Adelaide and Fern. Chantal checked in too. It became clear that all present at Thursday's debacle needed to see each other, to ask questions, to make some sense out of the outrageous. Marco and I decided to host the Supper Club members that following Saturday evening with the comfort food of an old-fashioned cocktail party, the sort our parents hosted years ago.

As I left for the grocery store, another call rang in. Ian Wilkes, begged me to meet him at the Seagrove Village Market.

We sat outside on the back patio at tables under the shade of the palms and oak trees alongside 30-A.

He began. "I had been working undercover for two years infiltrating that group. Colin, who I knew since college, resisted the most for the longest time. He never quite believed I could develop an interest in Civil War re-enactments and the Sons of Liberty since I made fun of them while in college. I could never believe he became the crook he is. Then you showed up with the coin and made the connection to Eliza's great great-grandmother. Wilson went wild with the possibilities. He knew Eliza had one hidden some where. It drove him crazy that she played dumb. Who knew there'd be a second? That was pure luck."

"You might have trusted me. Southern secession? You know I don't have a dog in that hunt. If had I known more, perhaps I could have prevented this crisis. Stopped Marco from being shot."

"I'm sorry, Harley. But I've been in this business a long time. It's harder to keep your cover intact than you think." His broad shoulders stiffened. "The agency recruited me long ago, when I was flat broke. They spotted my academic bent and lured me in with scholarships. It is what it is."

"Do you have a family, or is that a secret?"

"Past flames only. My work keeps getting in the way. You'll probably find this amusing, but since I cannot be fully honest about my work, it affects personal relationships. I don't lie very well to people I care about." Ian leaned back in his chair and stared out toward the blue Gulf of Mexico.

"And Jim Reed?"

"He's a friend and always does the right thing. He's not a spy if that's what you're asking. And Guillermo? He told me you figured him out quickly. Too bad he's retired."

"If he is retired." I was beginning to understand this game.

"Well, you never know with those types."

"Who is Han Li? You freaked out at the office when you learned I had never seen him."

"He's really an antiques expert. He works for the highest bidder. The Order of the Sons of Liberty got to him first. He didn't even have to see a coin. Just a picture of one from them. And a wad of cash. Certified the provenance which let them post all the coins, but since it was fake and he'll claim he didn't know, he'll squeal on the Order, and will likely never be charged. He burned his bridges with us. But I am more concerned about us. Friends? Colleagues? How many years have we been at that college and never connected?"

"Why did you have to hit Marco? You could have broken his face? Why couldn't you have trusted him? Who cares about being colleagues?"

"Hey, he threw the first punch! Marco wouldn't give me the coins. I couldn't wrap this up without them. He's a tough guy. I just reacted and my mission overrode any personal feelings. You have to remember it is not personal." He fixed his eyes on me. Two laser beams.

"You could have shot him by accident." I looked away, ripping a paper napkin into shreds, inch by inch.

"Truthfully, no. No bullets in the gun. The magazine was in my pocket so there was no way I'd shoot him. I didn't want any accidents. I sure did not expect him to be such a fierce adversary. He actually knows how to fight."

"Marco can do anything. Everything. He's no one's fool." I struggled to reconcile my hostility toward Ian and my instinct that he was telling me the truth. That he was, in fact, one of the good guys in this story.

"What can I do to make it up?"

"Nothing, I guess. Do you have other bad guys you are chasing?"

"That would be telling." He shot a quick smile at me.

"Well, the Supper Club gang, what's left of it, is coming tomorrow night for a post-game wrap-up of sorts. We just need to talk about what happened. Might be good for them to hear some explanation from you if that is not too top secret for your mission. Seeing as they all witnessed the arrest, the least you could do is give them the whole story."

"I don't usually do follow up. Besides, what will Marco say? I doubt he wants me in his home."

"He'll be civil. That's all. That's actually all you deserve. You would be coming for the Supper Club members."

"Let me think about it. On the subject of the coins, you never have figured out the numbers, have you? I never did."

"Not yet."

*

Saturday evening arrived and our friends arrived in waves, some at seven sharp, others by half past seven. The porch lights glowed through heavy muslin curtains and the horizontal louvers of the wraparound screen porch on our house. I fixed the appetizers. Our family favorites served in the late 50s and the 60s. Lots of dips and cheese and shellfish with baskets crammed with crackers and chips. The chilled white wine sat iced in a large copper bucket and the reds stood like bowling pins lined up on a bowling lane. The phone rang. Private Caller. I picked it up and spun around slowly in my ball chair.

"Hello?"

"Harley, it's Ian. Can't come."

"Where are you?"

"That would be telling. Won't be back in the fall at the college. Got a new gig. A promotion."

"To what? A desk job?"

"No. Very deep cover. Ever since the Oklahoma City bombing, homegrown terrorist cells are on the rise. Gotta keep all of you safe."

"So that's it? Will we ever cross paths again?" I kept Marco and the others in view. Thankfully, they were across the room.

"Be safe, Harley." The lined clicked off.

I put down the phone, which felt heavy in my hand. Someone spoke to me. "Harley, I brought you something." Eliza pulled me out of the chair. "I meant to give it to you a long time ago, but I kept forgetting. Guess there's been a lot going on." She handed me a book. A first edition of Florence Nightingale's *Notes on Nursing*. "My great great-grandmother would want you to have it."

"Eliza, no, I can't accept this. It should stay in your family, but leave it here for a few days, I'd love to read it."

"No, I insist because you are our best caregiver. Now, get me a glass of wine, before I expire."

I placed the treasure on the bookshelf near the desk and turned to survey the room. Mario had slid over to my ball chair and feeling a bump, pulled out my hidden novel from beneath the cushion. He spun around exhibiting the Starr Elliott book for all to see.

Spencer and Patricia perched on a pair of bar stools. Jean Louis and Marie Justine sat close on the couch, making space for Fern who had only decided at the last minute to attend. Eliza conferred with Consuela and Guillermo in a corner near the bookshelf. She shook her head at Guillermo's words which I could not hear. Darius, crisp in a striped shirt with his sleeves rolled back as was his custom, served the wine since Marco's arm was in a sling. Dana helped me add some fresh hot bacon, basil, tomato shells to a platter. The first round was quickly consumed by Walter and Reese. That made me happy.

Seven of our usual 24 are gone. Glen had disappeared. No one knew where he was, and his phone always goes to voice mail. The suspects, out on bail, and their angry spouses stayed away except for Fern and Eliza. Darius and Chantal said it helps that they are first offenders, but the scope of the fraud was vast. Interstate transport and international transactions. It won't help that the conspiracy has been active for several years.

Eliza, Chantal and I had agreed to bring the coins. Chantal brought along the Bible with the papers from both great great-grand parents, and the diagrams, yellowed with age bearing the cryptic words and a triangle.

We each recounted our part in the story. Eliza gloated with pride that Wilson never realized the authentic but invalid statement of her great great-grandfather had been snatched up by her. Sweet revenge for his swatting her while stealing her coin.

Jean Louis picked up the coins while Eliza spoke, turning them over and over in his hands. Chantal began to recount her great great-grandmother's adventures. He picked up the paper with the triangle, studying it in detail. Like civil engineers do. With analytical minds. He squinted at the triangle, eyes burning into it. Suddenly his face relaxed and his eyes grew wide. His cheeks pulled up in a satisfied smile. I watched him, holding my breath. He leaned to Marie Justine, whispering in her ear. She turned to him sharply. "Non!" escaped from her lips. "Yes." His grin could barely hold back words.

"What is it Jean Louis? You've seen something?" I scooted forward on the chair.

"From what you say, you concluded the numbers indicated longitude and latitude. Then you plotted the longitude and latitude of the three points. The center ended up in the Mediterranean Sea. Correct? That's what you found, yes?"

I looked at Eliza and Chantal. We said yes like a chorus.

"The drawing below made no sense at all," I said. "It was

just a triangle, with the longitude and latitude coordinates from each coin at one of the three points. A reddish brown X marked the exact center. The tiny maps held no geological cues or references. No hint of location. We always ended up plotting the X in the Mediterranean Sea just off the coast of Spain above Algeria. We once thought about running off to an obscure historical library to plod through old texts to uncover a secret postwar trade route to the Mediterranean. It didn't seem that far fetched given the way those Confederate supporters sailed away to Brazil."

"And, I suppose you used the typical map with the zero meridian, or the starting point for longitude, at Greenwich. Right?" He looked around the room at the faces intently staring at him, waiting for him.

"Right," I said. The others nodded.

"Wrong!"

"Wrong? What do you mean wrong?" Eliza stood up while Marco used his good arm to fill her wine glass. The pulse in my hand beat stronger than I ever remembered. When I rubbed it with my left hand, it was scorching hot to the touch.

"The zero meridian at Greenwich was not adopted until 1884 or thereabouts. In 1864, only seafarers used Greenwich. And not uniformly. In the U.S., at that time, for this sort of thing, people in America would use the Washington Meridian. The zero meridian running through the Capitol. Washington D.C.," Jean Louis said.

"So we have been calculating off the wrong zero? Where is the X if we use the Washington Meridian?" Chantal said. "Harley, is your computer handy?"

"Mine is," said Marco who hit the keyboard on the table nearby.

Jean Louis sat down in front and quickly brought up a map with longitude and latitude and adjusted for the historic zero meridian of the era. Next, from my coin, he entered Latitude 38.750949, Longitude 0.438901. Manassas, Virginia. Then from Chantal's coin, Lattitude 39.457599, Longitude 0.712516. Sharpsburg, Virginia. Eliza's coin read Latitude 38.895112, Longitude 0.0 The Washington Meridian.

"There is your diagram, ladies. Manassas, Sharpsburg, and Washington, D.C. Those are sites of important battles, if I am not mistaken. Any Civil War experts left here, that haven't gone to jail?"

"That's not funny. Be nice," said Marie Justine swatting him across the back.

"He's right. How do we interpret this?" I slid my hot, throbbing hand into a pocket. I feared losing control of it, that it might move on its own.

Eliza began to pace the room. "Manassas. The First Battle of Manassas in February 1861 was a significant Confederate victory."

"Why?" Mario spun around in the ball chair.

"Because it came soon after Fort Sumter and it was decisive. It set the Union on notice that the Confederacy was serious, not to be trifled with."

"What about Sharpsburg?" Jean Louis asked.

"That's more tricky. The Battle of Sharpsburg in September of 1862 was a Union victory but not a rout of the Confederates. Lee's army survived to fight again. It is said that it was enough of a victory to give President Lincoln the confidence to go ahead with the Emancipation Proclamation." Eliza stared off into space, concentrating on something.

"That leaves Washington D.C.," I said, "and the X in the middle. Eliza, the words on the diagrams are clues too. Do they relate to the battle sites at all?"

We read the words, "war no more, gold compounds" over and over again. Everyone agreed "war no more" meant "peace."

Eliza picked up the three coins and looked at each one. "My great great-grandmother hated the war. She had dedicated her own resources to the clinic to care for the wounded, all wounded, whatever side. She even freed her slaves during the war. Perhaps the points are important as symbols of balance. Manassas belongs to the

Confederates. Sharpsburg belongs to the Union. Washington D.C. belongs to us all. North and South, we are one."

"What if the X is not a geographical point as 'in x marks the spot'?" Marie Justine asked. "It's also a reddish color. Not black ink like the drawing."

The room fell quiet as everyone strained to find an answer. Eliza gasped. "Oh my God! Harley, where is that book I brought?" I fetched the book from the shelf as she continued. "It's not just a red X, it is a cross. It is a red cross."

"You mean *the* Red Cross?" asked Chantal.

"Yes. See, the initials C.B. on the paper? We couldn't figure them out. They stand for Clara Barton, the founder of the American Red Cross," said Eliza. She took the book from me and opened it to the title page. "*To Eliza Powell, with gratitude for your support and friendship over the years. Your gold compounds into care, into love, into peace. Inspired by F. Nightingale, may we continue in this blessed work for many years to come. Clara Barton. December, 1864.* I always knew that an inscription was there, but had never bothered to read it carefully."

"Gold compounds, meaning it grows over time, an investment. Your great great-grandmother spent the gold meant for more war, instead to alleviate suffering and pain, for all soldiers, like Clara Barton. War no more. An investment in people, in peace. Rather existential, but it makes sense," said Chantal. "Clara Barton's inscription shows she knew and supported Eliza Powell's actions."

"But the coins were made before the end of the war. How could she have known about the American Red Cross which wasn't founded until later, after the war ended?" Dana said. "And why Washington?"

"Washington, because Clara Barton operated from there during the war. She was famous and controversial because she cared for Confederate wounded as well as Union soldiers. She also helped families find missing soldiers, dead or alive, from both sides. My great great-grandmother was sending her money all along, to repatriate the fallen soldiers, and to support field hospitals and services needed by desperate families. Remember she had her own hospital on her property and way before Clara Barton founded the American Red Cross," said Eliza.

"What about the X? It's not a red cross, then." Chantal rubbed her coin with her fingers.

"It's a red cross, but not for the American Red Cross. That came later, in 1881," said Eliza.

"You sure know a lot about the history of the era," said Jean Louis "Impressive."

"I ought to. I am a proud daughter of the Old South." Eliza gripped the *Notes on Nursing* by Florence Nightingale in her hands. "The red cross on the papers probably signifies The International Committee for the Red Cross, founded in October, 1863 by Henry Dunant in Geneva, Switzerland. Eliza Powell and Clara Barton, aware of the Crimean War and Florence Nightingale, as proved by this book right here, would also have known about this new international organization and its aims, with an emblem of a red cross. My guess is that Eliza Powell put a red cross on these diagrams to tell us that she knew about the new organization and its aims which she supported. Because they were her aims too. This was the whole point of her clinic and the support to Clara Barton. She used her riches to care for the suffering, to work for peace." Eliza nodded to me. "That's what she wants us to do, too."

"But why the mystery?" Dana walked over to the clam dip and scooped some up. "So she chose to spend her money her own way, why the mini maps and coins?"

"Perhaps only secrecy allowed her, a widow of a Confederate officer to make such a noble contribution." I said. "Publicly supporting an initiative spearheaded by Clara Barton, a Union woman, could be dangerous. She devised the elaborate game to document her decision to break with her husband's folly, and chart her own destiny. She wanted us to know what she did and why. She couldn't have known it could take over a hundred years."

Then as strangely as it began, the pulsing throb in my hand

subsided. For the first time in months, it felt normal. My own pulse had been restored to me. The experience defies explanation. I have never spoken to anyone about it. There are many things in my life I have never spoken about. This will be one of them, as was my time in Egypt. I have always liked having my own stuff. My own secrets.

I stood back to observe the 30-A Supper Club members. The din of conversation filled the room. The brand new *Starr Elliott, Undercover Agent #V* novel lay on the coffee table for all to see, but I didn't care if that secret was out. The occasional clink of a wine glass popped against the copper tabletop. Walter McElwain and Mario Obstbaum were deeply engaged in some exchange, the Old South and New South. Marco slid over to be near me, wrapping his arm around me, offering me some M&M almonds.

I closed my eyes and revisited the September day we went for the walk on the beach. The story that began with a water-tossed coin, that took hold of me with an unearthly, physical grip had concluded. Its ending had always been written. The story had merely searched for its rightful actors for the telling of it. Tonight it retreated with the undercurrent of some mystical wave back to the depths of the great ocean. Such is the world of our beachside community, mysterious as the sea and unpredictable as the 30-A Supper Club.

The End

Acknowledgements

30-A Supper Club benefited from the input of many people along the way. Tom Elliott Jr. read early drafts and encouraged me to keep at it.

Liz Selden, Patricia Miller, and Melody Bogle actually set spectacular tables and prepare fine cuisine as is done in the novel. I am in their debt as I stole liberally from their recipe boxes and table settings. Mazy Holiday, who makes the best homemade marshmallows, and Doug Richey, a specialty caterer, provided menu suggestions.

Nancy Dinsmore read various drafts and provided insightful observations. Christine and Fred Tricker championed my efforts with shots of single malt scotch.

Mike Wright, author of *What They Didn't Tell You About the Civil War*, first pointed me toward Confederate secrets and ultimately gold.

My thanks to Sabrina Simon, who provided illuminating facts about the African-American history of communities in Mobile, Alabama.

The fascinating history of Union Springs, Alabama, and the context of travel in the post Civil War South, was brought alive by Dean Spratlan, a genuine Southern gentleman and historian, who graciously gave me his time and a tour of his collection of Southern artifacts.

Another son of the South, Neal Lambert, made sure all the weapons used in the novel fired correctly.

Jen and Rob Slocumb of Martha's Trouble generously provided one of their beautiful songs for the book trailer.

My editor, Virginia Caris, guided the project toward its completion with her wise, witty criticisms and lots of black coffee.

Carl Sanders Jr., friend and journalist, took a keen eye to the manuscript and made sure it looked good.

David Porter, artist and book designer, arranged all the pieces into a beautiful book, that is a pleasure to see and read.

And there is Pete, my sugar man. My most excellent strongman. He gives me everything.

I am grateful to you all.

L.E.

30-A Supper Club
Discussion Questions

1. Harley McBride keeps secrets. Do you keep secrets? What sort of secrets?

2. Are you a Southerner? Have you ever encountered the Old South, New South differences or similarities with people you have met in the South?

3. A supper club is supposed to foster the sense of community in a neighborhood. Do you think this existed in the 30-A Supper Club?

4. Which female character do you like the most and why? The least and why? Which male character do you like the most and why? The least and why?

5. What passage or section from the book stood out to you?

6. Are there situations, history and/or characters you can identify with, if so how?

7. Did you learn something you didn't know before?

8. Do you feel as if your views on a subject have changed by reading this book?

9. Have you had a surprising revelation from reading this text?

10. What major emotion did the story evoke in you as a reader?

11. At what point in the book did you decide if you liked it or not? What helped make this decision?

12. Name your favorite thing overall about the book. Your least favorite?

Made in the USA
Lexington, KY
11 December 2011